Payday Someday

And Other Sermons by Robert Greene Lee

Foreword by Adrian Rogers

Timothy and Denise George, Editors

Nashville, Tennessee

4212-57
0-8054-1257-3

Dewey Decimal Classification: 252
Subject Heading: Sermons
Library of Congress Card Catalog Number: 94-40564

Unless otherwise stated all Scripture quotations are from the King James Version.

Interior design by Leslie Joslin
Cover design by Steve Diggs & Friends

Library of Congress Cataloging-in-Publication Data

Lee, Robert Greene, 1886-1978
Payday—Someday / Timothy George, editor: Denise George, editor.
p. cm. (The Library of Baptist Classics; vol. 7)
Includes bibliographical references and index.
ISBN 0-8054-1257-3
1. Baptist Sermons. 2. Sermons, American. I. George, Timothy.
II. George, Denise. III. Title. IV. Series.
BX6333.L3953P38 1995
252'.06132—dc20 94-40564
CIP

Contents

General Editors' Introduction

The Baptist movement as we know it today began as a small persecuted sect in pre-Revolutionary England. One critic labeled them as "miscreants begat in rebellion, born in sedition, and nursed in faction." Excluded by law from the English universities, Baptists developed their own structures for pastoral training. They also wrote hymns, preached sermons, published confessions, and defended their beliefs against skeptics, detractors, and rival religious groups of all kinds. From the popular works of John Bunyan and Benjamin Keach to the learned theology of John Gill and Andrew Fuller, Baptists wrote with a passion and with a purpose. In time a large body of Baptist literature was developed, writings that both reflected and contributed to the emerging sense of Baptist identity.

The Southern Baptist Convention was organized in 1845 for the purpose of "eliciting, combining, and directing the energies of the whole denomination in one sacred effort, for the propagation of the Gospel." This was an ambitious undertaking for the 293 "delegates," as they were then called, who gathered in Augusta, Georgia, and embraced this far-reaching vision at the founding meeting of the convention. Through the years the SBC has suffered numerous setbacks and distractions—the Civil War, Reconstruction, the Great Depression, social unrest, denominational strife, and much more. But through it all God has graciously blessed Southern Baptists in ways that future historians will surely record as remarkable. By the end of the twentieth century, Southern Baptists had grown into America's largest Protestant denomination, a fellowship of some fifteen million members in nearly forty thousand congregations supporting more than nine thousand missionaries.

Drawing on this rich heritage, the Library of Baptist Classics presents a series of books reflecting the faith and vision of Southern Baptists over the past 150 years. We are republishing in fresh editions and with new introductions a collection of seminal writings. These works have proven their worth as classics among Southern Baptists in the past and still speak powerfully to Baptist and other evangelical Christians today.

The Library of Baptist Classics includes writings of pastors, theologians, missionary statesmen, and denominational leaders from the past. Some of them are popular, other scholarly in form. They include sermons, doctrinal treatises, missionary biographies, and an anthology of Baptist confessions, covenants, and catechisms. Most of these writings have long been out of print. We present them now in the fervent hope that the Lord will see fit to use them again, as He has in the past, not only to remind us of the great legacy we have received, but also to inspire us to be faithful shapers of the future under the lordship of Jesus Christ.

Timothy George and Denise George,
General Editors

Foreword

ADRIAN ROGERS

Robert G. Lee was a colossal man. When I first came to serve as pastor of Bellevue Baptist Church in Memphis, Tennessee, ever so often someone would ask me if I thought I could fill Dr. Lee's shoes. I was amused by that. There will never be another R. G. Lee. No one has or can fill his shoes.

I learned, however, that while I could not fill his shoes, I could stand upon his shoulders. The church I now pastor is, to a large degree, a testimony to the life and legacy of this great man and other of my predecessor pastors.

When I came to Bellevue Baptist Church, I found a fellowship that was convinced of three things: The Bible is the inerrant and infallible Word of God; the pastor is God's anointed and appointed leader; and the mandate of the church is to love the Lord, love the lost, and to love one another. What a legacy! I am forever grateful.

I was not only Dr. Lee's admirer, but I also became his pastor. We met and prayed together, ate together, laughed together, and wept together. I am thankful for the intimate privilege. If there were ever a man who loved the Lord Jesus Christ, the Word of God, and the church of our Redeemer, Dr. Lee was that man. He knew his members intimately. He had pet names for many of them, and they remind me of that to this day.

He expected much of others, but he gave much of himself. Dr. Lee was no compromiser. He had fearless conviction. He was absolutely undaunted by the opinions of others. Dr. Lee used to say, "If somebody preaches my funeral and says, 'Here lies Dr. Lee. He didn't have an enemy,' Then I'll kick the lid off that coffin, rise up, and say that's a lie." Little did I dream that I would be the one preaching his funeral.

What some may not know is this: Just before Dr. Lee stepped over into heaven, he had a vision of heaven. He had lapsed into a deep sleep, almost like a coma. Awakening, he reported that he saw into heaven. He said that in the vision he saw the Lord Jesus, he saw his mother, and he saw that golden city. When asked to describe what he had seen, this man, who more nearly than any of the rest of us had mastered the English language, said, "I can't describe it. My vocabulary is inadequate, and I never did it justice in my preaching."

If those in heaven know what is going on here on earth, and I believe they do, it is my desire that Dr. Lee will know the love, the admiration, and the gratitude we have for him.

Dr. Lee was bigger than Bellevue, bigger than the Southern Baptist Convention and the Baptist world. He was and is an evangelical legend. Southern Baptists, in particular, and the Christian world at large, owe this man so very much.

Introduction

TIMOTHY GEORGE

Robert Greene Lee first saw the light of day in a three room log cabin in York County, South Carolina, on November 11, 1886. When he died nearly one hundred years later, thousands of people streamed into Bellevue Baptist Church in Memphis, Tennessee, to pay tribute to a man who had risen from humble origins to become one of the most renowned preachers in the Christian world.

In the year of R. G. Lee's birth, most of the 488 messengers who attended the Southern Baptist Convention in Montgomery, Alabama, that year arrived by train or horse and buggy. There were no automobiles or airplanes, no radios or televisions, no computers or tape recorders. Patrick Hues Mell was president of the SBC, still a frontier denomination struggling to survive the rigors of Reconstruction. In 1886 Grover Cleveland was in the White House, the first Democratic president since the Civil

War. The shadow of slavery still fell across life in the rural South. Lee's family were sharecroppers and they had to eke out a living tilling the same rocky soil as the former slaves who lived in their district. One of those former slaves who knew the Lee family very well was a black woman called "Mam Lindy." She served at Lee's birth as a midwife to his mother. When the new baby was born at four o'clock in the morning, "Mam Lindy" exclaimed, "Praise God! Glory be! The good Lord has done sent a preacher to this here house!"

Lee was a product of this kind of world but he transcended its limitations to fulfill the midwife's prophecy in a remarkable way. In the lineage of great Baptist leaders of the past century, R. G. Lee stands tall among such giants as Carroll, Mullins, Gambrel, Truett, Sampey, Newton, Criswell, and Hobbs. Lee played many roles in extending the work of Christ's Kingdom. He was a writer, a pastor, a world evangelist, a denominational statesman. But above all else he was "the preacher God sent." No one before or since has equaled the passion and power, the eloquence and urgency, the dramatic presence and prophetic appeal of his pulpit work. It is appropriate that the *Library of Baptist Classics* include an anthology of his sermons. They are messages from above which have lost none of their verve with the passing of the years.

Young "Bob" was the fifth child of David Ayers and Sarah Elizabeth Lee. David's father, Robert Byrd Lee, had fought in the Civil War as a Confederate cavalryman, and the family could claim distant relation to two great military heroes of American history, Colonel "Light Horse Harry" Lee and the even more famous General Robert E. Lee. R. G. Lee never boasted of this lineage, but in later life, with his stately bearing, chivalrous manner, piercing blue eyes, and shock of silver hair, the famous preacher seemed to be a ministerial reincarnation of his revered forebear, Robert E. Lee.

Whatever the family connection, David Lee belonged to the poor side of the Lee clan. He and his sons toiled from dawn to dusk raising cotton, corn, and watermelons. In a good year they earned as much as $250. Lee's parents were strict Christians and they taught their children not only the virtues of honesty, thrift, and hard work, but also the values of worship, prayer, and a disciplined Christian life. R. G. Lee's older sister Fannie played the "pump" organ at the First Baptist Church in Fort Mill, South

Carolina, where he belonged to the Sunbeam Band. In July 1898, during the annual "protracted meeting" in this church, Bob Lee was convicted of his sin and publicly professed his faith in Christ as the congregation sang, "Out of my bondage, sorrow and night, Jesus I come, Jesus I come." He was baptized that summer and, twelve years later, he was ordained to the gospel ministry by that same church.

Two individuals had a great influence on Lee in his early life. The first was his mother, Sarah Elizabeth Lee, and the other was Dr. Edwin M. Poteat, then president of Furman University. Although Lee held his father in great respect, it was his mother who most encouraged him to pursue the things of God. At the age of twenty-one, Lee volunteered to work on the canal that was then being dug through the Isthmus of Panama in order to earn enough money to continue his education. From Panama he wrote the following letter to his mother:

> My dear and honored mother:
>
> I think you have been the best mother and the best woman in the world. I think often of all the years you have toiled so faithfully, and loved us so tenderly.
>
> Tonight, with the sweet music of the guitars in my ears and the tender songs of this far away land, I went out and looked at the beautiful moon and thought of you, and prayed for you. I think of the years you have toiled in the fields; of the nights, after the day's toil was over, you watched by the cradle of your babies, and now, we have grown big and old. Only God knows all you did for us.
>
> We children owe you more than money, Mother—more than honor and love. We owe you ourselves—our lives. Even now, mamma, I remember how I used to say my prayers at your knee, and now since I have gone out into the world and have learned of its awful sin, I wish sometimes that I could always be a child. I enclose a dollar for you. Take it and get something for yourself—just something to remember me by.
>
> Love,
> Your boy,
> Robert G. Lee

Lee first met E. M. Poteat at an associational meeting in Fort Mill. In his address to this Baptist gathering, Poteat said: "If Galileo knew the earth went around the sun, this country boy has a right to know it too." Lee was deeply impressed by this message and reported to his mother, "Ma, I want to learn something so I can be a preacher." Already Lee was a voracious reader. He immersed himself in the Bible and the few other books he could get his hands on. A novel by Ralph Conner called *The Sky Pilot* made a lasting impression on him. As much as anything, it confirmed his burning desire to serve Christ as a faithful minister of the gospel. He also devoured two books of sermons, one by T. DeWitt Talmadge, the famous pastor of the Brooklyn Tabernacle whose sermons were published in more than six hundred newspapers across the country; the other by Sam Jones, the fiery Methodist evangelist whose homespun stories and quaint expressions made him one of the most popular preachers of his generation. Lee's own preaching style would combine the biblical wisdom and oratorical skill of Talmadge with the down-to-earth applications and evangelistic fervor of Jones.

With Poteat's encouragement Lee entered Furman University where he excelled in both academics and athletics. He was captain of the Furman track team and also won the coveted gold medal in the senior oratorical contest. After graduating *magnum cum laude* in the Class of 1913, Lee married Bula Gentry, a young woman with whom he had been in love since he first heard her sing "Whispering Hope" during a revival meeting. When he had asked for her hand in marriage, she had said, "I can't say yes because I can't talk in public." To which Lee answered, "I am not asking you to be a public speaker. I am asking you to be my wife. I'll do the preaching. Will you marry me? Say so, here and now." They were married in November and, four years later, they were blessed with a beautiful daughter, whom they called Bula G. after her mother.

Soon after graduation Lee was faced with one of the most important decisions of his life. Lee had always loved literature and language. While still a boy, he would walk three miles each way to take Latin lessons from a retired professor. Now President Poteat and the Board of Trustees at Furman offered Lee the chair of Latin at the university. The offer was attractive and Lee at first accepted. However, when it became clear that he could not be a pastor and a professor at the same time, he faced a dilemma. To the consternation of his friends who had hoped for him a brilliant academic career, Lee resigned his position at Furman dedicating himself without reservation to the pastoral ministry. When he told his wife of this decision, she replied, "That's good! God never meant for you to dig around Latin roots. He meant for you to be a preacher."

Lee served several country churches and small-town congregations before being called as pastor of the First Baptist Church of Edgefield, South Carolina, in 1918. This was a historic church once served by William Bullein Johnson, first president of the SBC. A cup from which Johnson had drunk water was still on the pulpit stand and, at the urging of the congregation, the new pastor also drank "out of Dr. Johnson's cup, feeling that my lips were touching holy silver." Under Lee's ministry at Edgefield, the church paid off its debt, and built a new parsonage. It was also here, during a Wednesday night prayer service, that Lee first preached his world-famous sermon, "Payday—Someday."

After a brief pastorate in Chester, South Carolina, Lee was called to the First Baptist Church of New Orleans. More than one thousand new members were admitted to the fellowship of this church during his four-year ministry there, many of them received through believers' baptism. During these years Lee was becoming well-known in Baptist circles. He took an active role in promoting the Seventy-Five Million Campaign, the forerunner of the Cooperative Program. Although he had chosen pastoral ministry over a professorial career, Lee always had a great love for young preachers and never failed to encourage them to pursue the most thorough preparation possible in the service of Christ. While a pastor in the Crescent City, Lee became a strong supporter of the Baptist Bible Institute, later known as New Orleans Baptist Theological Seminary. Lee's four years in New Orleans were followed by two more back in South Carolina where he served as pastor of the historic Citadel Square Baptist Church in Charleston. While at Citadel Square Lee personally led his young daughter to faith in Christ and baptized her in a memorable outdoor service in the lake at Hampton Park. Here also he published his first book, *From Feet to Fathoms*, which contained the first printed version of "Payday—Someday."

On December 11, 1927, Lee began his phenomenal pastoral ministry at Bellevue Baptist Church in Memphis. Although Lee was already recognized as one of the leading preachers in the SBC, he also bore the reputation of being something of a "mover." After all, Bellevue was his fifth church within less than ten years! The skeptics doubted whether he would stay there for more than two or three years. In fact, his ministry at Bellevue would extend for thirty-three years, until February 1, 1960. During these years Lee was approached by many other churches—Truett urged him to join him in Texas at First Baptist, Lubbock; his lifelong friend Ellis Fuller wanted him to accept a call from the Baptist Tabernacle in Atlanta; many friends pressed him to go to Calvary Baptist Church in New York City where he could provide a biblical counterpoint to the famous liberal Baptist, Harry Emerson Fosdick. During these years he was also offered the presidency of New Orleans Baptist Theological Seminary and Union University in Tennessee. But his call was to stay at Bellevue which grew from a membership of 1,430 when he arrived to nearly 10,000 when he resigned.

Although millions of people knew R. G. Lee only as a great pulpiteer, a spellbinding preacher whose magic with words could move the hearts and minds of men and women as few others could, yet to the people of Bellevue their pastor was indeed a shepherd of souls who knew them personally and cared deeply about their spiritual standing before God. In an age when many large church pastors of Lee's stature were accustomed to shuffle off their responsibilities for visitation and personal work, Lee maintained a regular routine of pastoral labors and personal involvement with the souls entrusted to his care. The following entries from his diary during the war years of the 1940s reveal a man of amazing stamina and great pastoral sensitivity:

Friday, August 28, 1942

Up at 6:00. Worked on sermon. Prayed. Went to Negro Vacation Bible School. Taught there. Visited in all hospitals—twenty-two visits in all. Talked with Bill McBride about being a Christian. Visited Mrs. Dash and talked to her about living more for Christ. Talked to Mr. Frank Peltier about lovely memorial honor roll. Had conference with Mrs. Stone, Mrs. Toler, Mrs. Smith about Mrs. Stone's presidency of Homemakers' Bible Class.

Sunday, September 13, 1942

Up at 6:00. Prayer. Study. Evangelistic service for Junior Department. Had eleven to confess faith in Christ. Preached on "God of Jacob, Our Refuge." Service broadcast. Baptized two after morning service. Preached at night—thirty-three additions, baptized ten at night. Very tired when went to bed. Grieved over news of L.T. Perkins' being killed. First in our church membership to die.

January 2, 1944

Up early. Boogie's [his daughter's] birthday. My engagement day, 1913, thirty years ago. Conferences with several folks, conference with Negro Welfare Committee. Two funerals. Made twelve visits. Wrote an article. Had birthday supper with Bula G., Betty Lee, and Mother. Married a lovely young couple from Nashville. Visited Mrs. Cleveland in Baptist Hospital, new baby. Home, to bed.

February 3, 1944

Up early. Buddy Lee sick. Breakfast. Wrote some. Prayed. Prepared prayer meeting talk. Addressed Cotton Farmers Association of Shelby County. Made fourteen visits. Visited Judge Camille Kelly's Court. Went to teachers' meeting supper. Talked to teachers of Adult Department. Conducted prayer meeting. Had conferences afterward with four people. Left so many things undone—so much put on me today. I wonder if I can hold up. Oh Lord, help me to serve, and give me strength and wisdom. Good night Lord. We are on the same good terms, you and I. Please help me. I am "exceeding sorrowful unto death" about my people. Went home at 11:30, greatly in need of comfort.

If this sounds like the record of a workaholic pastor, it should be remembered that Lee jealously guarded his hours in the study and never entered the pulpit to talk to his people until he had first talked with God. John Gill, the first Baptist preacher to write a complete commentary on every verse in the Bible, regarded anyone who failed to labor over sermon preparation as "nothing less than idle and lazy." In no respect could this charge be leveled against R. G. Lee. But the preparation in his study was matched by his preparation among his people. Like Ezekiel, he sat where his people sat. The message of his lips was mirrored in the witness of his life and this, above all else, made his proclamation credible as well as compelling.

Had Lee done nothing more than serve as pastor of Bellevue Baptist Church for thirty-three years, he would have earned a stellar place among luminaries of Baptist history. But in fact Bellevue became a base of operations from which Lee exercised a profoundly influential ministry throughout the SBC and the wider evangelical world. From 1932 to 1936 Lee served an unprecedented four terms as president of the Tennessee Baptist Convention. From 1948 to 1951 he was elected to three consecutive terms as president of the SBC, a distinction again unparalleled in modern Baptist history. His friend Ellis Fuller, then President of Southern Seminary in Louisville, expressed his joy over Lee's election: "I have felt for a long time that somebody ought to come into our midst to take the place of George Truett. He had heart-power. He wielded a tremendous influence over all groups in the denomination. I know of no man better fitted to do this than you."

A measure of Lee's influence in the SBC can be seen from his handling of the Alldredge Amendment, a motion brought to the 1949 Convention to prohibit anyone related to the Federal Council of Churches or its local affiliates from serving on any board, agency, or institution of the SBC. Lee himself was staunchly opposed to the kind of easygoing ecumenism that resulted in doctrinal compromise. He had frequently spoken out against official Southern Baptist entanglement with the Federal Council of Churches. Still, he could not support the Alldredge Amendment because he felt that it violated the high principles of Baptist polity and would be needlessly divisive within the SBC. At a dramatic moment in the debate, Lee handed the gavel to the convention's vice-president and spoke to the motion on the floor. "I do not walk with the presumptuous step of a 'know-it-all,'" he said, "but, brethren, this motion is a mistake; therefore, I make a motion that it be tabled." When the question was called, the Alldredge Amendment was overwhelmingly defeated. Everyone agreed that Lee's simple declaration had carried the day.

Another historic moment occurred during that meeting of the SBC in Oklahoma City. Dr. E. W. Perry, an outstanding black preacher and leader of the National Baptist Convention, had been invited to address the SBC. Dr. Perry began his message by saying to Dr. Lee, "Mr. President, I've been more than sixty years coming from the log cabin where I was born to this high and exalted position. . . . Knowing that you are a stickler for time, I'm asking you in advance—please don't ring me down." Amidst great laughter Lee promised not to do so. When Perry had concluded his sermon, Lee invited him back to the podium, and said: "Dr. Perry, I want you to come here and stand by me and take my hand. I want this Convention to witness a parable in black and white, written in red. You said that over sixty years ago you were born in a log cabin in Mississippi. I, too, was born in a log cabin in South Carolina. The same Christ who saved you is the same Christ who saved me, and both of us have been washed clean in the precious Blood of the Lamb. This is the parable in black and white, written in red."

Although R. G. Lee was "Mr. Southern Baptist," his influence among Bible-believing Christians extended far beyond the bounds of his own denomination. At a time when many Southern Baptist leaders were afflicted with a kind of denominational myopia, Lee boldly extended the frontiers of fellowship among evangelical Christians of various affiliations. For example, he was one of two Southern Baptists present at the founding of the National Association of Evangelicals in 1942. He spoke often and was well received at Moody Bible Institute in Chicago, Billy Sunday's Winona Lake Bible Conference in Indiana, and, near the end of his life, Jerry Falwell's Liberty University in Virginia. He was willing to preach Jesus to anyone who would listen, even if this meant he had to color outside of the lines to do so.

Throughout his ministry Lee was an ardent advocate of world missions. Even in the debt-ridden days of the Depression, Lee led Bellevue to increase its annual giving to evangelistic and world missionary causes. Lee's compassion for the lost and his desire to preach Christ unto the ends of the earth led him to carry the gospel message to such faraway places as Korea, Egypt, India, and Russia. Years before when Lee had turned down Furman's offer to head their Latin Department, he had said to Dr. Poteat: "I would not give up my preaching to be president of the United States."

When he resigned his pastoral ministry at Bellevue, *The Commercial Appeal* of Memphis said of him, "For half a century he has thrown punches at the devil, punches containing the same power and vengeance as those of Billy Sunday, George Truett, or

C. H. Spurgeon. In all of these years, he has never quit slugging. He says, 'The devil never sleeps.' So he has worked night and day to bring the gospel to as many people as possible." Nor did that pace slacken during the next eighteen years as he traveled some 100,000 miles a year speaking in churches large and small, to gatherings at home and abroad, from campuses to camp meetings, declaring to all persons everywhere the good news of salvation through personal faith in the crucified and risen Redeemer.

R. G. Lee died in 1978. In the following year Adrian Rogers, then pastor at Bellevue, was elected president of the SBC vowing to lead the denomination back to the kind of conservative biblical theology Lee had championed throughout his ministry. A Southern gentleman of the old order and a model of civility in every respect, Lee managed to avoid the rough edges of controversy during most of his life. No doubt he would have winced at the asperities on both sides of the SBC squabbles which garnered so many headlines in the decade after his death. But there is no doubt that his theological sympathies were with those who warned against a liberal drift within America's largest Protestant denomination and sought to recall it to biblical fidelity and spiritual renewal.

Along with Herschel Hobbs, W. A. Criswell, J. D. Gray, and a host of other popular preachers, Lee had proclaimed the doctrine of biblical inerrancy as a non-negotiable tenet of Baptist identity. For a variety of reasons, many seminary professors and denominational elites were reluctant to use this controverted word *inerrancy* to describe their own view of the Bible. But Lee and others had given it wide currency among grassroots Southern Baptists. Thus Lee's positive proclamation of the total truthfulness of Holy Scripture and his persistent warnings against the inroads of unbelieving theology prepared the way for the conservative resurgence in the SBC.

W. B. Johnson, Lee's predecessor at Edgefield, once said of Richard Furman, "When *he* arose to speak . . . all eyes were turned upon him, with profound attention, and reverential awe." No less could be said of the effect of R. G. Lee on the masses who heard him preach. There was always an air of expectancy in every meeting he addressed. Though his sermons were frequently spiced with humor, there was nothing flippant or vulgar about them. There was a gravity about Lee's preaching which carried his listeners into the throne room of heaven. As he entered the sanctuary at Bellevue, dressed as he usually was in his white gaberdine suit and white shoes, kneeling to pray for several minutes beside the sacred desk, there was a holy hush and a sense of another world impinging upon this one for all those who had come that day to worship the Lord. Lee's sermons were sometimes more than an hour in length. "I preach until I wear out," he quipped, "I never wind down!" Yet he preached with such pathos, eloquence, and urgency that few grew restless and none were ever bored by his message. John A. Broadus, who published his famous *Sermons and Addresses* in the year Lee was born, once gave the following advice to aspiring preachers, "You must know how to unite breadth of view, and charity of feeling, with fidelity to truth." This dictum, as much as anything I know, is an apt description of the preaching of R. G. Lee and the secret of his appeal which is still evident in the reading of his sermons.

The sermon "Payday—Someday" was published three times during Lee's lifetime: in his first book of sermons in 1926, then as an appendix in his biography by E. Schuyler English in 1949, and again as a separate pamphlet in 1956. The sermon originated in 1919 as a prayer meeting devotional during his ministry at Edgefield. One of his deacons, E. J. Norris, said to the young preacher, "You've got something there, my boy. Why don't you make a full-length sermon out of it? I think it is wonderful." Lee stayed up until two o'clock the next morning enlarging and reworking this sermon based on 1 Kings 21 and 2 Kings 9. For more than three decades Lee delivered "Payday—Someday" every year at Bellevue. In all, Lee preached "Payday—Someday" 1,275 times—in the State Capitol in Texas, before the legislature in Tennessee, in baseball parks and football stadiums, in foreign lands and tent revivals. It was also filmed and made into a sacred opera. What is the theme of this classic sermon? It is the simple message of Jesus: "Repent or perish!" (see Luke 13:3). "Payday—Someday" is narrative preaching at its best, a dramatic retelling of the biblical story of King Ahab and his wicked wife Jezebel. Through the years more than eight thousand persons professed faith in Jesus Christ after hearing "Payday—Someday."

The sermon "The Bible—Not Broken and Not Bound" was first published in 1930. Before he had taken his first tentative steps in ministry, Lee had received a word of advice from his dear mother, "Always believe the Bible," she had said "all of it—no matter who doesn't believe it." Lee later recalled that the Bible was revered in his family with the same kind of reverence and awe as the Israelites looked upon the Holy of Holies or the Ark of the Covenant. This sermon reflects the depth of Lee's unswerving commitment to the Holy Scriptures, a stance from which he was never to stray throughout his long life. Even in his letter of resignation from Bellevue he reiterated this same theme: "You can count on me until my tongue is silent in the grave and until my hand can no longer wield a pen to keep my unalterable stand for the Bible as the inspired, infallible, inerrant Word of God—giving rebuke to and standing in opposition to all enemies of the Bible, even as I have done for fifty years."

But Lee did not worship the Bible. He would have agreed with Martin Luther that the Bible is so precious because, like the straw in Jesus' manger, it conveys to us the living Christ. Lee knew what Alexander Maclaren meant when he said that in building a sermon, "We have to drive a shaft clear down through all the superficial strata, and lay the first stones on the Rock of Ages." The next three sermons in this collection, "The Face of Jesus Christ," "What He Was Made," and "The Triumphant Tense" all focus on the christological foundation of the Christian faith. For Lee, Jesus Christ could never be a mere pretext or afterthought for the sermon. No, Jesus Christ is everything! His eternal preexistence with the Father, his supernatural conception in a virgin mother, his deity and humanity, His atoning death and triumphant Resurrection, His ascension and session at the Father's right hand, the promise of His coming again in glory—all of this is the substance of true Christian proclamation.

The next three sermons, "Blood on Ears and Hands and Toes," "The Tongue of the Human Body," and "Bed of Pearls: Constraint" show Lee at his best in dealing with practical issues of the Christian life. Duke George of Saxony once said of the Protestant faith: "It's a good doctrine to die with, but a sorry one to live by." But Lee believed that justification could not be divorced from sanctification. In other words, we are justified by faith alone, but the faith that justifies is not alone. It is faith alone, working by love, leading to holiness. This too was a constant theme in Lee's sermons as he exhorted believers who had been saved by God's sovereign grace to "press on toward the goal to win the prize for which God has called [us] heavenward in Christ Jesus" (Phil. 3:14, NIV).

The Word of God is perfect and unchanging: "Forever, O LORD, thy word is settled in heaven" (Ps. 119:89). But the preacher who proclaims that immutable word is a creature of time. The context into which it is spoken is marked by the anxieties and vicissitudes of mortal life. R. G. Lee was a keen student of history and understood well the changing patterns of social and political life in the modern world. Five times during his life the United States was thrust into bloody wars. Lee was three years older than Adolf Hitler and three years younger than Benito Mussolini. In the midst of violent and uncertain times, Lee pointed his listeners to the Almighty God who was both in history and beyond it. "The Whirlwinds of God," "God in History," and "This Critical Hour" were first preached to congregations trying to make sense of a world coming apart at the seams. Rather than offering leftover political advice, faddish predictions, or a rehash of the news, Lee set before them the divine mystery of divine providence. He proclaimed to them the God of the Bible, the God who "from eternity decrees or permits all things that come to pass, and perpetually upholds, directs, and governs all creatures and all events."

The final sermon in this collection, "Roses Will Bloom Again," was first preached during Lee's ministry in New Orleans. This sermon was overheard by a woman of the gutters who stood on the outside of the church building at the corner of Delachaise Street while Lee proclaimed this message of hope and new beginnings. Early the next morning she burst into his office and poured out the sordid story of her shame and sin. "Do you think there is any chance for a girl like me to get back, to get out of the ditch, and on the road again? Will God—*will* God—accept my surrendered desert and make it blossom? You said He would. Is it so?" Lee later recalled his reaction:

> The recital of things she had done seemed to daze me into speechlessness. I did not, could not, speak at first. She took my silence for reluctance and cried out, almost shrieked out, as though she wanted all the world to know: "If you don't think so, if what you said last night is a lie, then you will read of 'em fishing my body out of the river tomorrow, if they can find it!" Her voice had in it the wail that

> bordered on a snarl. She stood to her feet and was gripping the corner of my desk with trembling fingers. Her whole body was a-quiver.
>
> Then I spoke. I told her that all I said the night before was so—that Christ would be far more than words could tell to all who with repentance toward God and faith in Christ surrendered to Him. I told her that Christ would accept her surrendered desert and restore the years the locusts had eaten and make her, though smutty from contact with the devil's pots, to be as "a dove covered with silver, and her feathers with yellow gold" (Ps. 68:13).
>
> I will simply say that she accepted Christ, knelt in prayer, and promised to "see me again." Later I baptized her—nobody, not even my secretary, knowing of her terrible sin, knowing nothing of her having been the dirty toy of dirtier men for three years. The next day she telephoned me that she was "leaving town" to start anew.
>
> Five years later—in another city—she came to my house with a young man. She stood before me at the marriage hour in our home, a fine young man beside her, a young man whose life, while in his teens, was one of awful sin. He, too, had been redeemed. Both of them told me they were getting married "without any secrets," that they had opened all the pages of both books when they talked of marriage and became engaged. They said that they had forgiven what needed to be forgiven in each other and that they were forgetting the past, starting over in beginning life together.
>
> I saw them as they left our little home. They stopped on the edge of the sidewalk and looked up at the stars, as though they were praying to God; and then they kissed, and went away arm in arm, heart to heart, hand in hand, soul to soul. I know where they live now. Their surrendered deserts have become gardens of the Lord. And their little children are beautiful flowers in the garden.

Lee never shirked from portraying in all of its horror the reality of sin and its devastating effects in human life. But the devil never had the last word in his sermons. God did not send Jesus into the world to condemn it, but to save it instead. The Christian message is one of hope, of streams in the desert, of roses that will bloom again. Because R. G. Lee never forgot this truth, his preaching was marked by the optimism of grace.

Thomas Crosby, the first historian of the English Baptists, wrote a remarkable tribute for his father-in-law, Benjamin Keach:

> Preaching the gospel was the very pleasure of his soul, and his heart was so engaged in the work of the ministry, that from the time of his first appearing in public, to the end of his days, his life was one continued scene of labor and toil. His close study and constant preaching did greatly exhaust his animal spirits, and enfeeble his strengths, yet to the last he discovered a becoming zeal against the errors of his day; his soul was too great to recede from any truth that he owned, either from the frowns or the flatteries of the greatest. He, with unwearied diligence, did discharge the duties of his pastoral office.

No more appropriate assessment can be offered for the life and ministry of Robert Greene Lee. May these sermons from his pen, so mightily used of God in days gone by, encourage the rising generation of ministers to preach with such gravity and gladness that the lost may be saved, and the Body of Christ built up, and God glorified in every increasing measure.

Sources

English, E. Schuyler, *Robert G. Lee: A Chosen Vessel.* Grand Rapids: Zondervan, 1949.

Gericke, Paul, *The Preaching of Robert G. Lee: Adorning the Doctrine of God.* Orlando: Christ for the World Publishers, 1967.

Huss, John E., *Robert G. Lee: The Authorized Biography.* Grand Rapids: Zondervan, 1967.

Lee, Robert G., *Payday Every Day.* Nashville: Broadman Press, 1974.

Routh, Porter, *Meet the Presidents.* Nashville: Broadman Press, 1982.

CHAPTER ONE

Payday—Someday

Arise, go down to meet Ahab king of Israel,
which is in Samaria: behold, he is in the vineyard of Naboth,
whither he is gone down to possess it. And thou shalt speak unto him,
saying, Thus saith the LORD, Hast thou killed, and also taken possession?
And thou shalt speak unto him, saying, Thus saith the LORD,
In the place where dogs licked the blood of Naboth shall dogs lick thy blood,
even thine. . . . And of Jezebel also spake the LORD, saying,
The dogs shall eat Jezebel by the wall of Jezreel.
1 Kings 21:18–19, 23

I introduce to you Naboth, a devout Israelite who lived in the town of Jezreel. Naboth was a good man. He abhorred that which is evil. He clave to that which is good. He would not dilute the stringency of his personal piety for any profit in money. He would not change his heavenly principles for loose expediences. And this good man who loved God, his family, and his nation, had a little vineyard which was close by the summer palace of Ahab, the king—a palace unique in its splendor as the first palace inlaid with ivory. This little vineyard had come to Naboth as a cherished inheritance from his forefathers—and all of it was dear to his heart.

I introduce to you Ahab, the vile human toad who squatted upon the throne of his nation—the worst of Israel's kings. King Ahab had command of a nation's wealth and a nation's army, but he had no command of his lusts and appetites. Ahab wore rich robes, but he had a sinning and wicked and troubled heart beneath them. He ate the finest food the world could supply—and this food was served to him in dishes splendid by servants obedient to his every beck and nod—but he had a starved soul. He lived in palaces sumptuous within and without, yet he tormented himself for one bit of land more. Ahab was a king with a throne and a crown and a scepter, yet he lived nearly all of his life under the thumb of a wicked woman—a tool in her hands. Ahab pilloried himself in the contempt of all God-fearing men as a mean and selfish rascal who was the curse of his country. The Bible introduces him to us in words more appropriate than these when it says:

> But there was none like unto Ahab, which did sell himself to work wickedness in the sight of the LORD, whom Jezebel his wife stirred up. And he did very abominably in following idols, according to all things as did the Amorites, whom the LORD cast out before the children of Israel. . . . And Ahab made a grove; and Ahab did more to provoke the LORD God of Israel to anger than all the kings of Israel that were before him (1 Kings 21:25–26; 16:33).

I introduce to you Jezebel, daughter of Ethbaal, King of Tyre (1 Kings 16:31), and wife of Ahab, the King of Israel—a king's daughter and a king's wife, the evil genius at once of her dynasty and of her country. Infinitely more daring and reckless was she in her wickedness than was her wicked husband. Masterful, indomitable, implacable, a devout worshiper of Baal, she hated anyone and everyone who spoke against or refused to worship her pagan god. As blunt in her wickedness and as brazen in her lewdness was she as Cleopatra, fair sorceress of the Nile. She had all the subtle and successful scheming of Lady Macbeth, all the adulterous desire and treachery of Potiphar's wife (Gen. 39:7–20), all the boldness of Mary Queen of Scots, all the cruelty and whimsical imperiousness of Katherine of Russia, all the devilish infamy of a Madame Pompadour, and doubtless, all the fascination of personality of a Josephine of France. Most of that which is bad in all evil women found expression through this painted viper of Israel. She had that rich endowment of nature which a good woman ought always to dedicate to the service of her day and generation. But—alas!—this idolatrous daughter of an idolatrous king of an idolatrous people engaging with her maidens in worship unto Ashtoreth—the personification of the most forbidding obscenity, uncleanness, and sensuality—became the evil genius who wrought wreck, brought blight, and devised death. She was the beautiful and malicious adder coiled upon the throne of the nation.

I introduce to you Elijah, the Tishbite, prophet of God at a time when by tens of thousands the people had forsaken God's covenants, thrown down God's altars, slain God's prophets with the sword (see 1 Kings 19:10). The prophet, knowing much of the glorious past of the now apostate nation, must have been filled with horror when he learned of the rank heathenism, fierce cruelties, and reeking licentiousness of Ahab's idolatrous capital. Holy anger burned within him like an unquenchable Vesuvius. He wore the roughest kind of clothes, but he had underneath these clothes a righteous and courageous heart. He ate bird's food and widow's fare, but he was a great physical and spiritual athlete. He was God's tall cedar that wrestled with the paganistic cyclones of his day without bending or breaking. He was God's granite wall that stood up and out against the rising tides of the apostasy of his day. Though much alone, he was sometimes attended by the invisible hosts of God. He grieved only when God's cause seemed tottering. He passed from earth without dying—into celestial glory. Everywhere courage is admired and manhood honored and service appreciated, he is honored as one of earth's greatest heroes and one of heaven's greatest saints. He was a seer who saw clearly. He was a great heart who felt deeply. He was a hero who dared valiantly.

And now with the introduction of these four characters—Naboth, the devout Jezreelite; Ahab, the vile human toad who squatted befoulingly on the throne of the nation; Jezebel, the beautiful adder beside the toad; and Elijah, the prophet of the living God, I bring you the tragedy of "Payday—Someday."

And the first scene in the tragedy of "Payday—Someday" is

The Real Estate Request

"Give Me Thy Vineyard."

> And it came to pass after these things, that Naboth the Jezreelite had a vineyard, which was in Jezreel, hard by the palace of Ahab king of Samaria. And Ahab spake unto Naboth, saying, Give me thy vineyard, that I may have it for a garden of herbs, because it is near unto my house: and I will give thee for it a better vineyard than it; or, if it seem good to thee, I will give thee the worth of it in money (1 Kings 21:1–2).

Thus far Ahab was quite within his rights. No intention had he of cheating Naboth out of his vineyard or of killing him to get it. Honestly did he offer to give him its worth in money. Honestly did he offer him a better vineyard for it. Perfectly fair and square was Ahab in this request and, under circumstances ordinary, one would have expected Naboth to put away any mere sentimental attachment which he had for his ancestral inheritance in order that he might please the king of his nation—especially when the king's aim was not to defraud or rob him.

Ahab had not, however, counted upon the reluctance of all Jews to part with their inheritance of land. By peculiar tenure every Israelite held his land, and to all land-holding transactions there was another party, even God, "who made the heavens and the earth." Throughout Judah and Israel, Jehovah was the real owner of the soil; and every tribe received its territory and every family its inheritence by lot from Him, with the added condition that the land should not be sold forever.

> The land shall not be sold for ever: for the land is mine; for ye are strangers and sojourners with me. . . . So shall not the inheritance of the children of Israel remove from tribe to tribe: for every one of the children of Israel shall keep himself to the inheritance of the tribe of his fathers . . . but every one of the tribes of the children of Israel shall keep himself to his own inheritance (Lev. 25:23; Num. 36:7, 9).

Thus we see that the permanent sale of the paternal inheritance was forbidden by law. Ahab forgot—if he had ever really known it—that for Naboth to sell for money or to swap for a better vineyard his little vineyard would seem to that good man like a denial of his allegiance to the true religion when jubilee restoration was neglected in such idolatrous times.

So, though he was Ahab's nearest neighbor, Naboth, with religious scruples blended with the pride of ancestry, stood firmly on his rights—and, with an expression of horror on his face and with tones of terror in his words, refused to sell or swap his vineyard to the king. Feeling that he must prefer the duty he owed to God to any danger that might arise from man, he made firm refusal. With much fear of God and little fear of man, he said: "The LORD forbid it me, that I should give the inheritance of my fathers unto thee" (1 Kings 21:3).

True to the religious teachings of his father with loyalty to the covenant God of Israel, he believed that he held the land in fee simple from God. His father and grandfather and doubtless grandfather's father had owned the land before him. All the memories of childhood were tangled in its grapevines. His father's hands, folded now in the dust of death, had used the pruning blade among the branches, and because of this every branch and vine was dear. His mother's hands, now doubtless wrapped in a dust-stained shroud, had gathered purple clusters from those bunch-laden boughs, and for this reason he loved every spot in his vineyard and every branch on his vines. The ties of sentiment, of religion, and of family pride bound and endeared him to the place. So his refusal to sell was quick, firm, final, and courteous. Then, too, doubtless working or resting or strolling as he often did in his vineyard hard by the king's castle, Naboth had had glimpses of strange and alien sights in the palace. He had seen with his own eyes what orgies idolatry led to when the queen was at home in her palace in Jezreel; and Naboth, deeply pious, felt smirched and hurt at the very request. He felt that his little plot of ground, so rich in prayer and fellowship, so sanctified with sweet and holy memories, would be tainted and befouled and cursed forever if it came into the hands of Jezebel. So with "the courage of a bird that dares the wild sea," he took his stand against the king's proposal.

And that brings us to the second scene in this tragedy. It is

The Pouting Potentate

"He came into his house heavy and displeased."

Naboth's quick, firm, courteous, final refusal took all the spokes from the wheels of Ahab's desires and plans. Naboth's refusal was a barrier that turned aside the stream of Ahab's desire and changed it into a foiled and foaming whirlpool of sullen sulks.

> And Ahab came into his house heavy and displeased because of the word which Naboth the Jezreelite had spoken to him: for he had said, I will not give thee the inheritance of my fathers. And he laid him down upon his bed, and turned away his face, and would eat no bread (1 Kings 21:4).

What a ridiculous picture! A king acting like a spoiled and sullen child—impotent in disappointment and ugly in petty rage! A king, whose victories over the Syrians have rung through many lands—a conquerer, a slave to himself—whining like a sick hound! A king, rejecting all converse with others, pouting like a spoiled and petulant child who has been denied one trinket in the midst of one thousand playthings! A king, in a chamber "ceiled with cedar, and painted with vermilion" (Jer. 22:14), prostituting genius to theatrical trumpery.

Ahab went into his ivory house, while the sun was shining and the matters of the daytime were all astir, and went to bed and "turned his face to the wall"—his lips swollen with his mulish moping, his eyes burning with cheap anger-fire, his wicked heart stubborn in perverse rebellion against the commandment of God. Servants brought him his meal, plenteously prepared on platters beautiful, but he "would eat no bread." Doubtless, musicians came to play skillfully on stringed instruments, but he drove them all away with imperious gestures and impatient growlings. He turned from his victuals as one turns from garbage and refuse. The conqueror of the Syrians is a low slave to dirt-cheap trivialities. His spirit, now devilishly sullen, is in bondage.

What an ancient picture we have of great powers dedicated to mean, ugly, petty things. Think of it! In the middle of the day, the commander-in-chief of an army seized by Sergeant Sensitive. General Ahab made prisoner by Private Pouts! The leader of an army laid low by Corporal Mopishness! A monarch moaning and blubbering and growlingly refusing to eat because a man, a good man, because of the commandments of God and because of religious principles, would not sell or swap a little vineyard which was his by inheritance from his forefathers. Ahab had lost nothing—had gained nothing. No one had injured him. No one had made attempt on his life. Yet he, a king with a great army and a fat treasury, was acting like a blubbering baby. Cannon ability was expressing itself in popgun achievement. A massive giant sprawling on the bed like a dwarf punily peevish! A whale wallowing and spouting angrily about because he is denied minnow food! A bear growling sulkily because he cannot lick a spoon in which is a bit of honey! An eagle shrieking and beating his wings in the dust of his own displeasure like a quarreling sparrow fussily fighting with other sparrows for the crumbs in the dust of a village street! A lion sulkily roaring because he was not granted the cheese in a mouse trap! A battleship cruising for a beetle!

What an ancient picture of great powers and talents prostituted to base and purposeless ends and withheld from the service of God! What an ancient spectacle! And how modern and up-to-date, in this respect, was Ahab, king of Israel. What a likeness to him in conduct today are many talented men and women. I know men and women—you know men and women—with diamond and ruby abilities who are worth no more to God through the churches than a punctured Japanese nickel in a Chinese bazaar! So many there are who, like Ahab, withhold their talents from God—using them in the service of the devil. People there are, not a few, who have pipe-organ abilities and make no more music for the causes of Christ than a wheezy saxophone in an idiot's hands. People there are, many of them, who have incandescent light powers who make no more light for God than a smoky barn lantern, with smoke-blackened globe, on a stormy night. People there are—I know them and you know them—with locomotive powers doing pushcart work for God. People there are—and how sad 'tis true—who have steam-shovel abilities who are doing teaspoon work for God. Yes! Now look at this overfed bull bellowing for a little spot of grass outside his own vast pasture lands—and, if you are withholding talents and powers from the service of God, receive the rebuke of the tragic and ludicrous picture.

And now, consider the third scene in this tragedy of "Payday—Someday." It is

The Wicked Wife

"And Jezebel his wife."

When Ahab would "eat no bread," the servants went and told Jezebel. What she said to them, we do not know. Something of what she said to Ahab we do know. Puzzled and provoked at the news that her husband would not eat—that he had gone to bed when it was not bedtime—Jezebel went to investigate. She found him in bed with his face turned to the wall, his lips swollen with mulish moping, his eyes burning with cheap anger-fire, his heart stubborn in wicked rebellion. He was groaningly mournful and peevishly petulant—having, up to the moment when she stood by his bedside, refused to eat or cheer up in the least.

Looking at him then, she doubtless, as is the custom with women until this day, put her hand on his forehead to see if he had fever. He had fever—without doubt! He was set on fire of hell, even as is a wicked tongue (James 3:6). Then, in a voice of "sweet" solicitation, she sought the reason of his anger. She asked, to put it in the semi-slang language of our day: "What's the matter with you, Big Boy?" But, in the words of the Bible: "Why is thy spirit so sad, that thou eatest no bread?" (1 Kings 21:5). Then, with his mouth full of grouches, with his heart stubborn in rebellion against the commandment of God, he told her—his every word full of mopish petulance:

> Because I spake unto Naboth the Jezreelite, and said unto him, Give me thy vineyard for money; or else, if it please thee, I will give thee another vineyard for it: and he answered, I will not give thee my vineyard (1 Kings 21:6).

Every word he said stung like a whip upon a naked back of this wickedly unscrupulous woman who had never had any regard for the welfare of anyone who did not worship her god, Baal—who never had any conscientious regard for the rights of others, or for others who did not yield to her whimsical imperiousness.

Hear her derisive laugh as it rings out in the palace like the shrill cackle of a wild fowl that has returned to it nest and has found a serpent therein! With her tongue, sharp as a razor, she prods Ahab as an ox driver prods with sharp goad the ox which does not want to press his neck into the yoke, or as one whips with a rawhide a stubborn mule. With profuse and harsh laughter this old gay and gaudy guinea of Satan derided this king of hers for a cowardly buffoon and sordid jester. What hornet-like sting in her sarcasm! What wolf-mouth fierceness in her every reproach! What tiger-fang cruelty in her expressed displeasure! What fury in the shrieking of her rebuke! What bitterness in the teasing taunts she hurled at him for his scrupulous timidity! Her bosom with anger was heaving! Her eyes were flashing with rage under the surge of hot anger that swept over her.

"Are you not the king of this country?" she chides bitingly, her tongue sharp like a butcher's blade. "Can you not command and have it done?" she scolds as a common village hag who has more noise than wisdom in her words. "Can you not seize and keep?" she cries with reproach. "I thought you told me you were king in these parts! And here you are crying like a baby and will not eat anything because you do not have courage to take a bit of land. You! Ha! Ha! Ha! Ha! You, the king of Israel, allow youself to be disobeyed and defied by a common clodhopper from the country. You are more courteous and considerate of him than you are of your queen! Shame on you! But you leave it to me! I will get the vineyard for you, and all that I require is that you ask no questions. Leave it to me, Ahab!"

"And Jezebel his wife said unto him, Dost thou now govern the kingdom of Israel? arise, and eat bread, and let thine heart be merry: I will give thee the vineyard of Naboth the Jezreelite" (1 Kings 21:7).

Ahab knew Jezebel well enough to know that she would do her best, or her worst, to keep her wicked promise. So, as a turtle that has been sluggish in the cold winter's mud begins to move when the spring sunshine warms the mud, Ahab crawled out of the slime of his sulks—somewhat as a snake arouses and uncoils from winter sleep. Then Jezebel doubtless tickled him under the chin with her bejeweled fingers or kissed him peckingly on the cheek with her lips screwed in a tight knot, and said: "There now! Smile! And eat something. I will get thee the vineyard of Naboth the Jezreelite!"

Now, let us ask, who can so inspire a man to noble purposes as a noble woman? And who can so thoroughly degrade a man as a wife of unworthy tendencies? Back of the statement, "And Ahab the son of Omri did evil in the sight of the LORD above all that were before him" (1 Kings 16:30), and back of what Elijah spoke, "Thou hast sold thyself to work evil in the sight of the LORD" (1 Kings 21:20), is the statement explaining both the other statements: "Whom Jezebel his wife stirred up." She was the polluted reservoir from which the streams of his own iniquity found mighty increase. She was the poisonous pocket from which his cruel fangs fed. She was the sulphurous pit wherein the fires of his own iniquity found fuel for intenser burning. She was the devil's grindstone which furnished sharpening for his weapons of wickedness.

Search the pages of the Bible all you will; study history all you please. And you will find one truth that stands out above some other truths. What is that truth? The truth that the spiritual life of a nation, city, town, school, church, home never rises any higher than the spiritual life of women. When women sag morally and spiritually, men sag morally and spiritually. When women slump morally and spiritually, men slip morally and spiritually. When women take the downward road men travel with them. When women are lame morally and spiritually, men limp morally and spiritually. The degeneracy of womanhood helps the decay of manhood.

Yes—we ask again—who can so degrade a man as a woman of wicked tendencies and purposes? Is not a woman without spiritual religion and love of God in her heart like a rainbow without color—like a strong poisoned well from which the thirsty drink—like a heated stove whose heat is infection—like kissing lips spread with deadly poison?

What a tragedy when any woman thinks more of paint than purity, of vulgarity than virtue, of pearls than principles of adornment with righteous adoration, of hose and hats than holiness, of dress than duty, of mirrors than manners! What a tragedy when any woman sacrifices decency on the altar of degradation—visualizing the slimy, the tawdry, the tinseled!

We ask—just here—some questions. Who dominated the papacy in its most shameful days? Lucrezia Borgia—a woman. Who really ordered the massacre of Saint Bartholomew's day? Catherine de Medici—a woman. Who breathed fury through Robespierre in those dark and bloody days in France when the guillotine was chopping off the heads of the royalty? A woman—determined, devilish, dominant! Who caused Samson to have his eyes punched out and to be a prisoner of the Philistines, after he had been a judge in Israel for twenty years? Delilah—a woman! Who caused David to stake his crown for a caress? Bathsheba—a woman. Who danced Herod into hell? Herodias—a woman! Who was like a heavy chain around the neck of Governor Felix for life or death, for time and eternity? Drusilla—a woman! Who, by lying and diabolical stratagem, sent the spotless Joseph to jail because he refused her dirty, improper proposal? Potiphar's wife. Who suggested to Haman that he build a high gallows on which to hang Mordecai, the Jew? Zeresh—a woman—his wife! Who told Job in the midst of his calamities, financial and physical, to curse God and die? A woman—his wife. Who ruined the career of Charles Stewart Parnell and delayed Home Rule for Ireland in the good days of good Queen Victoria? Kitty O'Shea—a woman. Who caused Anthony to throw away the world at the battle of Actium and follow the enchantress of the Nile back to Egypt? The enchantress herself, Cleopatra—a woman—the lovely serpent coiled on the throne of the Ptolemies.

So also it was a woman, a passionate and ambitious idolatress, even Jezebel, who mastered Ahab. Take the stirring crimes of any age, and at the bottom, more or less consciously concerned, the world almost invariably finds a woman. Only God Almighty knows the full story of the foul plots hatched by women.

But we know enough to say that some of the foulest plots that have been hatched out of Satan's incubator were hatched out of eggs placed therein by women's hands.

But let me say, incidentally, if women have mastered men for evil, they have also mastered them for good—and we gladly make declaration that some of the fairest and most fragrant flowers that grow in the garden of God and some of the sweetest and most luscious fruit that ripens in God's spiritual orchards are there because of woman's faith, woman's love, woman's prayer, woman's virtue, woman's tears, woman's devotion to Christ.

But as for Ahab, it was Jezebel who stirred him up to more and mightier wickedness than his own wicked mind could conceive or his own wicked hand could execute.

Let us come to the next terrible scene in this tragedy of sin. The next scene is

A Message Meaning Murder

"She wrote letters."

Jezebel wrote letters to the elders of Jezreel. And in these letters she made definite and subtle declaration that some terrible sin had been committed in their city, for which it was needful that a fast should be proclaimed in order to avert the wrath of heaven.

> So she wrote letters in Ahab's name, and sealed them with his seal, and sent the letters unto the elders and to the nobles that were in his city, dwelling with Naboth. And she wrote in the letters, saying, Proclaim a fast, and set Naboth on high among the people: and set two men, sons of Belial, before him, to bear witness against him, saying, Thou didst blaspheme God and the king. And then carry him out, and stone him, that he may die (1 Kings 21:8–10).

This letter, with cynical disregard of decency, was a hideous mockery in the name of religion. Once get the recusant citizen accused of blasphemy, and, by a divine law, the property of the blasphemer and rebel went to the crown. "Justice! How many traitors to sacred truth have dragged the innocent to destruction!"

Surely black ink never wrote a fouler plot or death scheme on white paper since writing was known among men. Every drop had in it the adder's poison. Every syllable of every word of every line of every sentence was full of hate toward him who had done only good continually. Every letter of every syllable was but the thread which, united with other threads, made the hangman's noose for him who had not changed his righteous principles for the whim of a king. The whole letter was a diabolical death warrant.

The letters being written, must be sealed and the sealing was done, as all these matters of letter writing and sealing were done, by rubbing ink on the seal, moistening the paper, and pressing the seal thereon. And when Jezebel had finished with her iniquitous pen, she asked Ahab for his signet ring; with that ring she affixed the royal seal. She sealed the letters with Ahab's ring (1 Kings 21:8). When Ahab gave it to her he knew it meant crime of some sort, but he asked no questions. Moreover, Jezebel's deeds showed that when she went down to market, as it were, she would have in her basket a nice vineyard for her husband when she returned. She said to herself: This man Naboth has refused my honorable lord on religious grounds, and by all the gods of Baal, I will get him yet on these very same grounds. She understood perfectly the passion of a devout Jew for a public fast; and she knew that nothing would keep the Jews away. Every Jew and every member of his household would be there.

"Proclaim a fast!" Fasting has even been a sign of humiliation before God, of humbling one's self in the dust before the "high and lofty One that inhabiteth eternity." The idea in calling for a fast was clearly to declare that the community was under the anger of God on account of a grave crime committed by one of its members, which crime is to be exposed and punished. Then, too, the fast involved a cessation of work, a holiday, so that the citizens would have time to attend the public gathering.

"Set Naboth on high!" "On high" meant before the bar of justice, not in the seat of honor. "On high" meant in the seat of the accused, and not in the seat to be desired. "On high" meant that Naboth was put where every eye could watch him closely and keenly observe his bearing under the accusation. "And set two men, base fellows, before him." How illegal she was in bringing about his death in a legal way! For the law required two witnesses in all cases where the punishment was death. "At the mouth of two witnesses, or three witnesses, shall he . . . be put to death" (Deut. 17:6). The witnesses required by Jezebel were men of no character, men who would take bribes and swear to any lie for gain.

And let them "bear witness against him"! In other words, put him out of the way by judicial murder, not by private assassination. "And then carry him out, and stone him, that he may die." A criminal was not to be executed within a city, as that would defile it! Thus Christ was crucified outside the walls of Jerusalem! We see that Jezebel took it for granted that Naboth would be condemned.

And so one day, while Naboth worked in his vineyard, the letters came down to Jezreel. And one evening, while Naboth talked at the cottage door with his sons or neighbors, the message meaning murder was known to the elders of the city. And that night, while he slept with the wife of his bosom, the hounds of death let loose from the kennels of hell by the jewel-adorned fingers of a king's daughter and a king's wife were close on his heels. The message meaning murder was known to many but not to him, until they came and told him that a fast had been proclaimed—proclaimed because God had been offended at some crime and that His wrath must be appeased and the threatening anger turned away, and he himself, all unconscious of any offense toward God or the king, was to be set in the place of the accused, even "on high among the people," to be tried as a conspicuous criminal.

Consider now

The Fatal Fast

"They proclaimed a fast."

And what concern they must have created in the household of Naboth, when they knew that Naboth was to be "set on high," even in the "seat of the accused," even before the bar of "justice," because of a ferocious message calling religion in to attest a lie. And what excitement there was in the city when, with fawning readiness to carry out her vile commands, the elders and nobles "fastened the minds" of the people upon the fast—proclaimed as if some great calamity were overhanging the city for their sins like a black cloud portending a storm, and proclaimed as if something must be done at once to avert the doom. Curious throngs hurried to the fast to see him who had been accused of the crime which made necessary the appeasing of the threatening wrath of an angered God.

Yes, the rulers of Jezreel, "either in dread of offending one whose revenge they knew was terrible, or eager to do a service to one to whom in temporal matters they were so largely indebted, or moved with envy against their own iniquity, carried out her instructions to the letter." They were ready and efficient tools in her hands. No doubt she had tested their character as her "butcher boys" in the slaughter of the prophets of the Lord (1 Kings 18:4, 13).

And they did! "And there came in two men, children of Belial, and sat down before him" (1 Kings 21:13). Satan's hawks ready to bring death to God's harmless sparrow! Satan's eagles ready to bury their cruel talons in God's innocent dove. Satan's bloody wolves ready to kill God's lamb! Satan's boars ready with keen tusks to rip God's stag to shreds! Reckless and depraved professional perjurers they were! "And the men of Belial witnessed against him, even against Naboth, in the presence of the people, saying, Naboth did blaspheme God and the king" (1 Kings 21:13).

Then strong hands jerked Naboth out of the seat of the accused. Doubtless muttering curses the while, they dragged him out from among the throngs of people, while children screamed and cried, while women shrieked in terror, while men moved in confusion and murmured in consternation. They dragged him roughly to a place outside the walls of the city and with stones they beat his body to the ground. Naboth fell to the ground as a lily by hailstones beaten to earth, as a stately cedar uprooted by furious storm. His head by stones is crushed, as eggs crushed by the heel of a giant. His legs are splintered! His arms are broken! His ribs are crushed. Bones stick out from the mass of human flesh as fingers of ivory from pots of red paint. Brains, emptied from his skull, are scattered about. Blood splatters like crimson rain. Naboth's eyes roll in sockets of blood. His tongue between broken jaws becomes still. His mauled body becomes—at last—still. His last gasp is a sigh. Naboth is dead—dead for cursing God and the king as many were led to believe!

And we learn from 2 Kings 9:26, that by the savage law of those days his innocent sons were involved in his overthrow. They, too, that they might not claim the inheritance, were slain. And Naboth's property, left without heirs, reverted to the crown.

Thus it came to pass that in an orderly fashion, in the name of religion and in the name of the king, Naboth really fell, not by the king's hand, but by the condemnation of his fellow citizens. Yes, the old-fashioned conservatism of Naboth was, in the judgment of many, sorely out of place in that "progressive" state of society. No doubt Naboth's righteous austerity had made him extremely unpopular in many ways in "progressive Jezreel." And since Jezebel carried out her purpose in a perfectly legal and orderly way and in a "wonderfully" democratic manner, we see a fine picture of autocracy working by democratic methods. And when these "loyally patriotic citizens" of Jezreel had left the bodies of Naboth and his sons to be devoured by the wild dogs which prowled after nightfall in and around the city, they sent and told Queen Jezebel that her orders had been bloodily and completely obeyed! "Then they sent to Jezebel, saying, Naboth is stoned, and is dead" (1 Kings 21:14).

I do not know where Jezebel was when she received the news of Naboth's death. Maybe she was out on the lawn watching the fountains splash. Maybe she was in the sun parlor, or somewhere listening to the musicians thrum on their instruments. But, if I judge this painted human viper by her nature, I say she received the tragic news with devilish delight, with jubilant merriment. What was it to her that yonder, over twenty miles away, sat a little woman who the night before had her husband but who now washed his crushed and ghastly face with her tears? What did it matter to her that in Jezreel only yesterday her sons ran to her at her call but today were mangled in death? What did it matter to her that outside the city walls the dogs licked the blood of a godly husband? What mattered it to her that Jehovah God has been defied, His commandments broken, His altars splattered with pagan mud, His holy Name profaned? What mattered it to her that the worship of God had been dishonored? What did she care if a wife, tragically widowed by murder, walked life's way in loneliness? What did she care that there was lamentation and grief and great mourning, "Rachel weeping for her children because they were not"? What did she care if justice had been outraged just so she had gotten the little plot of land close by their palace, within which was evil dirt with diadem? Nothing! Did pang grip her heart because innocent blood had been shed? Just as well as if the ravenous lion mourns over the lamb it devours.

Trippingly, as a gay dancer, she hurried to where Ahab sat. With profuse caresses and words glib with joy she told him the "good" news. She had about her the triumphant manner of one who has accomplished successfully what others had not dared attempt. Her "tryout" in getting the vineyard was a decided "triumph." She had "pulled the stunt." She had been "brave" and "wise"—and because of this her husband now could arise and hie him down to the vineyard and call it his own.

In her words and manner there was jubilant elation bordering on the satanic: Arise! Get thee down and take possession of the vineyard of Naboth! I told thee I would get his vineyard for thee. And I got for nothing what thou wast going to give a better vineyard for!

> And it came to pass, when Jezebel heard that Naboth was stoned, and was dead, that Jezebel said to Ahab, Arise, take possession of the vineyard of Naboth the Jezreelite, which he refused to give thee for money: for Naboth is not alive, but dead (1 Kings 21:15).

It was the plot hatched in her own mind and it was her hand, her lily-white hand, her queen's hand, that wrote the letters that made this tragic statement true.

The next scene in this tragedy of "Payday—Someday" is

The Visit To The Vineyard

"Ahab rose up to go down to the vineyard."

How Jezebel must have paraded with pride before Ahab when she went with tidings that the vineyard which he wanted to buy was now his for nothing! How keen must have been the sarcasm of her attitude when she made it known by word and manner that she had succeeded where he failed—and at less cost! How gloatingly victorious were the remarks which she made which kept him warmly reminded that she had kept her "sacred" promise! What a love fabric, stained and dyed red with Naboth's blood, she spread before him for his "comfort" from the loom of her evil machinations!

> And it came to pass, when Ahab heard that Naboth was dead, that Ahab rose up to go down to the vineyard of Naboth the Jezreelite, to take possession of it (1 Kings 21:16).

Ahab rose up to go down—from Samaria to Jezreel. He gave orders to his royal wardrobe keeper to get out his king's clothes, because he had a little "business" trip to make to look over some property that had come to him by the shrewdness of his wife in the real estate market!

Yes, Naboth, the good man who "feared the Lord," is dead; and Ahab expressed no condemnation of this awful conspiracy, culminating in such a tragic horror. Though afraid or restrained by his conscience from committing murder himself, he had no scruple in availing himself of the results of such crime when perpetrated by another. He flattered himself that, by the splendid genius of his queen in bloody matters, he, though having no part in the crime which did Naboth to death, might, as well as another, "receive the benefit of his dying."

And you will notice just here that not one noble or elder had divulged the terrible secret which had given the semblance of legality to atrocious villainy. And, Ahab, rejoicing in the bloody garment woven on the loom of his wife's evil machinations, gave orders to those in charge of livery stables to get ready his royal chariot for an unexpected trip. Jehu and Bidkar, the royal charioteers, make ready the great horses such as kings had in those days. Jehu was the speed-breaking driver of his day, known as the one who drove furiously. The gilded chariot is drawn forth. The fiery horses are harnessed and to the king's chariot hitched. The outriders, in gorgeous garments dressed, saddle their horses and make ready to accompany the king in something of military state. Then, amid the clatter of prancing hoofs and the loud breathing of the chariot horses—eager-eyes, alert, strong-muscled, bellows-lunged, stouthearted, and agile of feet—Jehu drives the horses and the chariot up to the palace steps. Out from the palace doors, with Jezebel walking, almost strutting, proudly and gaily at his side, comes Ahab. Down the steps he goes while Jezebel, perhaps, waves a bejeweled hand to him or speaks a "sweet" good-bye. Bidkar opens the chariot door. Ahab steps in. Then, with the crack of his whip or a sharp command by word of mouth, Jehu sends the great horses on their way—away from the palace steps, away from the palace grounds, away through the gates, away, accompanied by the outriders, away down the road to Jezreel!

Where is God? Where is God? Is He blind that He cannot see? Is He deaf that He cannot hear? Is He dumb that He cannot speak? Is He paralyzed that He cannot move? Where is God? Well, wait a minute, and we shall see.

Over there in the palace Jezebel said to Ahab her husband: "Arise! Get thee down and take possession of the vineyard of Naboth." And over in the wilderness way, out where the tall cedars waved against the moon like green plumes against a silver shield, out where the only music of the night was the weird call of whippoorwill and the cough of coyote and the howl of wolf, out there God had an eagle-eyed, hairy, stouthearted prophet, a great physical and spiritual athlete, Elijah. "And the word of the LORD came to Elijah." And God said to Elijah: "Arise, go down."

Over here, in the palace, Jezebel said to Ahab: "Arise, get thee down!" And out there, near Carmel, God said to Elijah: "Arise!" I am so glad that I live in a universe where, when the devil has his Ahab to whom he can say, "Arise," God has His Elijah to whom He can say, "Arise!"

> And the word of the LORD came to Elijah the Tishbite, saying, Arise, go down to meet Ahab king of Israel, which is in Samaria: behold, he is in the vineyard of Naboth, whither he is gone down to possess it. And thou shalt speak unto him, saying, Thus saith the LORD, Hast thou killed, and also taken possession? And thou shalt speak unto him, saying, thus saith the LORD, In the place where dogs licked the blood of Naboth shall dogs lick thy blood, even thine (1 Kings 21:17–19).

As Ahab goes down to Jezreel, the voice of Jehu, as he restrains the fiery horses, or the lash of his whip as he urges them on, attracts the attention of the grazing cattle in adjacent pasture land. The sound of clanking hoofs of cantering horses resounds in every glen by the roadway. The gilded chariot catches the light of the sun and reflects it brightly, but he who rides therein is unmindful of the bloodstains on the ground where Naboth died. Dust clouds arise from the chariot's wheels and wild winds blow them across the fields where the plowman or the reaper wonders who goes so swiftly along the highway.

The neighing steeds announce to all that Ahab's royal horses tire not in carrying him down from Samaria to Jezreel. And soon many know that the chariot carried the king who was going down to possess what had reverted to the crown, even the vineyard of Naboth, which Naboth refused to sell to him. Would the "game" be worth the "candle"? Would Ahab learn that sin buys pleasure at the price of peace? We shall see—and that right soon!

And that brings us to the other scene in his tragedy of "Payday—Someday." It is

The Alarming Appearance

"The word of the LORD came to Elijah."

The journey of twenty-odd miles from Samaria to Jezreel is over. Jehu brings the horses to a stop outside the gate to the vineyard. The horses stretch their necks trying to get slack on the reins. They have stood well the furious pace at which they have been driven. Around the rim of their harness is the foam of their sweat. On their flanks are, perhaps, the marks of Jehu's whip. They breathe as though their great lungs were a tireless bellows. The outriders line up in something of military formation. The hands of ready servants open the gate to the vineyard. Bidkar opens the chariot door. And Ahab steps out in Naboth's vineyard. There, no doubt, he sees, in the soft soil, Naboth's footprints. Close by, doubtless, the smaller footprints of his wife he sees. Naboth is dead, and the coveted vineyard is now Ahab's through the "gentle scheming" of the queen of his house. Perhaps Ahab, as he walks into the vineyard, see Naboth's pruning hook among the vines. Or he notices the fine trellis work which Naboth's hands had fastened together for the growing vines. Perhaps, in a corner of the vineyard is a seat where Naboth and his sons rested after the day's toil, or a well where sparkling waters refreshed the thirsty or furnished water for the vine in time of drout.

Ahab walks around his newly gotten vineyard. The rows of vines glisten in the sunlight. Maybe a breeze moves the leaves on the vines. Ahab admires trellis and cluster. As he walks, he plans how he will have the royal gardener to pull up those vines and plant cucumbers, squash, garlic, onions, cabbage, and other vegetables that he may have his "garden of herbs."

And while Ahab strolls among the vines that Naboth tended, what is it that appears? Snarling wild beasts? No. Black clouds full of threatening storm? No, not that. Flaming lightning which dazzles him? No. War chariots of his ancient enemies rumbling along the road? No. An oncoming flood sweeping things before it? No; not a flood. A tornado goring the earth? No. A huge serpent threatening to encircle him and crush his bones in its deadly coils? No, not a serpent. What then? What alarmed Ahab so? Let us follow him and see.

As Ahab goes walking through the rows of vines, he begins to plan how he will have that vineyard arranged by his royal gardener, how flowers will be here and vegetables yonder, and herbs there. As he converses with himself, suddenly a shadow falls across his path. Quick as a flash Ahab whirls on his heels, and there, before him, stands Elijah, prophet of the living God. Elijah's cheeks are swarthy; his eye is keen and piercing; like coals of fire, his eyes burn with righteous indignation in their sockets; his bosom heaves; his head is held high. His only weapon is a staff: his only robe a sheepskin, and a leather girdle about his loins. Like an apparition from the other world, like Banquo's ghost at Macbeth's feast, Elijah, with suddenness terrifying, stands before Ahab. Ahab had not seen Elijah for five years. Ahab thought Elijah had been cowed and silenced by Jezebel, but now the prophet confronts him with his death-warrant from the Lord God Almighty.

To Ahab there is an eternity of agony in the few moments they stand thus, face to face, eye to eye, soul to soul! His voice is hoarse, like the cry of a hunted animal. He trembles like a hunted stag before the mouths of fierce hounds. Suddenly his face goes white. His lips quiver. He had gone to take possession of a vineyard, coveted for a garden of herbs; and there he is face to face with righteousness, face to face with honor, face to face with judgment. The vineyard, with the sun shining upon it now, is as black as if it were part of the midnight which has gathered in judgment. Like Poe's raven "his soul from out that shadow shall be lifted—nevermore."

"And Ahab said to Elijah, Hast thou found me, O mine enemy?" (1 Kings 21:20) and Elijah, without a tremor in his voice, his eyes burning their way into Ahab's guilty soul, answered: "I have found thee: because thou has sold thyself to work evil in the sight of the LORD." Then, with every word a thunderbolt, and every sentence a withering denunciation, Elijah continued:

> Hast thou killed, and also taken possession? . . . Thus saith the LORD, In the place where dogs licked the blood of Naboth shall dogs lick thy blood, even thine. . . . Behold, I will bring evil upon thee, and will take away thy posterity . . . and will make thine house like the house of Jeroboam the son of Nebat, and like the house of Baasha the son of Ahijah, for the provocation wherewith thou hast provoked me to anger, and made Israel to sin! (1 Kings 21:19, 21–22).

And then, plying other words mercilessly like a terrible scourge to the cringing Ahab, Elijah said:

> And of Jezebel also spake the LORD, saying, The dogs shall eat Jezebel by the wall of Jezreel. Him that dieth of Ahab in the city the dogs shall eat: and him that dieth in the field shall the fowls of the air eat (1 Kings 21:23–24).

And, with these words, making Ahab to cower as one cowers and recoils from a hissing adder, finding Naboth's vineyard to be haunted with ghosts and the clusters thereof to be full of blood, Elijah went his way—as was his custom so suddenly to appear and so quickly to disappear.

Ahab had sold himself for nought, as did Achan for a burial robe and a useless ingot, as did Judas for thirty pieces of silver which so burned his palms and so burned his conscience and so burned his soul that he found relief in the noose at the rope's end. And when Ahab got back in the chariot to go back to Jezebel—the vile toad who squatted upon the throne to be gain with the beautiful adder coiled upon the throne—the hoofs of the horses pounding the road pounded into his guilty soul Elijah's words: "Some day—the dogs will lick thy blood! Some day the dogs will eat Jezebel—by the ramparts of Jezreel." God had spoken! Would it come to pass?

And now we come to the last scene in this tragedy—"Payday—Someday." It is

Payday Itself

Did God mean what He said? Or was He playing a prank on royalty? Did payday come? "Payday—Someday" is written in the constitution of God's universe. The retributive providence of God is a reality as certainly as night follows day, because sin carries in itself the seed of its own fatal penalty.

Dr. Meyer said: "According to God's constitution of the world, the wrongdoer will be abundantly punished." The fathers sow the wind and the children reap the whirlwind. One generation labors to scatter tares, and the next generation reaps tares and retribution immeasurable. To the individual who goes not the direction God points, a terrible payday comes. To the nation which forgets God, payday will come in the awful realization of the truth that the "nations which forget God shall be turned into hell." When nations trample on the principles of the Almighty, the result is that the world is beaten with many stripes. We have seen nations slide into Gehenna—and the smoke of their torment has gone up before our eyes day and night.

To the home that has no room for the Christ, death and grave clothes are certain. "Ichabod" will be written about the church that soft-pedals on unpleasant truth or that stands not unwaveringly for "the faith once delivered"—and it will acknowledge its retribution in that it will become "a drifting sepulcher manned by a frozen crew."

A man can prostitute God's holy Name to profane lips if he will, but he is forewarned as to the payday in the words: "The LORD will not hold him guiltless that taketh his name in vain" (Exod. 20:7).

A man can, if he will, follow the way of some wicked woman; but God leaves him not without warning as to the payday, in the words:

> He goeth after her straightway, as an ox goeth to the slaughter, or as a fool to the correction of the stocks; till a dart strike through his liver; as a bird hasteth to the snare, and knoweth not that it is for his life. . . . For she hath cast down many wounded: yea, many strong men have been slain by her. Her house is the way to hell, going down to the chambers of death (Prov. 7:22–23, 26–27).

People can drink booze, if they will, and offer the damnable bottle to others, if they will, but the certainty of "Payday—Someday" is read in the words: "No drunkard shall inherit the kingdom of God," and in the words: "At the last it biteth like a serpent, and stingeth like an adder." The certainty of "Payday—Someday" for all who regard not God or man is set forth in the words of an unknown poet:

> You'll pay. The knowledge of your acts will weigh
> Heavier on your mind each day.
> The more you climb, the more you gain,
> The more you'll feel the nagging strain.
> Success will cower at the threat
> Of retribution. Fear will fret
> Your peace and bleed you for the debt;
> Conscience collects from every crook
> More than the worth of what he took,
> You only thought you got away
> But in the night you'll pay and pay.

Churchill expressed the certainty of God's retributive justice when, speaking of Mussolini, he said:

> Mussolini is swept into the maelstrom of his own making. The flames of war he kindled burn himself. He and his people are taking the stinging lash of the whip they applied to Ethiopia and Albania. They pay for Fascist sins with defeat, despair, death. Mussolini's promise of life like a lion turned into the existence of a beaten cur!

Years before the statesman, Winston Churchill, spoke these words, Ralph Waldo Emerson in his *Compensation* wrote:

> Crime and punishment grow out of one stem. Punishment is a fruit that unsuspected ripens within the flower of the pleasure that concealed it. Cause and effect, means and ends, seed and fruit, can not

be severed, for the effect already blooms in the cause. The end pre-exists in the means—the fruit in the seed.

Paul Lawrence Dunbar showed wisdom as great as the wisdom of Churchill and a knowledge of Nature's laws as great as Emerson's knowledge when he wrote the autobiography of many individual sinners in these poetic and potent words:

This is the price I pay—
Just for one riotous day—
Years of regret and of grief,
And sorrow without relief.

Suffer it I will, my friend,
Suffer it until the end,
Until the grave shall give relief.
Small was the thing I bought,
Small was the thing at best,
Small was the debt, I thought,
But, O God!—the interest.

All these statements are but verification of Bible truth:

Whoso diggeth a pit shall fall therein: and he that rolleth a stone, it will return upon him (Prov. 26:27).

Therefore shall they eat of the fruit of their own way, and be filled with their own devices. For the turning away of the simple shall slay them, and the prosperity of fools shall destroy them (Prov. 1:31–32).

Even as I have seen, they that plow iniquity, and sow wickedness, reap the same (Job 4:8).

For they have sown the wind, and they shall reap the whirlwind (Hos. 8:7).

The gods are just—and of our voices make instruments to scourge us.

When I was pastor of the First Baptist Church of New Orleans, all that I preached and taught was sent out over the radio. In my "fan mail" I received letters from a young man who called himself "Chief of the Kangaroo Court." Many nasty, critical things he said. Sometimes he wrote a nice line—and a nice line was, in all the vulgar things he wrote, like a gardenia in a garbage can. One day I received a telephone call from a nurse in the Charity Hospital of New Orleans. It was about this fellow who so often dipped his pen in slop, who seldom thrust his pen into nectar. She said: "Pastor, there is a young man down here whose name we do not know, who will not tell us his name. All he will tell us is that he is chief of the Kangaroo Court. He is going to die. He says that you are the only preacher in New Orleans that he has ever heard—and he has never seen you. He wants to see you. Will you come down?" "Yes," I replied. And I quit what I was doing and hurried down to the hospital.

The young nurse met me at the entrance to the charity ward and took me in. A glance around showed me cots on the north side, cots on the south side, beds on the east side and beds on the west side—and clusters of cots in the center of the huge ward. In a place by itself, somewhat removed from all other cots and beds, was a bed on which lay a young man about nineteen or twenty years of age—big of frame, though the ravages of disease had brought a slenderness. The nurse, with little ado, introduced me to the young man, saying: "This, sir, is the chief of the Kangaroo Court."

I found myself looking into two of the wildest eyes I have ever seen. As kindly as I could, I spoke, saying "Hello." "Howdy do?" he answered in a voice that was a discourteous and furious snarl—more like the voice of a male wolf than the voice of a rational man. "Is there something I can do for you?" I asked as kindly as I could speak.

"No. Nothing! Not a thing. Nothin' 'tall!—unless you throw my body to the buzzards when I am dead—if the buzzards will have it!" he said, with half a shout and with a sort of fierce resentment that made me wonder why he had ever sent for me.

Then his voice lost some of the snarl—and he spoke again. "I sent for you, sir, because I want you to tell these young fellows here something for me. I sent for you because I know you go up and down the land and talk to many young people. And I want you to tell 'em, and tell 'em every chance you get, that the devil pays only in counterfeit money."

Oh! I wish I could tell all men and women and all boys and girls everywhere to believe the truth that Satan always pays in counterfeit money, that all his pearls are paste pearls, that the nectar he offers is poisoned through and through. Oh, that men would learn the truth and be warned by the truth that if they eat the devil's corn, he will choke them with the cob.

I stayed with this young man nearly two hours. Occasionally he spoke. There was a desperate earnestness in the young man's voice as he looked at me with wild eyes where terror was enthroned. Afterwhile I saw those eyes become as though they were glass as he gazed at the ceiling above. I saw his huge lean chest heave like a bellows. I felt his hand clutch at mine as a drowning man would grab for a rope. I held his hand. I heard the raucous gurgle in his throat. Then he became quiet—like a forest when the cyclone is long gone.

When he died, the little nurse called me to her, excitedly. "Come here!" she called.

"What do you want, child?" I asked.

"I want to wash your hands!" She meant she wanted to wash my hands with a disinfectant. Then she added—with something of fright in her words, "It's dangerous to touch him!"

The devil had paid the young man off in counterfeit money.

But what about Ahab? Did payday come for him? Yes. Consider how. Three years went by. Ahab was still king. And I dare say that during those three years Jezebel had reminded him that they were eating herbs out of Naboth's vineyard. I can hear her say something like this as they sat at the king's table: "Ahab, help yourself to these herbs. I thought Elijah said the dogs were going to lick your blood. I guess his dogs lost their noses and lost the trail."

But I think that during those three years, Ahab never heard a dog bark that he did not jump.

One day Jehoshaphat, king of Judah, visited Ahab. The Bible tells us what took place—what was said, what was done:

> And the king of Israel said unto his servants, Know ye that Ramoth in Gilead is ours, and we be still, and take it not out of the hand of the king of Syria? And he said unto Jehoshaphat, Wilt thou go with

> me to battle to Ramoth-gilead? And Jehoshaphat said to the king of Israel, I am as thou art, my people as thy people, my horses as thy horses (1 Kings 22:3–4).
> So the king of Israel and Jehoshaphat the king of Judah went up to Ramoth-gilead" (1 Kings 22:29).

Ahab, after Jehoshaphat had promised to go with him, in his heart was afraid, and had sad forebodings, dreadful premonitions, horrible fears. Remembering the withering words of Elijah three years before, he disguised himself—put armor on his body and covered this armor with ordinary citizen's clothes.

> And the king of Israel said unto Jehoshaphat, I will disguise myself, and enter into the battle; but put thou on thy robes. And the king of Israel disguised himself, and went into the battle (1 Kings 22:30).

The Syrian general had given orders to slay only the king of Israel—Ahab.

> But the king of Syria commanded his thirty and two captains that had rule over his chariots, saying, Fight neither with small nor great, save only with the king of Israel (1 Kings 22:31).

Jehoshaphat was not injured, although he wore his royal clothes.

> And it came to pass, when the captains of the chariots saw Jehoshaphat, that they said, Surely it is the king of Israel. And they turned aside to fight against him: and Jehoshaphat cried out. And it came to pass, when the captains of the chariots perceived that it was not the king of Israel, that they turned back from pursuing him (1 Kings 22:32, 33).

While war steeds neighed and war chariots rumbled and shields clashed on shields and arrows whizzed and spears were thrown and swords were wielded, a death-carrying arrow, shot by an aimless and nameless archer, found the crack in Ahab's armor.

> And a certain man drew a bow at a venture, and smote the king of Israel between the joints of the harness: wherefore he said unto the driver of his chariot, turn thine hand, and carry me out of the host; for I am wounded. And the battled increased that day: and the king was stayed up in his chariot against the Syrians, and died at even: and

> the blood ran out of the wound into the midst of the chariot . . . And one washed the chariot in the pool of Samaria; and the dogs licked up his blood; and they washed his armour; according unto the word of the LORD which he spake (1 Kings 22:34–35, 38).

Thus we learn that no man can evade God's laws with impunity. All of God's laws are their own executioners. They have strange penalties annexed. Stolen waters are sweet. But every ounce of sweetness makes a pound of nausea. Nature keeps books pitilessly. Man's credit with her is good. But Nature collects. And there is no land to which you can flee and escape her bailiffs. Every day her bloodhounds track down the men and women who owe her.

But what about Jezebel? Did her payday come? Yes—after twenty years. After Ahab's death, after the dogs had licked his blood, she virtually ruled the kingdom. But I think that she went into the temple of Baal on occasions and prayed her god Baal to protect her from Elijah's hounds.

Elijah had been taken home to heaven without the touch of the deathdew upon his brow. Elisha had succeeded him.

> And Elisha the prophet called one of the children of the prophets, and said unto him, Gird up thy loins, and take this box of oil in thine hand, and go to Ramoth-gilead: and when thou comest thither, look out there Jehu the son of Jehoshaphat the son of nimshi, and go in, and make him arise up from among his brethren, and carry him to an inner chamber; then take the box of oil and pour it on his head, and say, Thus saith the LORD, I have anointed thee king over Israel. Then open the door and flee, and tarry not. So the young man, even the young man the prophet, went to Ramoth-gilead. And when he came, behold, the captains of the host were sitting; and he said, I have an errand to thee, O captain. And Jehu said, Unto which of all us? And he said, To thee, O captain. And he arose, and went into the house; and he poured the oil on his head, and said unto him, Thus saith the LORD God of Israel, I have anointed thee king over the people of the LORD, even over Israel. And thou shalt smite the house of Ahab thy master, that I may avenge the blood of my servants the prophets, and the blood of all the servants of the LORD, at the hand of Jezebel. . . . And I will make the house of Ahab like the house of Jeroboam the son of Nebat, and like the house of Baasha the son of Ahijah: and the dogs shall eat Jezebel in the portion of

> Jezreel, and there shall be none to bury her. And he opened the door, and fled. (2 Kings 9:1–7, 9–10)

Jehu was just the man for such an occasion—furious in his anger, rapid in his movements, unscrupulous, yet zealous to uphold the law of Moses.

> Then Jehu came forth to the servants of his lord: and one said unto him, Is all well? wherefore came this mad fellow to thee? And he said unto them, Ye know the man, and his communication. And they said, It is false; tell us now. And he said, Thus and thus spake he to me, saying, Thus saith the LORD, I have anointed thee king over Israel. Then they hasted, and took every man his garment, and put in under him on the top of the stairs, and blew with trumpets, saying, Jehu is king (2 Kings 9:11–13).

Mounting his chariot, commanding and taking with him a company of his most reliable soldiers, furiously did he drive nearly sixty miles to Jezreel.

> So Jehu rode in a chariot, and went to Jezreel; for Joram lay there. And Ahaziah king of Judah was come down to see Joram. And there stood a watchman on the tower in Jezreel, and he spied the company of Jehu as he came, and said, I see a company. And Joram said, Take an horseman, and send to meet them, and let him say, Is it peace? So there went one on horseback to meet him, and said, Thus saith the king, Is it peace? And Jehu said, What hast thou to do with peace? turn thee behind me. And the watchman told, saying, The messenger came to them, but he cometh not again. Then he sent out a second on horseback, which came to them, and said, Thus saith the king, Is it peace? And Jehu answered, What hast thou to do with peace? turn thee behind me. And the watchman told, saying, He came even unto them, and cometh not again: and the driving is like the driving of Jehu the son of Nimshi; for he driveth furiously. And Joram said, Make ready. And his chariot was made ready. And Joram king of Israel and Ahaziah king of Judah went out, each in his chariot, and they went out against Jehu, and met him in the portion of Naboth the Jezreelite. And it came to pass, when Joram saw Jehu, that he said, Is it peace, Jehu? And he answered, What peace, so long as the whoredoms of thy mother Jezebel and her witchcrafts are so many? And Joram turned his hands, and fled, and said to Ahaziah, There is treachery, O Ahaziah. And Jehu drew a bow with his full strength, and smote Jehoram between his arms, and the arrow went

> out at his heart, and he sunk down in his chariot. Then said Jehu to Bidkar his captain, Take up, and cast him in the portion of the field of Naboth the Jezreelite: for remember how that, when I and thou rode together after Ahab his father, the LORD laid this burden upon him; surely I have seen yesterday the blood of Naboth, and the blood of his sons, saith the Lord; and I will requite thee in this plat, saith the LORD. Now therefore take and cast him into the plat of ground, according to the word of the LORD" (2 Kings 9:16–26).

"And when Jehu was come to Jezreel, Jezebel heard of it." Pause! Who is Jehu? He is the one who, twenty years before the events of this chapter from which we quote, rode down with Ahab to take Naboth's vineyard, the one who throughout those twenty years never forgot those withering words of terrible denunciation which Elijah spoke. And who is Jezebel? Oh! the very same who wrote the letters and had Naboth put to death. And what is Jezreel? The place where Naboth had his vineyard and where Naboth died, his life pounded out by stones in the hands of ruffians. "And when Jehu was come to Jezreel, Jezebel heard of it; and she painted her face, and tired her head, and looked out at a window" (2 Kings 9:30).

Just here I think of what the poet, Leslie Savage Clark, wrote:

> From the palace casement she looked down,
> Queenly, scornful, proud,
> And watched with cold indifferent eyes
> The weary ragged crowd.
>
> Of the wage of sin she never thought,
> Nor that a crown might fall . . .
> Nor did she note the hungry dogs
> Skulking along the wall.

And as Jehu, the new king by the will and word of the Lord, entered in at the gate, she asked: "Had Zimri peace who slew his master?" And Jehu lifted up his face to the window and said, "Who is on my side? who? And there looked out to him two or three eunuchs. And he said, Throw her down" (2 Kings 9:32–33).

These men put their strong men's fingers into her soft feminine flesh and picked her up, tired head and all, painted face and all, bejeweled fingers and all, silken skirts and all—and threw her down. Her body hit the street and burst open. Some of her blood splattered on the legs of Jehu's horses, dishonoring them. Some of her blood splattered on the walls of the city, disgracing them.

And Jehu drove his horses and chariot over her. There she lies, twisting in death agony in the street. Her body is crushed by the chariot wheels. On her white bosom are the black crescent-shapes of horses' hoofs. She is hissing like an adder in the fire. Jehu drove away and left her there.

> And when he was come in he did eat and drink, and said, Go, see now this cursed woman, and bury her: for she is a king's daughter. And they went to bury her: but they found no more of her than the skull, and the feet, and the palms of her hands (2 Kings 9:34–35).

God Almighty saw to it that the hungry dogs despised the brains that conceived the plot that took Naboth's life. God Almighty saw to it that the mangy lean dogs of the back alleys despised the hands that wrote the plot that took Naboth's life. God Almighty saw to it that the lousy dogs which ate carrion despised the feet that walked in Baal's courts and then in Naboth's vineyard.

These soldiers of Jehu went back to Jehu and said: "We went to bury her, O king, but the dogs had eaten her!"

And Jehu replied:

> This is the word of the LORD, which he spake by his servant Elijah the Tishbite, saying, In the portion of Jezreel shall dogs eat the flesh of Jezebel. And the carcass of Jezebel shall be as dung upon the face of the field in the portion of Jezreel; so that they shall not say, This is Jezebel (2 Kings 9:36–37).

Thus perished a female demon, the most infamous queen who ever wore a royal diadem.

"Payday—Someday!" God said it—and it was done! Yes, and from this we learn the power and certainty of God in carrying out His own retributive providence, that men might know that His justice slumbereth not. Even though the mill of God grinds slowly, it grinds to powder.

Yes, the judgments of God often have heels and travel slowly. But they always have iron hands and crush completely.

And when I see Ahab fall in his chariot, and when I see the dogs eating Jezebel by the walls of Jezreel, I say, as the Scripture saith: "O that thou hadst hearkened to my commandments; then had thy peace been as a river, and thy righteouness as the waves of the sea" (Isa. 48:18). And as I remember that the gains of ungodliness are weighted with the curse of God, I ask you: "Wherefore do ye spend money for that which is not bread? and your labor for that which satisfieth not?" (Isa. 55:2).

And the only way I know for any man or woman on earth to escape the sinner's payday on earth and the sinner's hell beyond—making sure of the Christian's payday—is through Christ Jesus, who took the sinner's place upon the cross, becoming for all sinners all that God must judge, that sinners through faith in Christ Jesus might become all that God cannot judge.

CHAPTER TWO

The Word of God—Not Broken and Not Bound

*If he called them gods, unto whom the word of God came,
and the scripture cannot be broken.
John 10:35*

*Wherein I suffer trouble, as an evil doer, even unto bonds;
but the Word of God is not bound.
2 Tim. 2:9*

The Bible is a wonderful Book of sixty-six books, a vast library in one volume, written by forty men of different capacity and temperament and position over a period of 1,600 years, having one message, progressive, constructive, complete. All who wrote are immortalized by their writing of this great Book, supernatural in origin, divine in authorship, human in penmanship, infallible in authority, infinite in scope, universal in interest, personal in application, regenerative in power, inspired in totality. It is a miracle Book of diversity in unity, of harmony in infinite complexity.

The Masterpiece of God

This Word of God, the masterpiece of God, the Book above and beyond all books as a river is beyond a rill in reach, as the sun is beyond a candle in brightness, as Niagara is above and beyond a mud puddle in glory, is immortal in its hopes, a complete code of laws, the most entertaining and authentic history ever published, the best covenant ever made, the best deed ever written, the best will ever executed, it comes to us drenched in the tears of millions of contritions, worn with the fingers of agony and death, expounded by the greatest intellects, steeped in the prayers of many saints, stained with the blood of martyrs. The accuracy of its statements and prophecies is substantiated by every turn of the excavator's spade in Bible lands, by history, by multitudinous inscriptions deciphered among classic ruins, by the unlocking of Egyptian hieroglyphics.

From rusty coins and corroded marbles we find confirmation of its own veracity. Infinite in height, infinite in depth, it is and will forever be. Volumes that would fill the shelves of many libraries have been written on single chapters, single verses, single words. Yet those chapters and verses are as fresh, as fertile, as inexhaustible as ever. The fountain in which dying martyrs cooled their hot faces, the pillow on which saints of all ages have rested their heads, it breaks the fetters of the slave, takes the heat out of life's fierce fever, the pain out of parting, the sting out of death, the gloom out of the grave.

Thus Saith the Lord . . .

Addressing itself to the universal conscience, speaking with binding claims, commanding the obedience of all mankind, the one and only hope of information concerning divine revelation, the world's creation, the soul's salvation, human destiny, and the realities of eternity, it offers the first and demands the last by its unequivocal "Thus saith the Lord."

We wonder at the wonder of its indestructibility when we know how it has been severely abused in the hands of its enemies and sorely wounded in the house of its friends. Our faith in its eternal indestructibility is strengthened when we read: "Forever, O LORD, thy word is settled in heaven" (Ps. 119:89). Isaiah wrote: "The word of our God shall stand for ever" (Isa. 40:8). Jesus said: "Heaven and earth shall pass away, but my words shall not pass away" (Mark 13:31).

Wonderful in its inspiration, translation, preservation, unification, salvation, sanctification, and consummation, it makes nations and civilizations, homes and individuals, to breathe and grow. Free from earthly mixtures—original, unborrowed, solitary in its greatness—outliving all other books as a mighty factor in civilization, it is unique and peerless. It is always identified with the promotion of liberty.

Wonderful in its authority, it is the companion of pioneers in commerce, the foundation of civil government, the source and support of learning—always containing and fostering the best literature.

Given by Inspiration

> All scripture is given by inspiration of God, and is profitable for doctrine, for reproof, for correction, for instruction in righteousness (2 Tim. 3:16).

All sacred writings are given by inspiration, inspired not according to the ordinary theory which says that the Bible writers were inspired as were Homer, Tennyson, Browning. This prostitutes inspiration to the level of human genius. Nor is the Bible inspired according to the theory which states that only parts are divinely inspired. This theory of inspiration leaves us in the plight of incompetence to decide which parts are inspired. It eliminates the truth. I like what Dr. DeWitt Talmage said on this:

> I never so much as now felt the truth in the entire Bible. I prefer the old robe which has kept so many warm amid the cold pilgrimage of this life and amid the chills of death. Give me the old robe rather than the thin gauze offered us by the wiseacres who believe the Bible in spots.

Nor is the Bible inspired according to the thermometer theory which claims that parts of the Bible are more inspired than other parts. But we must remember that a thing is true or not true. And one truth cannot be more truthful than another truth. Psalm 23 is not more inspired than Proverbs 7. To say that Lindbergh flew to Paris is not more truthful than the truth that Benjamin Franklin had a tail to his kite.

Nor is the Bible inspired according to the moral theory held by some. This theory declares that the moral and spiritual teachings of the Bible are inspired, but that the historical elements may be true or false. This is inconsistent and would have us believe the Bible only when it speaks on certain subjects.

The Apostle

The apostle Paul pulled in the poles of the world of his day and bound them to the cross. Sacrifice and suffering was his life's law. Calvary was his passion. His moral grandeur casts its shadow across our times, and his head and shoulders are seen above the most mountainous of men.

On the way to Damascus, he met Jesus and made a voyage from the teacup of himself into the ocean of God's self. For Christ his life was in peril in Damascus. For Christ he was coldly suspected by his fellow believers in Jerusalem. For Christ he was stoned in Lystra. For Christ he was beaten with many stripes and put in jail in Philippi. For Christ he was assaulted in Iconium. For Christ he was pursued by callous enmity in Berea. For Christ, he was attacked by the lewd and envious crowd in Thessalonica. For Christ he was blasphemed in Corinth. For Christ he was despised in Athens. For Christ, he gave his life in Rome. For Christ Paul made the mightiest journey and crossed the widest distance ever accomplished by mortal man, the distance between Jewish exclusiveness and pagan liberalism. Passing out of the realm of narrow provincialism, he entered the broad realm of a dying and needy world.

In hard labors abundant, Paul received thirty-nine stripes from the Jews, beaten three times with rods, in frequent journeyings, in perils of robbers, in perils of waters, in perils from the heathen, in perils in the city, in perils in the wilderness, in perils in the sea, in perils among false brethren, in weariness, in pain, in watchings often, in hunger and thirst, in frequent fastings, in cold and nakedness. He bore the burden of the care of the churches and he counted all things but loss that he might know Jesus and "the power of his resurrection, and the fellowship of His sufferings, being made conformable unto his death" (Phil. 3:10).

He himself said concerning himself:

> But what things were gain to me, those I counted but loss for Christ. Yea, doubtless and I count all things but loss for the excellency of the knowledge of Christ Jesus my Lord: for whom I have suffered the loss of all things, and do count them but dung, that I may win Christ (Phil. 3:7-8).

Paul's Assertion

Paul—this mightiest of all missionaries, this valiant soldier of Christ's Cross, this great preacher who compassed the earth with the truths of redemption and left a trail of glory across the Gentile world, this marvelous man who dotted plains and cities with churches he built, this profound theologian, this tender-hearted pastor, this great hero wrote with frenzied pen. His letters are now Bible books, wellsprings of doctrine, the scaffolding of church theology. Gospel truths dropped from his pen like golden pollen from the stems of shaken lilies. His pen is inactive now, but his Epistles speak. They speak as softly sometimes as a mother's lullaby, as loudly often as the thunder cloud's voice, as wooingly sometimes as a lover's voice.

Wonderful and weighty the assertion he made after he stated that he suffered trouble as though he were an evildoer, that he was treated as if he were a criminal, as if he were one of the world of lawless malefactors. He said: "The word of God is not bound."

Happy and triumphant this assertion of Paul. It shows his kinship with the thought and words of Jesus who, in verbal combat with His enemies, said: "The scripture cannot be broken" (John 10:35).

Still the Bible is unbound, as glorious as a starry night, as fresh as the break of day. As God made man and breathed into him the breath of life and he became a living soul, so God made the Scriptures and breathed into them the breath of life.

A Living Book

God is in this Book. His thoughts, His feelings, His heart are there. His anger blazes from its pages of power. His love trembles in its tones. His lamentations sigh and sob in its sentences. His power and wisdom throb in the whole of it.

It is a living Book. In reading it, we come into contact and communion with Him who is Lord over all and blessed forever. Book of the church militant is the Bible. Book of the church triumphant! Book our mothers stained with grateful tears. Book our fathers touched with reverent hands. Book that unrolls the panorama of creation. Book that gives the lofty imagery of the prophets. Book that gives the portrait of Christ. Book that gives the philosophy of salvation. Book that gives the facts of sin and the fact of the Savior. Book that gives the truth of man lost and man redeemed. Book that gives the fact of death as "the wages of sin." Book that gives the truth of eternal life as the "gift of God." In breadth and sweep of theme it is more vast than any other book, in flight more lofty, in depth more profound. Upon it Reformers fed the holy fires which flamed in their bosoms.

In this Word of God which can never be bound or imprisoned, the historian has found his most thrilling chapters, the artist his loveliest conceptions, the poet his loftiest themes, God's prophets their divinest messages, ethics its greatest authority, philosophy its profoundest inspiration, oratory its most beautiful quotations to bejewel its grandest flights, and many writers multitudinous themes and suggestions that blossom like rare and fragrant flowers in the world's vast garden of literature.

Paul in Bonds

Paul was in bonds. To King Agrippa he had said: "I would to God, that not only thou, but also all that hear me this day, were both almost, and altogether such as I am, except these bonds" (Acts 26:29).

His feet and ankles were accustomed to stocks, his wrists were weighted with chains. But the Word of God could not be bound! There, as now, it traveled many highways, walked many bypaths, knocked at many doors, and spoke to many people in their mother tongue. The Word, marvelous and mighty, could not be fettered and imprisoned. The Word circulated with freedom. No chains could weigh it down. No shears could clip its wings. No enemy could put it behind penitentiary walls or on the executioner's block. No yoke could enslave the Word, even though Paul, appointed to preach the Word, spoke of how his "bonds in Christ" were "manifest in all the palace, and in all other places," enabling the brethren to wax confident and become more bold to speak the Word without fear (Phil. 1:13–14). And that the gospel should be unfettered was the great matter. His own imprisonment was of comparatively little consequence.

"Not bound." What an antithesis to his own imprisonment. The gospel is preached in spirit of the imprisonment of Paul, not now by and through himself but by others. "Therefore . . . glory" because the Word of God is not bound. The unimpeded course of the gospel is to the apostle proof of its all-embracing power. Such thoughts inspired him to suffer. Fettered was Paul, but not the Word. Imprisoned was Paul, but not the Word. It went abroad giving freedom. In years past, martyr's blood reddened the mouths of lions or simmered in the fire, but the Word goes on.

The Authority

God is the authority. Men who summon the Bible to appear at the bar of human reason and substitute a "Thus saith the mind of man" for a "Thus saith the Lord" forget that fact. The Word of God is the voice of the Almighty.

Since God is infinite, His Book will be independent of those finite limitations which characterize man's work.

Since God is immutable, His Book, however long the period of its production, will reveal changeless elements, and be throughout essentially consistent.

Since God is one, however varied the human writers of His Book and the times in which prepared, or the themes of which it speaks, it will be one Book and will reveal a definite and homogeneous plan. That is why I so often call it the miracle Book of diversity in unity, the Book so harmonious in infinite complexity.

Since God is omniscient, we can expect His Book to deal with facts of past history or future destiny with equal certainty as the present.

Since God is wise, never errs and is never chargeable with folly, His Book will be marked by convictions, conclusions, and counsels according to the highest truth and wisdom.

Since God is almighty, His Book will display and record achievements far beyond the unaided powers or possibilities of human strength.

Since God is the Creator of all things, we may expect to find in His Book the marks of a creative hand and mind.

Since God is righteous, His Book will exhibit a high standard of moral teaching and practice, and be consistent with the unchangeable principles of right and wrong.

Since God is holy, His Book will be a revelation of His holiness, of infinite beauty and excellence, of highest sympathy with what is faultlessly perfect for its own sake.

Since God is benevolent, His Book will both teach and exemplify unselfish goodness and love, inculcate forgiveness, mercy, self-sacrifice.

Since God is mysterious and incomprehensible, His Book will probably contain mystery, paradox, and apparent contradiction. It will deal with infinite magnitudes as well as moral certitudes.

Since God is superhuman and supernatural, His Book will speak as the language of one who knows man and the secrets of his whole being, and of the universe, and to whom what man deems marvelous and impossible is possible and simple.

Since God is unimpeachable, we can expect His Book to be instinct with vitality, to be a living Book, indestructible by man, divinely preserved by the Author.

Since God is a God of absolute faithfulness, His Book will be an uncompromising rebuke of human falsehood, vice, inconsistency, catering never to human sin, pandering never to vice, compromising never with evil.

Since God is a God of purpose, His Book will have a plain design consistent with Himself.

Since God is omnipresent, His Book is independent of the limitations of locality.

Since God is a God of divine providence, His Book represents God as both controlling the present and future, having oversight of all persons and events.

Since God is Judge, His Book reveals Him as judicially dealing with men, rewarding virtue and punishing vice, partially in this life and fully and finally in the life to come.

Since God is sovereign, His Book represents Him as supreme, even over foes. He makes even the wrath of man to praise Him, and restrains the remainder. He performs all His pleasure, despite all His enemies and their plots.

Since God is Spirit, His Book shows Him as independent of physical organs and limitations.

Though all this be true, there is still manifest toward the Bible devilish antagonisms.

The Bible Has Its Enemies

The Bible has had and still has many enemies. Considering the persecution the Bible has encountered, its survival is the miracle of history and the history of miracle.

1. There was the pagan persecution under Diocletian in A.D. 303, when this infamous scoundrel set forth his sanguinary persecution of Christians.

2. There was the papal persecution of the Bible in a different form, locking it up from the common people and putting the key in the hands of the priests. Rome became the jailer of the Word of God. Human legends and traditions took its place until the Reformation. Then once more it was let out of captivity and made accessible to humble believers. It was increasingly translated and diffused in various vernaculars.

3. Then another enemy of the Bible stood up as Goliath of Gath challenging Israel: rationalism, the deification of human reason. This enemy, asserting that whatever is above the reach of reason is unreasonable and incredible, attacked and still attacks the Bible with cogent weapons. The Bible miracles are denied, as contrary to the uniformity of natural laws. Prophecy at best is "sagacious human guesswork," but shrewd conjecture, and can never be the inspired forecast of the future.

   The deity of Jesus is denied. Myths are the incarnation and resurrection. Rationalism admits the excellency of the Bible as a mere book and sometimes assigns it a foremost place in all literature but this enemy of the Bible persistently treats the Bible as a mere human book. Thus does rationalism rob the Bible of every supernatural and superhuman element.

   With the polite and patronizing attitude that becomes occasionally rude and coarse and denunciatory, rationalism prostitutes divine inspiration to the level of human genius, and compares the inspiration of the Scriptures with that of Homer and Shakespeare. Whether rationalism be calmly philosophical or boisterously infidelic, whether it sometimes praises and exalts or sometimes derides and degrades, whether it appears to be sometimes openly hostile and sometimes professedly Christian, it is an avowed enemy of the Bible as the one unique Book.

No matter under what veils of pretense it makes its assault, rationalism regards the Bible as a human product.

4. Pantheism, making the divine element to pervade all things, even matter, lowers and degrades God's Word by lifting everything else to a divine level, declaring with a sort of reluctance that God is in the Book, but in the Book like He is in all things else.

5. Modernism, which mutilates the Bible and minimizes sin, and humanizes God and deifies man, assaulting the Word of God, claims to be friendly toward the Bible. But, with perverse persistence and persistent perversity, it points out what it calls errors and defects plausibly accounting for its "blemishes and mistakes" on the ground of human weakness and the fallibility of its writers. The attitude of modernism, making maybes mighty in many minds, is the practical denial of any really supernatural and superhuman elements in the Bible.

"Infidelity With a Fancy Name"

A study of modernism, or liberalism, which is infidelity with a fancy name, reveals men, under the guise of scholarship, from behind some pulpit stands and from professorship chairs, asking people to believe:

- that Adam just dreamed about the rib being taken from his side to make a helpmeet for him;
- that Eden's tree of the knowledge of good and evil was some sort of vegetable poison, a sort of poison ivy;
- that Adam and Eve were driven out of the garden by a terrific thunderstorm;
- that Moses built a fire on the top of the mountain and the people in the valley below thought it was supernatural fire;
- that Bible writers had unbalanced minds and rabid imaginations;

- that Mary mistook the Angel Gabriel for a passing stranger;
- that, at the Transfiguration, two strangers passed by at rosy dawn and Peter and James and John, in their heightened religious experience, mistook them for Moses and Elijah;
- that Jesus did not walk on the water, but walked on the sea shore and the disciples thought he was walking on the water; that Methuselah's age was incompatible with the physical structure;
- that Jesus' virgin birth is unthinkable to the modern mind;
- that Jesus fainted on Calvary's cross, and when He was taken down, He was not dead but in a swoon;
- that the coolness of the grave revived Him, and He escaped, appeared to His disciples, but died soon afterward.

How refreshing to turn from the garbage can of modernists and eat at the table of scholarly men who believe the Bible and who speak, wisely. Note:

- Dr. D. S. Fisher of Harvard: "No excavation I know of in Palestine has done anything thus far but confirm in a remarkable way the statements of Holy Writ, and I have no fear that any excavation ever will."
- Dr. Grayce of Oxford: "A skeptical attitude toward the words of the Old Testament and New Testament is today usually the mark of ignorance or semi-knowledge."
- Dr. Robert Dick Wilson, the greatest Biblical linguist of modern times, says: "I have come to the conviction that no one knows enough to assail the truthfulness of the Old Testament."
- Sir William Ramsey, scholar, archaeologist, historian: "The longer I study the New Testament, the more I am convinced of its absolute trustworthiness. The Christian religion is not founded on falsehood nor on misrepresentation of facts, nor on legend, nor on half-forgotten and exaggerated tales.

Christianity is a religion of truth, absolute and perfect truth."

Yes, the Bible has had many enemies in years gone by. It has many enemies today, though it is the original code of the republic. Kings and rulers have tried to destroy it. Philosophers have tried to drown it in the muddy waters of their philosophy and ignorance. Science has tried to laugh it out of court. Two hundred and fifty years ago, or thereabouts, with skeptical battle shouts, Voltaire said: "Fifty years from now the world will hear no more of the Bible."

The archaeologist with his crowbar, the geologist with his hammer, the physicist with his battery, all these have fought against the Book. Some scientists and astronomers lifted up haughty mouths, "darkening counsel by words without wisdom," against the Book. The dissecting knives of some theological anatomists have cut at its milk veins. Inexorable censors have sat, and sit now, like Jehoiakim before the fireplace in his summer-house, Bible on knee, penknife in hand, calmly mutilating the only reliable franchise of our Christian hopes. Snipers, some from behind pulpit stands, some from behind college chairs, some from behind editorial desks, are accustomed to aim ill-grounded propositions against the Scriptures.

We have many open and avowed leaders of infidelity, organizations which are definitely against the Bible and God. We have troops of Ulysses hurled against the wall of Troy and the enemy in the belly of the wooden horse. We have not only those who are skeptically close kin disgracefully with Bradlaugh of England and Ingersoll and Darrow of America, but the body of militant critics, some of them wearing the sacred garb of the theological professor, who attempt to draw the bolts of the citadel from the inside.

Ancient and modern are its enemies. Diocletian, as I have said, tried to exterminate it in the third century. Celsus tried to undermine its message. The astute Pophyry hurled his venomed shafts. Hume with rare sublety, wielded cogent weapons against the Bible. He said: "Me thinks I see the twilight of Christianity." The trouble with Hume in his fuming was that he could not tell what time of day it was. What he thought was sundown going toward midnight was sunup going toward noonday.

In England in the time of Henry the Fifth, Bible reading was made a crime. A law was enacted saying: "That whosoever they were that should read the Scriptures in the mother tongue, they should forfeit land, life, and goods from their heyres forever, and so be condemned for heretics to God, enemies of the crown and more errant traitors to the lands."

Yet, the Bible lives. It is the Book that lives forever.

The earth shall pass away some day.
But My Word shall not pass away;
The sun may fade, the moon decay,
But God's Word lives forever!
The flags of nations may be furled,
The mountains to be seas be hurled,
One thing will still outlast the world
God's Word will live forever!

A Woeful and Tragic Attitude: Practical Indifference

In our homes, the Bible is often the least read, not to say anything about it being so little studied and so little understood. The daily newspaper and monthly magazine and movies practically crowd God's Word out, or into a spiderweb corner.

Professor J. A. Carlson, in his book *Your Body*, speaks of hunger. He says most birds can go nine days without food, most dogs twenty days, turtles five hundred days, snakes eight hundred days, some fishes one thousand days, some insects twelve hundred days, and a man twelve days, without death. But food is necessary for all God's creatures.

Moreover, according to Professor Carlson, the human body in the process of starvation does not emaciate equally. The loss in percentage to the brain is thirty-five percent; to the lungs fourteen percent; to the bones fourteen percent; to the kidneys twenty-six percent; to the heart twenty-seven percent; to the liver, fifty-four percent, and fat, ninety-seven percent.

I think that we are not unkind to say that there are some "turtle" Christians who go five hundred days without a solid meal of real Bible meat. And many "bird" Christians who go more than nine days without Bible food. And some "fish" Christians of malicious arrows of scorn and jeers, and sniffs and sneers. But the Book lives on!

He that sitteth in the heavens shall laugh at those who think they destroy His Word and its triumphs. Agnostics who kindled their bonfire upon it burned not away one thread of its garments. Atheists have not been able to steal one flower from its gorgeous flower gardens. Unbelieving scientists, with microscope and telescope and test tube, have not been able to dilute one drop from its sweetness. Theological smoke-screeners who have tried to hide in clouds and thick darkness the Cross and the blood and the empty tomb in Joseph's garden, have not been able to invert its torch or to quench one ray of its light. Still it is our "pillar of fire" among all books. Not one jot or one tittle of its moral code has perished in the last century. Self-elected scholarship, with the presumptuous step of a know-much has pronounced the Bible out of date and dead.

Dr. Haldeman told about the doing of their self-styled scholarship: "Again and again the Bible's funeral services are held. Kind and condescending eulogies are uttered over its past history and its good intent. With considerate hands it is lowered into its grave. But before the critical mourners have returned to their homes, it has risen from the dead, passed with surprising speed the funeral coaches and is found—as of yore— in the busy centers of life, thundering against evil, offering consolation to the sorrowing and hope to the dying."

The Bible's Great Attraction: Jesus

The name of Jesus, the Supreme Personality, the center of the world's desire, is on every page, in expression or symbol, or prophecy, or psalm, or proverb. Through the Bible, the name of Jesus runs like a line of glimmering light. The thought of Jesus—literature's loftiest ideal, philosophy's highest personality, criticism's supremest problem, theology's fundamental doctrine, spirituality's cardinal necessity, the desire of all nations threads the great Book like a crystal river winds its way through a continent.

This living Word of our living God stars Jesus. And you cannot hold on to Christ and give up the Bible. You cannot believe in the Cross and surrender the infallible authority of the Bible. Faith in the deity of Christ is married to faith in the inspiration of the Bible.

Yes, Jesus Christ, the Creator of all things in earth and heaven, the one Mediator between God and man, the Redeemer who "bore our sins in his own body on the tree" (1 Pet. 2:24), the Conqueror of everyone and everything opposed to God, is the glorious One whose personality vitalizes and energizes the Word of God. The center of the Book is the Cross of Christ. The circumference of the Book is the glory of Christ.

All the Bible's types, all the Bible's analogies, all the Bible's pictures, all the Bible's truths are so related to Christ Jesus that He alone explains them. And the explanation is filled with such perfection of harmony in every detail, the relationships between them and our Lord Jesus is so strikingly self-evident, that any discussion of it would be useless. No one ought to have to argue with anyone to get them to see that the diversified and systematic sacrifices of the Jews, the significant shadows of redemptive entity still ahead, the adumbrations of a substance yet to come, were elemental, preparatory, rudimental, introductory, and pointed to Christ, the propellent Center to which the faith of mankind, before and since, gravitated. The promises to fallen man in Eden and the ceremonies of Judaism mean Christ. The music of Israel's sweetest harps and the light that burns in prophecy mean Christ.

Jesus is the vital substance that gives meaning to the Bible's genealogies, meaning to its histories, meaning to its chronologies. Take Jesus out of the Bible and it would be like taking calcium out of lime, carbon out of diamonds, truth out of history, invention out of fiction, matter out of physics, mind out of metaphysics, numbers out of mathematics.

Christ Jesus alone is the secret of the Bible's strength, beauty and unity. Christ Jesus, sometimes called "one hour of God on earth," the full, comprehensive, all-sufficient, ultimate revelation of God, is the foundation and keystone of the arches of the great Bible building.

Jesus Himself said:

> Search the scriptures; for in them ye think ye have eternal life: and they are they which testify of me. . . . Do not think that I will accuse you to the Father: there is one that accuseth you, even Moses, in whom ye trust. For had ye believed Moses, ye would have believed me: for he wrote of me. But if ye believe not his writings, how shall ye believe my words? (John 5:39, 45-47).

Dr. Haldeman preached: "Take Christ out of the Bible, and it is a harp without a player, a song without a singer, a palace with all doors locked and all windows removed."

But the Christ Jesus as the supreme theme of the Bible, it is "an organ whose full breath is thunder beneath God's fingers pressed."

With Christ Jesus as the center, the Bible is the music of all Scriptural choirs poured forth in one anthem.

With Christ Jesus occupying the throne in the Bible, which the Bible assigns to Him, the Bible is a palace every door of which has His truth inscribed on it, and every window of which pours forth light to His honor.

With Christ Jesus assigned His rightful place in the Bible, it is a garden where all flowers cluster around Him who is the Lily of the Valley and the Rose of Sharon, "the fairest of ten thousand and the One altogether lovely."

With Christ as the central theme, the Bible is a starry sky where all stars do obeisance to Him, who is the "Bright and Morning Star," even as, in Joseph's dream, he and his brethren were "binding sheaves in the field, and Joseph's sheaf arose and stood upright," and the sheaves of his brethren "stood round about and made obeisance to Joseph's sheaf" (Gen. 37:7).

Applying the Bible to All of Life

The Bible truths we should apply to every interest in life, whether personal, social, commercial, political, domestic, civil, or religious.

Oh! Let all mourners read and study the Word; it will wipe away their tears.

Let all bereaved read and study it; it will give assurance that a father of the fatherless and a husband of the widow is God in His holy habitation.

Let the poor read and study it; it will soothe them under their privations.

Let the rich read and study it, it will sanctify their abundance.

Let the old read and study it, it will support their tottering age.

Let the young read and study it; it will help them walk in that path which grows brighter and brighter unto the perfect day.

Let us heed these words urging us to give strength and time to the words in the Word of our God:

> And thou shalt teach them diligently unto thy children and shalt talk of them when thou sittest in thine house, and when thou walkest by the way and when thou liest down, and when thou risest up (Deut. 6:7).

> Bind them continually upon thine heart, and tie them about thy neck. When thou goest, it shall lead thee; when thou sleepest, it shall keep thee; when thou awakest, it shall talk with thee. For the commandment is a lamp; and the law is light; and reproofs of instruction are the way of life (Prov. 6:21–23).

Then we will be wise to know the Word in the head, to stow it in the heart, to sow it in the world, and to show it in the life.

CHAPTER THREE

The Face of Jesus Christ

The face of Jesus Christ.
2 Cor. 4:6

The Bible is a vast portrait gallery. In it God has preserved imperishably for us sketches and pictures which give vivid and wonderful ideas and mental photographs of the leaders of the people and of those less known but no less worthy.

How splendid are the pictures that look down upon us from the ancient scriptural walls as we wander through the great rooms in the vast art gallery of the Bible. There we see Adam in his loneliness. And Eve in her dialogue with the devil. And Cain, flying from the crimson spots of blood on the ground where, for no cause except his own foolish envy, he slew his brother, Abel.

And Abraham welcoming angels at his door. And Daniel, the greatest man of a thousand years, in the lions' den. And Daniel's fellow exiles Shadrach, Meshach, and Abed-nego, in the fiery furnace. And Joseph coming down from the throne to greet his brothers. And Moses, the mighty lawgiver, walking across the fields of achievement with the stride of a giant. And David with his harp, at once king, poet, prophet, and musician. And Elijah, a seer who saw clearly, a great heart who felt deeply; a hero who dared valiantly. And John the Baptist, descending upon the iniquities of his day with a torch in one hand and a sword in the other. And Paul, the great Aristotle and Demosthenes of the Jewish race. And John, marooned on Patmos while his mind traveled the ranges of a new heaven and a new earth. And on and on we might wander in this awe-inspiring, worship-begetting observation journey through the Bible art gallery unsurpassed indeed.

In the Vatican at Rome, the largest of earth's art galleries, there are eleven thousand rooms. There, with walls of speaking pictures on either side, and on all sides, one may wander for days. But the Bible is an art gallery greater than the Vatican. In the corners and continents of this marvelous Book one may wander for centuries and not see all its glories. But on every page we will get evidence that all its portraits lose their splendor in the greater glory of the face of Jesus Christ. Of His face, His blessed face, His sweet face, His dear face, we would speak now. What kind of face was it?

A Sad Face

Yes, the face of Jesus was a sad face, sometimes.

Sad, because men were often deaf to the significance of His teaching. Sad, because men were often unresponsive to the magnanimity of His nature. Sad, because men were often ungrateful before His ministries of mercy. Sad, because men were often so stupidly blind to the beauty of His life. Sad, because He knew men, even as He knows the end from the beginning and understands our thoughts afar off, and knew how deceitful above all things and desperately wicked were their hearts. Sad, because, with a perception that no human ever had, He saw the unneighborliness, the unbrotherliness, the ungodliness of men's motives. Sad, because He knew the false standards and the false motives and the false and unworthy ideals of men and women. Sad, because He saw the low slavery in which men lived who were in inward bondage to bad motives and sordid objectives. Sad, because He saw men making poor choices between things of value and things of no worth—emphasizing the things that matter but little, if at all, neglecting the things that matter most in eternity and in time. Sad, because He saw man eagerly pursuing his own disadvantage, his own shame, his own sorrow.

Truly, in more ways than one, He was a man of sorrows and acquainted with grief. Because He was a man of sorrows His face was often sad. His face reflected the sadness of His heart. And His face was sad because His heart knew that many were believing that a man's life consisteth in the abundance of things which he possesseth. Sad because He saw men measuring themselves by themselves and were not wise. Sad because so many were building their houses on the sand—houses that would stand against no wind, no rain, no flood, no storm.

Sad was His face because His heart had compassion on the great multitudes who were as sheep without a shepherd. Sad was His face because He knew so many were loving darkness rather than light because their deeds were evil. Sad was His face because He saw many who were participants in the degradation of love. But the sadness of His face was not the sadness that takes on the stamp of a heart torn with remorse. Not the sadness of a face that takes on the hue of a heart that holds some abiding bitterness. Not the sadness of a face that gives reflection from a heart that nurses some bitter resentment. Not the sadness of a face that testifies to a heart that stamps itself in cynicism and doubt and unbelief on the face. But the sadness that came from a heart, a sinless heart, that grieved over men and sorrowed over their foolish and perverse ways.

A Shining Face

Yes, the face of Jesus was a shining face, sometimes.

> And after six days Jesus taketh Peter, James, and John his brother, and bringeth them up unto an high mountain apart, and was transfigured before them: and his face did shine as the sun, and his raiment was white as the light (Matt. 17:1–2).

He brought them "up into an high mountain apart"—Mount Hermon, 9,200 feet above the level of the sea—and there, in transfiguration, the face of Jesus did shine as the sun. And only the sun could express the radiant glories of the face of Jesus when His heavenly nature shone through the veil of the flesh—when His deity, with shining brightness and heavenly glory, glowed and shone through His body.

There He was, the One through whom God has spoken to us in these last days, by whom also He made the worlds, His face shining as the sun, because He was the brightness of God's glory and the express image of His person (Heb. 1:2–3). And they beheld the glory of His shining face, the glory of the only begotten of God!

Then, too, John, marooned on Patmos, saw seven golden candlesticks:

> And in the midst of the seven candlesticks one like unto the Son of man, clothed with a garment down to the foot, and girt about the paps with a golden girdle. His head and his hairs were white like wool, as white as snow; and his eyes were as a flame of fire; and his feet like unto fine brass, as if they burned in a furnace; and his voice as the sound of many waters. And he had in his right hand seven stars: and out of his mouth went a sharp two-edged sword: and his countenance was as the sun shineth in his strength (Rev. 1:13–16).

There His face shines like the sun when no cloud is upon it. There, like the brightness of the sun at hot and high noonday of longest summer, His face shines. His face, like a fire at full heart, shines—until John falls at His feet as one dead before the brightness of it all. To gaze upon His face, bright and shining like the sun in full strength, struck the eyes blind. And John, breathed upon by the Holy Spirit, symbolized the glory of His shining face by the strongest symbol the world affords! "His countenance was as the sun shineth in His strength." So, the face of Jesus was a shining face, sometimes.

And again:

> And Saul, yet breathing out threatenings and slaughter against the disciples of the Lord, went unto the high priest, and desired of him letters to Damascus to the synagogues, that if he found any of this way, whether they were men or women, he might bring them bound unto Jerusalem. And as he journeyed, he came near Damascus: and suddenly there shined round about him a light from heaven: and he fell to the earth, and heard a voice saying unto him, Saul, Saul, why persecutest thou me? (Acts 9:1–4)

The light that shone round about Saul of Tarsus, a light from heaven, was the light of the glory of God in the face of Christ Jesus.

On that journey to Damascus, as Matthew tells us, the strong, majestic Mount Hermon of white peacefulness was his companion—gleaming pink in the dawn as he started each day, silhouetted in royal purple as the sun set over its shoulder. On that last day of his journey, the dawn came out of the desert land eastward, and the Mount Hermon height glowed as they pressed forward over the volcanic tableland which at last drops down on the plain of Damascus. "The sun lifted slowly in the shadeless land. The hour of noon drew near, when the power of the sun is like a burden bowing the shoulders of the traveler."

The road stretched ahead of them across the plain or orchards, beyond which the walls of Damascus rose. There, just ahead, was the city in which Saul, in the strength of the full flood of his boundless energy, was to win his spurs!

> Suddenly there shined round about him a light from heaven: and he fell to the earth, and heard a voice saying unto him, Saul, Saul, why persecutest thou me? And he said, Who art thou, Lord? And the Lord said, I am Jesus whom thou persecutest: it is hard for thee to kick against the pricks. And he trembling and astonished said, Lord, what wilt thou have me to do? And the Lord said unto him, Arise, and go into the city, and it shall be told thee what thou must do (Acts 9:3–6).

And Paul arose—stood up. But he could not see. Gone was Damascus. Gone was the plain. Gone was the white crest of Hermon. Gone the rooftops out yonder. Gone the walls of Damascus. Gone the green of the orchards. Gone the white, hot road. Gone the blazing sun. All were gone. He was blind. Gropingly he reached out his hands. Those who were with him led him over the last lap of the journey (Acts 22:11).

The night of blindness had shut Saul in upon himself. He could not see the curious peasants who gazed at this white-robed young rabbi being led along the road. But there was one thing he could see, for it was burned into his brain by the blaze that smote him to his knees. It was the light of the glory of God in the face of Jesus Christ.

A shining face, Matthew says.

A shining face, Luke testifies.

A shining face, John vouches for.

A shining face, Paul declares.

I love to think of the shining face of Jesus as Peter, James, and John saw it on the Mount of Transfiguration. And as John saw it in exile on Patmos—a face shining "like the sun . . . in his strength." I know that the face of Jesus was a shining face, though not bright as the sun shining in his strength, when the blind looked at Him with new-seeing eyes, when the deaf listened to the world of sound He had opened to them, when the mute talked after He had untied the knots in their tongues, when the crippled went away whole, when the lepers went on their way cleansed, when the crazy men went on their way with their reason restored, when funeral processions were broken up. His face shone because of the joy He had brought to others!

And because of the sympathy and the sweetness and the tenderness and the gentleness and the kindness and the indignation which He so quickly felt in the presence of injustice and evil, His face shone. A shining face indeed was His face, oftentimes!

A Stained Face

Yes, the face of Jesus was a stained face, sometimes.

Once, in Bethany, His face was stained with tears.

To this little town He came where in the grave for four days Lazarus had been sleeping the sleep that no noise can disturb, no life arouse, no power molest. All the shadows of a reality darker than midnight's darkest blackness were focused upon that little house. And death, whose only music is the sob of broken hearts, had boldly and defiantly robbed their treasure house of the dearest object of their affection.

> When Jesus therefore saw her weeping, and the Jews also weeping which came with her, he groaned in the spirit, and was troubled, and said, Where have ye laid him? They said unto him, Lord, come and see. Jesus wept. Then said the Jews, Behold how he loved him! And some of them said, Could not this man which opened the eyes of the blind, have caused that even this man should not have died? (John 11:33–37)

Jesus, weeping, came to the grave. "It was a cave, and a stone lay upon it" (John 11:38). Stained with tears was His blessed face, in Bethany!

Not only there, but at another time and at another place, His face was stained with tears. During the days of that last week that sloped up to Calvary's bloody top like rough steps that lead to a height where storms howl and rage, He came one day around Olivet's brow, in His one and only hour of royal pomp. Then and there His eyes, like clouds that suddenly burst into floods, washed His face with tears.

"And when he was come near, he beheld the city, and wept over it" (Luke 19:41).

"Eklausen!" He wailed aloud, the tears streaming down His face. What wretchedness in that city. What wickedness! What future calamities awaited Jerusalem! He knew the end from the beginning, and His tender heart revealed itself through tearful eyes. No wonder. Wherever He looked He found unhappiness. Discontented and bitter the upper classes. Sullen and hopeless the lower classes! Insecure was life. Insecure was property. The city was filled with alarming rumors, jealousies, suspicion, fierce debates. There poverty added horror to horror. He saw Jerusalem as she was in her sorrow. Behind her pageants was the heart of the city burdened with care. Amid the playgrounds the heart of the city was smitten with sin. He saw that despite the theaters, the processions, the games, the festivals, the heart of the city was wrung with anguish. Looking into the future with His omniscient eyes, He saw the hillsides covered with Roman encampments and more crosses than there were trees in the king's forest, and the bodies of thousands upon thousands of Jews festering thereon while the sky was darkened with vultures feeding upon these bodies, and Titus Vespasian exulting in bloody victories and cruelties.

Stained with tears His dear face. But with blood, too.

In Gethsemane's garden the roots of His divine emotion put forth like flowers their crimson tears. Let the Book tell us about it. Listen!

> And he was withdrawn from them about a stone's cast, and kneeled down, and prayed, Saying, Father, if thou be willing, remove this cup from me: nevertheless, not my will, but thine, be done. And there appeared an angel unto him from heaven, strengthening him. And being in an agony he prayed more earnestly: and his sweat was as it were great drops of blood falling down to the ground (Luke 22:41–44).

Behold the weeping Christ's face stained with tears. Behold the suffering Christ's face stained with blood. "His sweat was as it were great drops of blood."

He gave His blood for me. Yes. Blood oozed from the holes in His palms where nails went. Blood spurted from the feet where spikes were driven raggedly through. Blood dripped from His back where the merciless scourge cut His back to shreds. Blood gushed from His side where the savage Roman spear went its unholy way. Blood trickled from the thorn punctures in His brow. Yes, all this. And blood stained His face when, in the shadow of the old olive trees, He listened to the shuddering necessity of a world's sin utter itself in agony of soul no words can express.

Stained with tears. Yes.

Stained with blood. Yes.

But more. Stained with spit.

In the Book of Mark one bold, bare, cruel statement stands out in all those darkening scenes like a flash of lightning that rips the black vestments of the storm cloud. "They smote him on the head with a reed, and did spit upon him" (Mark 15:19). Isaiah had prophesied, "I hid not my face from shame and spitting" (Isa. 50:6). And here, in indignity heaped upon indignity, it came to pass. In close kinship with Mark's statement is Matthew's statement, which seems to shriek itself with all the wildness of delirium into our souls: "What think ye? They answered and said, he is guilty of death. Then did they spit in his face, and buffeted him" (Matt. 26:66–67).

But shudderingly, as one passes by a ghastly sight by the roadside, shall we not pass from the sight of that face befouled with spit? But, when we pass, may we never forget that His face was stained with spit—for us. With tears, too—for us. And with blood!

A Smitten Face

Yes, a smitten face was His.

The old prophet, whose words flamed in the darkness of ignorance like forest fires at night, eight hundred years before heaven put out its brightest star to ark the birthplace of the Messiah, he said:

> I gave my back to the smiters, and my cheeks to them that plucked off the hair: I hid not my face from shame and spitting (Isa. 50:6).
>
> Surely he hath borne our griefs, and carried our sorrows: yet we did esteem him stricken, smitten of God, and afflicted" (Isa. 53:4).

Matthew has told us this:

> Then did they spit in his face, and buffeted him; and others smote him with the palms of their hands, saying, Prophesy unto us, thou Christ, Who is he that smote thee? (Matt. 26:67–68).

And Luke, by the Holy Spirit, even as the others, said:

> And the men that held Jesus mocked him, and smote him. And when they had blindfolded him, they struck him on the face, and asked him, saying, Prophesy, who is it that smote thee? (Luke 22:63–64).

And John writing as one who speaks weepingly, said:

> Then Pilate therefore took Jesus, and scourged him. And the soldiers plaited a crown of thorns, and put it on his head, and they put on him a purple robe, and said, Hail, King of the Jews! and they smote him with their hands" (John 19:1–3).

Think of it! Smitten the face where never dwelt a trace of indwelling hate. Beaten with their hard knuckles the face that never for one moment bore trace of sin. Smitten with their hard fists the face where no hypocrisy ever stamped itself. Smitten with callous palms the face whereon no evidence of scorn of the high and holy was ever seen. Smitten with rough buffeting the face where no deceit, no insincerity, no sin, no dishonesty, nor anything evil ever held for one fleeting second reign or rule. Surely with a sort of spiritual nausea at the thought of such malicious hate, we turn from looking upon the face smitten and bruised with blows from hard fists and tough knuckles and callous palms!

No wonder in Isaiah 52:14 we find these words: "His visage was so marred more than any man."

God forbid that we should forget that face more marred than any man's!

Down South, where his memory is still revered, they tell this story of the late General John B. Gordon:

> Years after the Civil War, Gordon was a candidate for the United States Senate. The day came when his name was to be put in nomination in his state legislature. In that body was a man who had been Gordon's comrade during the war. But for some reason the latter had incurred his resentment and the man had decided to vote against the general. When the time came, the roll was being called for the voting. Presently this old soldier's name was reached and he arose to cast his vote against the man with whom he had fought through the great struggle of four years. General Gordon was seated at the time upon the speaker's platform in full view of all legislators. As the man rose, his eyes fell upon a scar on Gordon's face, the mark of his valor and suffering for the cause to which he had literally given his lifeblood in battle. Immediately the old soldier was stricken with remorse. As he saw this token of the sacrifice and suffering of the man by whose side he had himself fought, he cried with great emotion, "I cannot vote against him. I had forgotten the scar. I had forgotten the scar!"

Some of us have forgotten the scars. We have forgotten the sacred brow dripping crimson from under its thorny crown.

We have forgotten the wounded side where the savage Roman spear drank deep the costly libation of His blood.

We have forgotten the hands and feet pierced with the nails and stretched and torn with the weight of the precious body of the Suffering One.

We have forgotten what a claim these scars constitute upon every life they have redeemed from death, and the tender appeal of their mute lips.

A Set Face

Looking not and turning not to the right or to the left, He walked deliberately down that road that was blocked yonder by a bloody cross.

Significant words indeed are those we find in Isaiah 50:7, where Isaiah speaks of the "patient endurance of reproach" as shown by Christ. We find these words which show us the set face of Christ. "Therefore have I set my face like a flint, and I know that I shall not be ashamed."

Significant words in Luke 9:51:

> And it came to pass, when the time was come that he should be received up, he stedfastly set his face to go to Jerusalem, and sent messengers before his face.

And then in Luke 9:53, we find, "And they did not receive him, because his face was as though he would go to Jerusalem."

We think of the pioneer fathers who set their faces to the wilds and the wilderness!

We think of Columbus with his face set across an uncharted, unknown, wild, and awful ocean!

We think of Judson with his face set toward a heathen land where he suffered valiantly for Christ in foul and filthy prisons!

We think of Livingstone with his face set toward the jungles of Africa where people were in the darkness of heathenism; where he started the road that become a highway over which Ethiopia stumbles with hands stretched out toward God.

We see Paton with his face set toward islands of cannibalism—set toward those islands when people warned him that the cannibals would make a drinking cup of his skull.

We see Luther with his face set toward the Diet of Worms.

We see Washington with his face set toward the east when there was no shining of the yet unrisen sun of liberty.

But none of these, nor all of these, means what it meant for Jesus to set His face "like a flint" toward the Cross of Calvary, where He was to give His body to the nails and "make His soul an offering for sin."

Jesus came to die—not to teach, not merely to live a beautiful life, not merely to be a miracle worker, but to die, and He would not be turned aside.

> From that time forth began Jesus to shew unto his disciples, how that he must go unto Jerusalem, and suffer many things of the elders and chief priests and scribes, and be killed, and be raised again the third day. Then Peter took him, and began to rebuke him saying, Be it far from thee, Lord: this shall not be unto thee. But he turned, and said unto Peter, Get thee behind me, Satan: thou art an offense unto me: for thou savorest not the things that be of God, but those that be of men (Matt. 16:21–23).

And Jesus heard in Peter's voice the hiss of the serpent. He heard again the voice of him who, in the wilderness, said: "Command that these stones be made bread"; who, from the pinnacle, said, "Cast thyself down"; who, from the mountaintop, said, "Fall down and worship me."

But Jesus would not be turned aside from the Cross. He kept His face set "like a flint" as the sun will not cease its shining because of the clouds—as a mighty river will not be stayed by sand piles on its way to the sea—as a great giant will not be stopped in his march by straws men put in his way.

Jesus set His face to walk the last foot of the Calvary road, to bleed the last drop of Calvary agony, to suffer the last minute of Calvary pain, to drink the Calvary cup to the last bitter dregs, to tread the wine press until the last cluster was trodden dry. And He had to be heroic to have and to hold that set face, for rough indeed the road that ran from Bethlehem to Calvary. And sometimes I wonder how even the strength of the Son of Man could endure it and keep on walking in it. No wonder there came hours when He was so tired He could sleep through a storm that lashed the sea into fury. I am not surprised that He sat down upon a well curb to rest. And somehow, I seem to catch some of the pathos of the statement that he has put into a song:

Thou didst leave Thy throne and Thy kingly crown,
When Thou camest to earth for me;
But in Bethlehem's home there was found no room
For Thy holy nativity.
Heaven's arches rang when the angels sang,
Proclaiming Thy royal degree;
But in lowly birth didst Thou come to earth,
And in great humility.
The foxes found rest, and the birds their nest,
In the shade of the forest tree;
But Thy couch was the sod, O Thou Son of God
In the desert of Galilee.
Thou camest, O Lord, with thy living Word,
That should set Thy people free;
But with mocking and scorn, and with crown of thorn,
They bore Thee to Calvary.
When heaven's arches shall ring, and her choirs shall sing,
At Thy coming to victory,
Let Thy voice call me home, Saying "Yet there is room,
There is room at My side for thee."

No wonder they had to call on Simon from Cyrene to carry Christ's Cross that awful day. How He could carry it so far is a reality that holds our hearts wrapped in wonder and awe.

And long, long centuries had His face been set. Mysterious but true it is that His face was set toward Calvary before light ever came from the sun, before any wave ever broke in white foam on any shore. Before any wind ever murmured among the forests of earth, the blessed face of Christ was set for our salvation—set bravely toward a bloody hill. Was He not the Lamb, the Lamb of God slain from the foundation of the world?

O blessed, love-set face! Call us to more heroic living. Our modern religion is so at fault as to matters of heroic. It speaks too often in terms of contentment, of success, of comfort. As a consequence, many languish with spiritual diabetes—too much sugar. Never hid Jesus the sharp stone. Never did He soften the shadows. Never did He guild the Cross for the sake of winning followers.

Turn Thou the light of Thy set face upon us, O Christ of God!

A Scorching Face

"Whom do men say that I the Son of man am?" (Matt. 16:13)

We turn to an aspect of the face of Jesus that we seldom consider. The Jesus of popular thought is a meek and mild-eyed saint who was always saying gracious things and always doing gentle deeds. He was a man who spoke always with a wooing note—indeed almost a cooing note—and who was unwilling to appear stern at any time. The Christ of history, the Christ with eyes of flame and feet of brass, as John saw Him, is a stranger to them. We do not feel the awe which the exile on Patmos felt.

> And when he had made a scourge of small cords, he drove them all out of the temple, and the sheep, and the oxen; and poured out the changers' money, and overthrew the tables; and said unto them that sold doves, Take these things hence. . . . And his disciples remembered that it was written, The zeal of thine house hath eaten me up" (John 2:15–17).

In popular thinking much is thought of His tenderness and of His sympathy and of His joyfulness and of His prayerfulness, but little evidence of thought of His severity is shown.

In popular speech much is said of His sinlessness, of His sufferings, of His forbearance, but little is said of His severity.

In popular writing today much is written of His patience and His humanity and His divinity and His wisdom and His power, but few pages about His severity!

In popular education, much is thought concerning His lovableness and His love and His faith and His hopefulness, but little concerning His severity.

Many look upon Him as a lamp glowing softly—never as a furnace burning fiercely. Many look upon Him as a zephyr ever whispering gentle, never as lightning flaring furiously, or as a storm full of fury! Many look upon Him as a river smoothly flowing—never as a whip hissing wrathfully. Many look upon Him as a balm sweet-scented—never as acid stringently cleansing. Many look upon Him as a hearthstone comfortably burning, never as a consuming fire. Many look upon Him as Mount Everest, quiet among snows of age, never as Vesuvius flaring forth in volcanic eruptions; as Lake Geneva never stirring, never as Niagara thunderous and righteously indignant; as a gentle mother speaking calm consolations—never as a mouth holding a two-edged sword. Jesus was a man of indignation. His eyes flashed. His words burned. There were men in Jerusalem who never forgot the glance of His angry eyes. The men who were nearest to Him and who called Him holy, often thought of the times when they had seen Him angry. They did not hesitate to tell about it in the narratives written for the instruction of all believers!

Hearken to Him there when every word falls with the scorching power of fire, with the burning power of lightning! They, His enemies, withered before Him—like flowers wither in a furnace. Somebody said when Wilberforce spoke in Parliament his face took on a new light and burned with some mysterious glow. Somebody said that when Daniel Webster spoke on one occasion, his eyes "emitted sparks." Somebody said when Patrick Henry spoke in the little Virginia courthouse, his face was "bright like a torch, slowly kindling, then flashing." A New York editor said of Henry Grady, "He was an animated aurora with all the variations of a luminous sunset!" And Jesus when He spoke that twenty-third chapter of Matthew had His face to catch the fire of His heart. Nobody could speak as He spoke then without his face "catching on fire from his heart."

> And I saw a great white throne, and him that sat on it, from whose face the earth and the heaven fled away; and there was found no place for them (Rev. 20:11).

We ought to keep clear in our hearts' vision the face of Jesus as our Lord. When the order for action was given in Dewey's fleet on that memorable May morning in Manila Bay, one of the powder boys hastily took off his coat, and it slipped from his hand into the water. In the inside pocket was a photograph of his mother. The boy had just been looking at it, and had restored it to what seemed to be a safe place. He asked to be allowed to jump overboard and recover the coat, and when he was forbidden to do this, he went to the other side of the ship, leaped into the water, swam to the coat, and rescued it. Because of his disobedience he was put in irons and held for punishment. Commodore Dewey wondered why he risked his life and disobeyed orders for the sake of a coat, for the boy had said nothing about the photograph. In answer to Commodore Dewey's kind questions, the lad disclosed his motive. The commodore's eyes filled with tears, and he clasped the boy in his arms. Orders were given that the little fellow should be released. "A boy who loves his mother enough to risk his life for her picture," said Dewey, "cannot be kept in irons on this fleet." This is the kind of feeling we ought to have about keeping clear in our mental vision and in our hearts the beautiful and wonderful face of the Divine Savior! At some glorious time "we shall see Him as He is"—one of God's days!

A Shrouded Face

What a day that was when Jesus died! If I knew all languages and had an eloquence that excelled the sweetness of heaven's music, I could not adequately talk about it. But He died. And Joseph of Arimathea, a rich man, went to Governor Pilate and begged the body of Jesus (see Matt. 27:58). And Pilate, marveling that He was so soon dead (see Mark 15:44), gave consent that they should take that body off the Cross.

I do not know who pulled the nails out of those cold icy hands and from those blue-veined feet. Maybe Nicodemus did it. Maybe Joseph of Arimathea himself did it. Maybe John. Maybe poor distracted Peter back from the scenes of the wild tortures of his denial. Anyway, the dear Christ was taken down from the cross. They wrapped His dear face in the graveclothes and carried Him out to the rich man's tomb and left Him there, all marred and scarred, where for the first time in thirty-three years the cruel world left Him alone. And that night when He, who had been born among cattle in a borrowed stable, and who died between two thieves on a cross of crucifixion, slept in that borrowed tomb, there was not a man or a woman among all the men and the women who had ever heard His name who believed He would live again. That shrouded face would be a banquet for worms. He was dead. No darker night ever shadowed human lives or ever gloomed a world.

Back, Mary Magdalene, and all ye weary women—back to the petty round of household duties. Jesus is dead.

Back, ye disappointed fisherman, James and John, sons of Zebedee, who left your nets to follow Him. Buy ye other nets now and take up your fishing again. Jesus is dead!

Back to your tax gathering Matthew. There were those who said you were foolish to leave your government position to follow the long-haired fanatic from Nazareth. And they were right. Wisdom was in their words, though you would not believe it. Back, Matthew. Jesus is dead.

Back, Mary, mother of Jesus, and see if you can find healing for the hurt of your soul. He, thy firstborn, whom thou didst carry in thy womb, is now an occupant of the tomb. Back, Mary, mother of the Christ. Thy Son is dead.

Back, Lazarus, to Bethany where everything about the Bethany home will make you think of Him. Back and someday you, the widow's son, and the nobleman's daughter may go in the garden and mingle your hot tears on the stone rolled against the tomb of Him who, not so long ago, took you from the embrace of the skeleton arms of death to the embrace of loving arms of flesh—back from the dark of death's night to the light of life's day. Jesus is dead.

Back, Simon Peter, to the old job. And from the old job to bed. And when, in the nightmaric grip of troubled dreams you swear again you never knew the mighty One from Nazareth, awake to joy. Your denial can wound Him never again and shame you no more. He who washed thy feet is dead.

Back, Governor Pilate, back to your court. Others will enter thy judgment hall. But none sinless like He. Look no more with horror upon your hands with the bloodstains that water will never wash away. The strange One, who said that you would have no power to crucify Him or release Him except it were given you from above, is dead.

Back, John, to your home. And fulfill the son's vow you made to the desolate mother at His bidding at the cross out yonder. Back, John. The bosom on which you leaned at the supper is as still as the deepest hush of whisperless silence. He is dead.

Back, ye women of Galilee. And you can come with spices not half so fragrant as the service He rendered you in Galilee—and maybe the soldiers who sit to guard the tomb will let you enter with the linen Joseph brought in which to wrap His body. He is dead now.

Back, ye Roman soldiers, who drove the nails and gambled at the foot of the cross. Remember that never before did you see one pray in the agonies of crucifixion for those who killed Him.

Go back, O centurion, who testified that He was a righteous man. Go back to supervise other bloody butcheries! Jesus is dead. But every storm cloud that drenches the earth with rain will turn your thoughts to Golgotha where midnight reigned on noonday's throne.

Back, ye Jewish authorities. Have no more controversies concerning His Messiahship. You have buried Him. Now bury your disputes. Dead He is—dead with strange scars on His body.

Go back, Simon of Cyrene, to your own country. But know thou that the load thou didst carry, when from His falling shoulders to thine it was placed, is the tree which, made into a cross, yielded blood and beareth fruit which is for the healing of the nations—a tree in the shape of a crossbeam around which gathereth all the light of sacred story.

A Seen Face

A seen face? Yes. Really? Here? No—not here. For "now we see through a glass darkly; but then face to face" (1 Cor. 13:12).

What a thrilling satisfaction to see the faces of those we love! We cherish their photographs when they are absent, and in quiet moments we gaze upon the pictures. They write us letters, and how we long for them! In greater hours they communicate by wireless. But when the door opens, and we see the loved one's face, what an exquisite and thrilling satisfaction—and so, says the Scripture, shall it be in heaven!

Here we have His photograph. Here we have His love letters. Here often do we catch His wireless message in the silence and secrecy of the regenerate heart. But there we shall see Him as He is, face to face, without a cloud between—and we shall be satisfied when we awake in His likeness.

"We shall see Him as He is!"

That's enough—that's all we can stand here. We shall all look upon the face of Jesus. We are assured that "every eye shall see him . . . they also which pierced him," (Rev. 1:7). And if we are steadfastly pressing on in His way, we may sing with the psalmist, "As for me, I will behold thy face in righteousness: I shall be satisfied when I awake, with thy likeness" (Ps. 17:15).

The reunion of the saints above will not be limited to the little circle that makes the family here. We belong to a bigger family than the one we live with in the flesh. "Many shall come from the east and west, and shall sit down with Abraham, and Isaac, and Jacob, in the kingdom of heaven." Like elder children born out in the world before the younger children appear, the poets, prophets, painters, and martyrs preceded us. We never saw them in the flesh, never heard their voices, but they will be with us in the great family reunion in the Father's house.

Time, like a doting father, has told us of his older children, and we feel as though we knew them. But there they shall tell us face to face the stories of their lives. Moses will tell us of the forty silent days on Sinai. Enoch will tell us how he rambled into glory. David will tell us the story of the Psalms. Daniel will tell us of the night in the lions' den.

Can you imagine yourself in the great throng that will crowd the Father's house, hearing the blessed Savior saying, "We will now hear Paul on the story of his conversion"? And later, "We will now listen to Judson on his work in Burma"? Can you catch the thrill that will vibrate when Luther, Wycliffe, Carey, Moody, Wesley, rise to speak?

The true and the great will all be there, and we shall see them and hear them at their best. Not at all the cold distance of a concert hall, but in the warm, unrestrained fellowship of home. They will not be to us members of another race, demigods of another era. Neither shall we be to them scions of a weak, degenerate age. The years will be miles, and we shall simply have come from near and far to our Father's house.

Like every family reunion, there shall be One, however, whose personality shall be dominant. What would the gathering of all the saints amount to if He would not be there who went to prepare the place? It would be a palace without a hearth. It would be a tree without foliage. It would be a sky without a sun.

We all want to see the loved ones with whom we walked the dusty miles. We all want to see the immortals who went on before us. But far above and beyond all cravings I desire to see our Lord and our Master.

We have seen Him in the sacred page. We have seen Him on the artist's canvas. We have seen Him in the light of faith. But we want to see Him as He is.

We have often heard Him in the multitude. The services of the sanctuary are the sweetest experiences we have ever known. But we want to know Him as the family of Bethany knew Him. We want to hear Him as the group at Emmaus heard Him. Free from all restraints of mortality and time, we want to grasp the nail-pierced hand, hear the love-filled voice of our Savior in His heavenly home.

The joy of fellowship with our Savior will not obliterate the joy of fellowship with each other, but it will subordinate it as the enjoyment of a soul-stirring sermon or chorus subordinates minor relations. Through eternity we shall be together in our Father's house, each real enough to each other, yet entranced by his Lord.

> Friends will be there I have loved long ago,
> Joy like a river around me will flow;
> Yet, just a smile from my Saviour I know,
> Will through the ages be glory for me.

CHAPTER FOUR

What He Was Made

"He was made"—
John 1:14; Rom. 8:3; Isa. 7:14; Gal. 4:4–5; Heb. 7:22; 2 Cor. 5:21

We make bold to say that none of the days gone forever into the tomb of time had or held more glorious opportunities and more stupendous responsibilities than do these days in which you and I are privileged to live. In these very recent years the titanic potencies accumulating through the centuries came to a sudden head. And when they did so, they toppled over old thrones, swept away ancient dynasties, burst through venerable creeds, snapped the rusty chains of tradition, smashed impregnable institutions, uprooted century-entrenched falsehoods—leaving us to face and to deal with a head-dizzy, body-weary, heart-sick, soul-famished world. And we acknowledge that today we are face to face with great giants of iniquity, with many subtle antagonisms, with many treacherous flatteries that come but to steal and to kill and to destroy. While the forces of righteousness are alive today—and powerful—so also are the forces of evil.

We are not "pale slaves of depression and pessimism" when we say that mightily existent today are all the forces of decay and all the powers of treacherous evil which, in the centuries gone by, wrought havoc!

Today, alive and active in our land, are all the haughty evils that made Babylon a "vermin-infested, briar-possessed, spider-hung, animal-prowling jungle where the hanging gardens once bloomed."

All the besmirching iniquities that made Nineveh a dirty doormat for irreverent feet thrive in our world today.

All the sin diseases that made glorious Tyre a meatless skeleton ghastly with grins exist today.

All the corrosive ills that made Assyria a rusty hinge on a doorless door fatten in our land today.

All the sins and sinning that made mighty Rome a branchless tree dishonorably fruitless are defiantly rampant now.

All the evils that made Greece—cultured, poetic, musical, philosophic, artistic, athletic, aesthetic Greece—a crumb in history's rubbish heap are at work in America today, silently as moths in chests of fine clothes, secretly and destructively as mice in a writer's desk, boldly as drunken men speaking in the wild nightmares of disordered brains.

All the blatant unrighteousness that made Egypt a shabby sexton of splendid tombs, today, in this land where the Pilgrim fathers prayed and Jonathan Edwards preached, "loose wild tongues that hold not God in awe."

All the greedy selfishness and craze for gold that made Spain a drowsy beggar watching a broken clock ply their trade with the effrontery of a thief who comes but to steal and to kill and to destroy—iniquities reeking with Pharisaic self-applause, iniquities that would "lead our greatest graces to the grave and leave the world no copy," as the debates superciliously conducted in scientific, psychologic, and philosophic kindergartens testify. Yes, the ageless problems of human sin and mischoice, black, menacing, terrible, big with possibilities of world destruction, are with us. Moreover, all the perversions of true religion and all the devices of all false religions assail us today.

We Have God's Book

But what rejoicing is ours that we have today God's Book—the Bible—the strangest, the mightiest, the weirdest, the loveliest, the best of all books, to guide us in our glooms, to prompt us in our perplexities, to help us in our hazards, to direct us in our doubts, to be a "lamp unto our feet and a light unto our path." Wondrous Book! Book above and beyond all books as a river is beyond a rill in reach, as the sun is above and beyond the tallow dip in brightness, as Niagara is above and beyond the mill pond in power, as the oak is above and beyond the roadside weed in majesty, as the wings of an eagle are beyond the wings of a sparrow in strength, as a tree is beyond a twig in fruit-bearing. Book that has withstood storms of fire! Book against which tyranny has issued its edicts! Book against which Mohammedanism has hurled its anathemas! Book against which infidelity has thrown its sharpest shafts and strongest spears of scorn and ridicule! Book which the dissecting knives of modernistic "intellectuals" have whacked at, like butchers, and do whack at now like savages on a midnight raid! Book against which snipers from behind some pulpit stands and some college chairs have aimed their ill-grounded propositions.

But withal, all its enemies have not torn one hole in its holy vesture nor stolen one flower from its wondrous garden nor diluted one drop of honey from its abundant hive nor broken one string on its thousand-stringed harp nor drowned one sweet word in infidel ink nor made dim one ray of its perpetual light nor stayed its triumphant progress by so much as one step nor shortened its life by so much as one brief hour! It is still the pilgrim's staff, the pilot's compass, the soldier's sword! And more besides!

Now Jesus, our preventative and curative Christ, is the grand subject of the Bible. Christ Jesus who was ever tender without being weak, strong without being coarse, lowly without being servile, mighty in His conviction but never intolerant, enthusiastic but never fanatical, ever holy but never Pharisaic, passionate for the truth but never tainted with prejudice—never making a false step never striking a jarring note, never speaking a false word. And about this Jesus, in the Bible, three simple and mightily significant words—"He was made"—are frequently written.

"He Was Made . . . "

"He was made"—three words that sound forth like a sweet old organ whose "full breath is thunder" in the stately cathedral of John's Gospel!

"He was made"—three words that gleam like radiantly rare jewels in the treasure house of Romans.

"He was made"—three words that burn their way into our attention, like forest fires at midnight, in the mountain ranges of Hebrews.

"He was made"—three words that sound forth in the Book of Galatians like the music of all choirs, visible and invisible, poured forth in one anthem.

"He was made"—three words that bloom like the flowers of ten thousand springtimes in one bouquet in the fertile gardens of 1 and 2 Corinthians.

"He was made." "He was made"—what? WHAT?

He Was Made Flesh

"In the beginning was the Word, and the Word was with God, and the Word was God" (John 1:1). "In the beginning"! Those words teach His eternity. "And the Word was with God"! Those words teach His equality. "And the Word was God"! Those words teach His deity. "The same was in the beginning with God"! Those words teach His preexistence.

"And the Word was made FLESH, and dwelt among us" (John 1:14, emphasis added). "For what the law could not do, in that it was weak through the flesh, God, sending his own Son in the *likeness* of sinful *flesh*, and for sin, condemned sin in the flesh"

(Rom. 8:3, emphasis added). "Made of the seed of David according to the flesh" (Rom. 1:3).

Here we behold the preexistent Christ. But this preexistent Christ Jesus was not flesh back yonder when the morning stars serenaded the advent of our infant earth as it lay, "wrapped in swaddling clothes of light," in the arms of the great Jehovah, for "all things were made by him; and without him was not anything made that was made" (John 1:3).

He was not flesh back in creation days when there was the gathering together of the waters called the seas for "the world was made by him" (John 1:10).

He was not flesh when the first ray of light shone, when the first bird sang, when the first lion "panted in the jungles of roses," when the first flower bloomed, when the first fire burned, when the first river flowed, when the first rose opened wide its rubied heart, when the first wind blew, when the first lily bared its white bosom. "For by him were all things created that are in heaven and that are in earth . . . and he is before all things, and by him all things consist" (Col. 1:16–17).

But! But "He was made flesh"—and every nerve was divine handwriting, every bone was divinely sculptured, every muscle was a pulley divinely swung! Jesus, "born not of blood, nor of the will of the flesh, nor of the will of man"—yet "made flesh," "made of a woman." As Milton puts it:

> That glorious form, that light insufferable,
> And that far-beaming blaze of majesty,
> Wherewith he wont at heaven's high council table
> To sit the midst of Tribal Unity,
> He laid aside; and here with us to be,
> Forsook the courts of everlasting day,
> And chose with us a darksome house of clay!

And only as we get some conception of the mystery and marvel and miracle of the truth that He "was made flesh" do we have some proper and adequate conception of His sufferings in the *physical realm* on the cross. It was upon flesh, flesh as tender as a little woman's flesh, that the merciless steel fingers of

Pilate's scourge fell. It was into flesh, flesh sensitive to pain, that the thorns that composed His crown of thorns bored. It was through flesh, tender flesh, that the nails of His death couch were driven. It was from flesh that the crimson tides of blood flowed. It was upon flesh that the hard palms of the slappers and mockers fell with strength and cruelty. It was in the flesh that He conquered the sins of the flesh, healed the diseases of the flesh, drove away the fever fires that burn up human bodies, conquered the loathsome leprosy that lays waste the flesh of the body, and straightened out the crippled bones of lame bodies. "It behooved him to be made like unto his brethren" (Heb. 2:17). For the Book says:

He Was Made of a Woman

A virgin irreproachable! A virgin having "found high favor with God"! A virgin "blessed among women," with child (see Luke 1:28). A virgin!—and the "holy thing born of her was the Son of God!" (see Luke 1:35). Event that has occurred once, only once, one marvelous once, in the history of the world.

"Therefore the Lord himself shall give you a sign; Behold, a virgin shall conceive, and bear a son, and shall call his name Immanuel" (Isa. 7:14).

> And the angel said unto her, Fear not, Mary: for thou hast found favor with God. And, behold, thou shalt conceive in thy womb, and bring forth a son, and shall call His name JESUS. . . . Then said Mary unto the angel, How shall this be, seeing I know not a man? And the angel answered and said unto her, The Holy Ghost shall come upon thee, and the power of the Highest shall overshadow thee: therefore also that holy thing which shall be born of thee shall be called the Son of God! (Luke 1:30–31, 34–35).

Then this: "But when the fulness of the time was come, God sent forth his Son, made of a woman, made under the law, to redeem them that were under the law, that we might receive the adoption of sons" (Gal. 4:4–5).

And of all the women who have been honored with motherhood, during all the centuries when women have gone down to the gates of death to bring human lives in being, Mary has had the highest honor placed upon her. For He who lived long before Mary was born chose to be "made of her," to be born of her, a woman; He who was loved of God before the foundation of the world (John 17:24), accepted God's choice of Mary as the channel through which He, the preexistent One, should become flesh and dwell among men; He who is the "firstborn of every creature" (Col. 1:15) became the firstborn of Mary, Mary the virgin who had not known a man.

His supernatural birth is the Alpha of our Christian faith. Let that be accepted and the whole alphabet follows as a matter of course. Deny it and, like a planet that leaves its orbit, there is no telling where unbelief will carry you. The virgin birth is the seal of the Father's approval affixed to the claims of Jesus as His only begotten Son!

His birth into our world by a virgin was a translation at the same time it was an incarnation. It was a transfer of His person from a previous condition of existence to this earthly one. It was His being clothed upon with our human nature. He saith, "A body hast thou prepared me" (Heb. 10:5). Before incarnation Jesus was God's instrument in creation. During incarnation Jesus was God's instrument in redemption. Then it is not just poetry and rhetoric and fiction when we say: "When the Lord of power determined to forsake His royal chariot and to alight on this earth, He undressed Himself first. He gave to the clouds His bow! He gave to the sky His azure mantle! He gave to the stars His jewels! He gave to the sun His brightness, AND, receiving instead of these the strange homespun clothes of One who had not where to lay His head," He was "made flesh," "made of a woman"! His incarnation meant, and means, that the preexistent Christ was embodied in human flesh, demonstrated in human life, exemplified in human action, crystalized in human form.

But He was not originally a human being, but the Divine One! He was not the offspring of woman as is man. He was the Mighty God, the Inhabitor of Eternity, the Creator made of the creature woman. He was Son of Man. He was Son of God! And both in one! And just as much Son of Man as though He were not Son of God and just as much Son of God as though He were not Son of Man!

He was so human He got tired. He was so divine He said "Come unto me all ye that labor and are heavy laden, and I will give you rest" (Matt. 11:28).

He was so human He got hungry. He was so divine He took five loaves and two fishes and fed thousands.

He was so human He got thirsty. He was so divine He walked on the stormed-tossed sea—so divine He said to the woman at the well: "Whosoever drinketh of the water that I shall give him shall never thirst; but the water that I give him shall be in him a well of water springing up into everlasting life" (John 4:14).

He was so human He felt the need to pray. He was so divine that in all of His praying there is no confession of sin.

He was so human He had to sleep. He was so divine He arose from sleep and stilled the raging tempest.

He was so human He accepted a village girl's invitation to her wedding. He was so divine that at this wedding He changed water into wine.

He was so human He got lonely and was pained at the slowness of human recognition. He was so divine He could say, "The Father hath not left me alone" (John 8:29).

He was so human He was "tempted in all points like as we are." He was so divine He asked, "Who convinceth me of sin?" (see John 8:46).

He was so human He yearned for human sympathy. He was so divine He "trod the winepress alone" (see Isa. 63:3).

He was so human He wept. He was so divine He stood at the grave where He wept and raised the dead brother and gave him back to the empty arms and aching hearts of the sisters.

He was so human He grew in wisdom and stature. He was so divine He "upholdeth all things by the word of his power" (see Heb. 1:3).

But yet again it was stated that He was:

He Was Made Under the Law

"To redeem them that were under the law, that we might receive the adoption of sons" (Gal. 4:5). This the high and holy purpose!

"He was made under the law." He was made under the law which was made for sinners and not for the righteous. He was made under the law which could not claim Him for Himself but claimed Him for us, for when He was made of a woman He was made under the law and His incarnation brought Him under our condemnation—Him who had no cause in Him for condemnation. The cause of condemnation was in us who had sinned and "come short of the glory of God"—in us who had "turned everyone to his own way"—in us who had lifted high hands of rebellion against God—in us, who, like sheep, had gone astray—in us who despised the goodness of God—in us who preferred darkness to light because our deeds were evil. So, for us who deserved death, Christ was made under the law and died under the law, but His death was the "end of law for righteouness." Made under the law, He bore the penalty of the law, grievous as it was. As someone says, "He arranged His own death sentence when He made the law and then bore His own fixed penalty in His own body on the tree."

But joy superlative it is to know that the Lord has fully dealt, for us, with the Law's claim that man shall deserve acceptance. Legal satisfaction is forever taken out of our hands by Christ. Jesus Himself dealt, in the sinner's interest, with the law, honoring its holy claims to the uttermost under the human conditions which He freely undertook, so that, by faith, the community between Jesus and sinners is real, the community of their debt on one side and Christ's merit on the other side!

He became one of us that He might become our King as well as our Savior. He clothed Himself in our dust that we might wear His royal robe. He lay in our grave that we might sit on His throne. He "emptied Himself of the glory He had with the Father before the world was" that we might be "filled with all the fulness of God." Again, He was:

He Was Made a Curse

God says so. And that truth presses itself down upon our hearts with the weight of a thousand worlds, when we consider it aright. Christ hath redeemed us from the curse of the law. Being made a curse for us, for it is written, "Cursed is every one that hangeth on a tree" (Gal. 3:13).

We pitch our mental tents on this verse, we gather our hearts' meditations about this statement, as those who approach a holy-white sanctuary where unanointed feet cannot walk! "Made a curse for us"! Jesus, so finely strung, so unutterably keyed to truth, mercy, justice, love, quickly feeling the sorrow, sympathy, and indignation which injustice and wrong invariably elicit for all high souls, "made a curse"!

Jesus, Inhabitor of Eternity—"made a curse"! Jesus, Teacher come from God—"made a curse"! Jesus, "Image of the invisible God, the firstborn of every creature"—"made a curse"! Jesus, "Light of Light," hanging in darkness when "the sun went down at noonday and the earth was darkened in the clear day"—"made a curse"! Jesus, "Poet's Poet, Wisdom's Tongue, Man's Best Man, Good Paragon, Crystal Christ"—"made a curse"! Jesus, Miracle greater than all His miracles,—"made a curse"! Jesus, "who had the glory with the Father before the world was," "giving His back to the smiters and His cheeks to them that plucked off His beard, and hiding not His face from shame and spitting"—"made a curse"! Jesus, "the Father's comprehensibility and visibility"—"made a curse"! Jesus, "Heir of all things," "fairer than all the fair who fill the heavenly train"—"made a curse"! He who was earth's greatest blessing was "made a curse"!

Never a curse TO anybody. "Made a curse" FOR everybody.

He was the blessed Son of God bringing blessing wherever He went. Into the midst of earth's night He came to give light! Into the midst of earth's sorrow He came to give joy! Into the midst of earth's strife He came to give peace! Into the midst of earth's death He came to give life! He never met a blind man that He didn't give him sight! He never met a deaf man that He didn't make him hear! He never met a dumb man that He didn't loose his tongue! He never met a crippled man that He didn't make him walk! He never met a leper that He didn't make him whole! He never went into a sick room that He didn't heal the sick! He never met a funeral procession that He didn't break it up! He never went into the cemetery that He didn't raise the dead!

He was never a curse TO anybody! He was "made a curse" FOR everybody! The curse due us fell crushingly on Him, for God laid on Him the iniquity of us all. Deuteronomy records the penalty of the curse. It reads: "His body shall not remain all night on a tree, but thou shalt in any wise bury him that day; (for he that is hanged is accursed of God;) that thy land be not defiled, which the LORD thy God giveth thee for an inheritance" (Deut. 21:23).

> I took a day to search for God,
> And found Him not. But as I trod
> By rocky ledge through woods untamed,
> Just where one scarlet lily flamed
> I saw His footprint in the sod!
> Then suddenly, all unaware,
> Far off in the deep shadows, where
> A solitary hermit thrush
> Sang through the holy twilight hush—
> I heard His voice upon the air.
> And even as I marveled how
> God gives us heaven and now,
> In a stir of wind that hardly shook
> The poplar leaves beside the brook—
> His hand was light upon my brow.
> At last with evening as I turned
> Homeward and thought what I had learned
> And all that there was still to probe—
> I caught the glory of His robe
> Where the last fires of sunset burned.

Now we do not agree with the pantheistic tendencies or teachings of the verses just quoted. But we do agree in believing that wherever Jesus walked, whether in dusty highways, by Galilee's shores, up mountain slopes or on city pavements, His were the footprints of God. "God manifest in the flesh." When He spoke, whether in teaching as "One who had authority and not as the scribes" or in wooing love that drew sinners to Him, or in rebuke, or in flaming and righteous wrath when His every sentence was a flash and flare of verbal lightning, His was the voice of God. When His hand touched the loathsome leper or blind eyes or deaf eardrums or crippled limbs or the brow hot with fever fires or the hand cold with the ice of death, the touch of His hand was the touch of God, for "God was in Christ" (2 Cor. 5:19). Wherever He went He was "the glory of the invisible God," the brightness of God's glory. This is He who was "made a curse." Truth that overawes us with its solemnity—"Christ was made a curse for us"! The only sinless One was made a curse for the vile and sinful ones.

My sins laid open to the rod,
The back which from the law was free;
And the eternal Son of God
Received the curse once due to me!
The sponge of vinegar and gall
By me was placed upon His tongue;
And when derision mocked His call
I stood the mocking crowd among!

Wonderful that the Son of God, "Wonderful, Counselor, The mighty God, The everlasting Father, The Prince of Peace" was, for us, "made a curse"!

Not only so. But Jesus was:

He Was Made Sin

"For he hath made him to be sin for us, who knew no sin; that we might be made the righteousness of God in him" (2 Cor. 5:21).

The fact of His sinlessness is beyond all challenge. John the Baptist had not hesitated to condemn with unpitying severity the religious leaders of those times and to demand of them repentance and baptism, but to Christ Jesus he said, "I have need to be baptized of thee, and comest thou to me?" (Matt. 3:14). Several times Pilate, with an emphasis and an earnestness no one could overlook, said "I find no fault in him!" Pilate's wife called Him "this just man!" Judas, refusing to die with a lie on his lips, said "I have betrayed the innocent blood!" The centurion who saw Him die when every breath He drew was a pang of pain and when every beat of His heart was a throb of agony, said, "Surely this man was the Son of God." The worst things His enemies could say about Him was that "He made himself the Son of God" and "this man receiveth sinners and eateth with them!"

When, on one occasion, the Jews sought to throw slurs on His birth, Jesus, with a question that flares like lightning, asked, "Which of you convinceth me of sin?" (John 8:46). And yet again we read: "Ye know that he was manifested to take away our sins; and in him is no sin" (1 John 3:5).

Marvelous that He was "made of a woman." Marvelous that He was "made under the law to redeem them that are under the law!" Marvelous that God "sending His own Son in the likeness of sinful flesh and as an offering for sin condemned sin in the flesh that the righteousness of the law might be fulfilled in us who walk not after the flesh but after the Spirit!" But more wonderful even than that, more triumphantly transcendent, is the truth that God "hath made him to be sin for us who knew no sin; that we might become the righteousness of God in him." This verse is a fortune in a single diamond; the glories of many flowers in one flower; the eloquence of much eloquence in one utterance. By the truths it reveals, some luminous with noonday brightness, some dark with midnight blackness, it is one of the stateliest cathedrals of human speech. By the mercy and mystery it testifies to, it stands among the real sublimities of Bible vocabulary. By the tragedy it acknowledges it is a pathos of language that defies all definition. By the victories it assures, it contains a splendor of revelation that leaves little to be said.

"MADE SIN! THE SINLESS ONE MADE SIN!" "IN HIM NO SIN" yet "MADE SIN."

Holy of holies this into which unhallowed eyes cannot look, behind the veil of which none dare to intrude with cheap scorn. I know of nothing more vastly vast!

Terrible Truth This in Face of the Terribleness of Sin

Sin, the darkest, saddest fact in God's universe. Tragedy back of every tragedy! SIN is folly, disorder, devastation, death. Sin, an opiate in the will, a frenzy in the imagination, a madness in the brain, a poison in the heart, is the intolerable burden of a soul that is destined to live forever, a black darkness that invests man's whole moral being—the sum of all terror, all horror, all cruelty. "By one man sin entered into the world, and death by sin; and so death passed upon all men, for that all have sinned" (Rom. 5:12).

Greedy as worms, merciless as an octopus, relentless as a serpent, poisonous as a viper, SIN is no "disagreeable hindrance to the smooth on-going of the social machinery" no "upward stumble in man's progress," as say some; no skin wound, but a fatal mischief of the heart; no light discord but a thunderbolt that crashes the organ into splinters and leaves it without shape or tone. A death's-head set amid life's feast—a desert breath that drinks up every dew!

And sin identifies itself with beauty. Not as a leper in sackcloth crying "Unclean," but with the glories of the rainbow it oft approaches. Not as a locust, but as a butterfly; not as a hornet, but as a hummingbird it oft appears. Not with the vulture's filthy beak and blood-fouled feathers, but with the peacock's train it oft comes to us. Whoever said the foregoing spoke mighty truths.

Like Mokanna, the prophet of the silver veil, it seems like some angel "Sent to free the world from every bond and stain/ And bring its primal glories back again."

But when the silver veil is torn away and its hideous features are revealed, it may well say with the veiled prophet to Zelica: "Here, judge if hell, with all its power to damn/ Can add one curse to the foul thing I am."

Terrible This Fact That He, the Sinless One, Was "Made Sin" in View of God's Hatred of Sin!

Behold this picture: It is night time. A little child, wearied with much play, falls asleep. The father and mother, the light of love beaming in their eyes, the tone of love in their whispering voices, the inexhaustible wonder of parental sacrifice burning in their hearts, put their darling into the trundle bed. With deft and tender hands the mother smooths the pillow and spreads the coverlets, the father taking in every detail of the scene with admiring eyes. Child of phenomenal beauty that, its voice sweeter to their ears than chiming bells, its eyes bluer than violets dew-wet, its luxuriant curls golden like sunshine, its face on the pillow dainty like a pink rose in a snowbank, its soft sleep-breathings like faint whispers of a harp touched by angel fingers. What mighty hold those baby hands, wee and dimpled, have upon human hearts! They kneel, those parents, a minute beside the trundle bed, pure thoughts holding high and holy carnival in their minds. Then, before they go to seek for themselves rest and sleep, they pray that God will give them wisdom to rear that child in the nurture and admonition of the Lord.

And then, in the night, while they sleep, a rattlesnake with stupid audacity and vile intrusion, crawls in through an open window and into the bed of the child. The hideous reptile coils itself into a circular pile and lies there apparently in a stupor until, at the movement of a dimpled hand or a turn of the curly head, the rattler, his buttons buzzing with diabolical effrontery, strikes out madly. And the poisonous fangs are buried in the cheek of the child. In awful agony it dies—while the parents sleep. The next morning they awake. They go to the bed and find their approach challenged by the rattler whose head sways ominously while his buttons sing with raucous warning. They see their child swollen, dead, its little face bearing the evidences of its frightful death agonies.

Now—if you will magnify the attitude and the hatred of that vile rattler by that father and that mother a million times a million times you will have a faint conception of how God Almighty looks toward sins and upon sin. You will know in some slight measure His perpetual attitude toward sin, His eternal hatred of sin. Yet it is said that our holy God made Jesus "to be sin for us who knew no sin that we might be made the righteousness of God in him!"

"Made Sin"—What Does It Mean?

What do they mean, these two words, "made sin," that stagger under a weight of agony?

It means that God dealt with Him as He must deal with sin—in severe and unrelenting judgment!

It means that God sentenced sin, ordered sin to execution in the person and death of His Son. Jesus has made up before God for all we failed to do and be. Jesus takes all our sin and sins upon Himself and bestows all His righteousness upon us. Jesus took sin's place on the cross! Took the guilty culprit's place there! Took *my* place there! It means that He, the perfectly righteous One, was made sin that we, the unrighteous ones, might be made righteous. For God meted out to Jesus the full measure of punishment sin deserves.

It means—"He stood before God with all our sin upon Him that we, through faith, might stand before God with none of our sin on us."

He who was righteous was judged before God as unrighteous that we who are unrighteous should be judged before God as righteous!

"He was made for us all that God must judge AND we are made in Him by faith all that God cannot judge."

And this could not be through physical suffering alone! By the bloody drops of sweat in Gethsemane, by the dirty sputum, "contempt materialized in a liquid," by the rough hands that plucked off His beard, by the merciless steel fingers of Pilate's scourge, by the thorns that punctured His brow veins, by the nails that pinned Him to the tree, by His mouth hot like an oven, I know, you know, all of us know, He suffered physically on the cross.

But! To speak of Jesus' suffering as intense physical torture only is a species of spiritual stupidity and intellectual clownishness. Because of the depths and vastnesses of sin's malignant nature, which caused the feet of Deity to draw back with trembling, terms like bravery, courage, martyrdom, physical agony have no place because they contain no meaning big enough to fit His experience, when He "made his soul an offering for sin"—when He died a spiritual death as well as a physical death. He founded our joy in the deep bitterness of His own soul.

The pangs of hell got hold upon Him! God turned Him into the slime pits of hell! The thirst of hell was upon Him! The lightest of His sufferings were physical! The tortures of the damned were upon Him. "The soul of His suffering was the suffering of His soul." He bore the burdens of sin on His sinless soul. And He did this for all—ALL!

    That night when in the Judean skies
The mystic star dispensed its light,
A blind man moved in his sleep—
And dreamed that he had sight!
    That night when shepherds heard the song
Of hosts angelic choiring near,
A deaf man stirred in slumber's spell—
And dreamed that he could hear!
    That night when in the cattle stall
Slept child and mother cheek by jowl,
A cripple turned his twisted limbs—
And dreamed that he was whole!
    That night when o'er the newborn babe
The tender Mary rose to lean,
A loathsome leper smiled in sleep—
And dreamed that he was clean!
    That night when to the mother's breast
The little King was held secure,
A harlot slept a happy sleep—
And dreamed that she was pure!
    That night when in the manger lay
The sanctified who came to save,
A man moved in the sleep of death—
And dreamed there was no grave!

And let it be counted folly, or frenzy, or fury, or whatsoever it is our wisdom and comfort to know that for those blind in sin, for those deaf in sin, for those crippled in sin, for those impure with the harlotry of sin, for those loathsome with the leprosy of sin, for those "dead in trespasses and sins," Him who knew no sin did God make to be sin in their behalf that they might be made the righteousness of God in Him.

The death of Christ was for us. Therefore Christ was condemned to death instead of us. To condemn us now after we have put our faith in Christ and surrendered personally to Him, would be to say that the death of Christ was not sufficient and that there was no justice with God, for He would get two payments for one debt, two payments for one offense. But, thank God, the death of Christ is sufficient and God is not possessed of the injustice that demands two payments for one debt—and we can truly say, "There is therefore now no condemnation to them which are in Christ Jesus, who walk not after the flesh, but after the Spirit" (Rom. 8:1). We can find no knowledge in the world better than this: That man hath sinned and God hath suffered; that God in Christ made Himself the sin of men; that men are made the righteousness of God!

In view of this let us ask: Is any distance too great to go—for Him—who went to the Cross for us? Is any burden too heavy to bear—for Him—who bore the heavy weight of the world's sins on our heart? Is any sacrifice too severe to make—for Him—who was "made a curse" for us? Is any obligation too heavy to assume—for Him—who was "made sin" in our behalf that we might become the righteousness of God in Him? Is any service too great to render—for Him—who was made for us all that God must judge and punish? Is it not time that we say: "I count all things but loss, that I may know him, and the power of his resurrection, and the fellowship of his sufferings"?

He Was Made Alive

"He showed himself alive after his passion" (Acts 1:3). "When they had heard that he was alive" (Mark 16:11). "If the Spirit of him that raised up Jesus from the dead" (Rom. 8:11).

Everybody thought He was dead. As the day went dark, as the sun went down at noonday upon the skull-shaped hill, they named Him a dead king. To them His day was ended. His glory departed. "Whatever He was, He is dead!" they said. The smug scribes and elders whose cautious creeds and ritualistic shows, so utterly void of inward reality, He had condemned, said He was dead! The religious leaders whose religion was "faultily faultless, icily regular, splendidly null" said He was dead. The soldiers who drove the nails into His hands said He was dead. AND "the little group who gazed through weeping eyes on that spectacle had a judgment different in quality but not in character. They saw a beloved form stiffen; eyes that had so often looked upon them with vast yearning, glaze; hands that had so often carried to the suffering multitudes the touch of healing become lifeless; the voice that had spoken as never man spake, grow dumb!" "And as they watched and wept, hope saw no star, for hope was dead, and listening love heard not even the rustle of an angel's wing!" "For as yet they knew not the Scriptures that He must rise from the dead!"

A tragedy for them! The throne of their beloved had disappeared in a tomb. His regal robes had changed to a dreary shroud. His own crown was a crown of thorns. His kingdom had shrunk to the narrow dimensions of a grave. His only throne was a cross of wood. His only inaugural cry "My God, my God, why hast thou forsaken me?" (Mark 15:34). His only scepter a weed. His only companions in inauguration two thieves. His only reign six hours physical and soul agony on the cross. His only inaugural splendor the darkness that shrouded the earth. His only "king's cup" a sponge filled with vinegar and gall. These sorrowful ones, in upper rooms and dark retreats, thinking of Him who, marred and scarred, was sleeping in Joseph's garden, whispered to each other, "We trust that it had been He who would have redeemed Israel!" But their expectation had been shattered by envious death. He who was "the Ancient of Days" was "cut off in the midst of His days."

But, He resumed His power; He recovered His challenged rights; He regained His waning influence; He reasserted His sacred grandeur! And answering thus His malignant enemies, He sent echoing down the ages the blest assurance that there is something in the universe higher than its laws, namely, a Christ who, born in denial of the laws of death, saith: "Behold, I am he that was dead and am alive forever more" (see Rev. 1:18). SO He is no mere shadow Christ of legend, no mere dream Christ of culture and romance, no mere immanent Christ of nature, no mere ideal Christ of the painter's canvas and the sculptor's chisel, no mere hero Christ of song and story, but a living Christ, for the tomb in Joseph's garden is empty.

But we would not have to know of the empty tomb to know that Jesus is "made alive from the dead!" We know, you and I, people in whom Christ lives today, daily, hourly. We know some, maybe more than the world's arithmetic allows, concerning whom we can testify, as Paul spoke of himself;

> they are "crucified with Christ: nevertheless [they] live; yet not [they], but Christ liveth in [them]; and the life which [they] now live in the flesh they live by the faith of the Son of God, who loved [them] and gave himself for [them]" (Gal. 2:20).

No dead king! No! As Dan Poling puts it, though I may add to and take from his words:

> He was not a dead king who commanded the intrepid saints of the early church, who led them out to light a gospel lamp in the palace of the Caesars and to set the banner of the Cross above the screaming eagles of Rome. No dead king He who lit the signal fires of the Pentecostal upper room, who held the gaze of Stephen, when, through the showering stone, the first Christian martyr lifted his dying eyes to the opening heavens and claimed forgiveness for his murderers! No dead king He who took command of Saul of Tarsus, blinded him with lightnings and then thrust him forth to compass the earth with the truths of redemption! No dead king He who made out of the heathen Coliseum a Christ church! No dead king He who tamed the fires for Savonarola, who enabled Luther to see a corrupt church broken and rebuked, who let Wycliffe see the first rays of the morning star of Reformation ere he "put out to sea," who led the Ironsides of Cromwell, who eased those waves that washed the decks of the "Mayflower" and calmed the seas that broke about the prow of the "Half-Moon," who enabled Florence Nightingale to bandage the world's battle wounds, who gave to the first missionaries the islands of the sea for an inheritance! No dead king He who led the

> scholarly William Screven, driven out of New England by persecution, to establish the first Baptist church in the South in Charleston in 1683. No dead king He who enabled William Carey to land in Calcutta on November 11, 1793 (the very day the French Revolutionists tore the Cross from Notre Dame, smashed it in the streets, and abjured Christianity), and claim a new continent for Christ.
>
> No dead king who inspired the great John A. Broadus, once as penniless as the Seminary was poor, to turn deaf ears to a call to a great Northern church that paid $10,000, to fasten his flag to the mast of what seemed to many to be a sinking Seminary ship. No dead king who gave John Anderson—a Sir Galahad from Furman University—courage to choose a mud grave in a Chinese river rather than the comforts of a life of ease. Not dead! No! Alive forevermore! Wesley, Carey, Paton, Morrison, Livingstone, Adoniram Judson, and that numberless company of their faith who went forth to make the waste places of idolatry blossom with the flowers of salvation, followed not the banner of a dead king, but marched in the train of a living Lord!

And this Christ Jesus, who was "made flesh," "made of a woman," "made a curse," "made sin," and "made alive from the dead" is the same Christ Jesus "who of God *is* made unto us wisdom, and righteousness, and sanctification, and redemption." "Christ in you, the hope of glory" (Col. 1:27). Not the glory of the future, but the glory of Christly character here and now, the glory of deliverance from the smiling ease with which old faiths are chucklingly thrown off and doubts grinningly taken on, the glory of deliverance from the intellectual conceit unaware of the rattle of its dry bones, the glory of deliverance from the superficial mental illumination that lacks the urge of sacrificial passion, the glory of dominion over sin, the glory of Christ enunciating Himself in the precincts of personality, the glory of deliverance from the tragedy of contracting spiritual boundaries after we have extended intellectual frontiers! And, beyond these, the glory of the reality and the fruits of a regenerate heart!

And we must remember that all this centers in Calvary's Cross. The salvation of every believer rests upon three facts. First, the fact that justice has been satisfied. Second, the fact that the law has been honored. Third, the fact that God has been glorified. And all this is done at and in and by the Cross of Jesus. At and in and by

His Cross justice has been fully and completely satisfied, the law has been gloriously honored, and God has been mightily glorified.

Somewhere, from some mouth touched as with fire from God's altar, I remember to have heard this, which stirred my heart, though I may not recall the exact words:

> The history of human guilt culminates in the Cross. The purposes of divine love are made intelligible at the Cross. The rays of glory emanating from Christ are focussed in the Cross. The fingers of prophecy point to the Cross. The mysteries of prophecy are unraveled at the Cross. The hieroglyphics of the types find their key at the Cross. The great problem of human redemption is solved at the Cross. The serpent's head is bruised at the Cross. The door of Heaven is opened at the Cross. The fountain of salvation is unsealed at the Cross. The streams of civilization rise at the Cross.
>
> AND—all the great events of the gospel yield in importance to the Cross. The Incarnation was preparatory to the Cross. The Transfiguration foreshadowed the Cross. The Resurrection was the Complement of the Cross. Pentecost was the fruit of the Cross. Bethlehem and Nazareth, Galilee and Jerusalem, Tabor and Olivet, gleam only in the light of the Cross. All the great doctrines of grace revolve around the Cross. Our new life with its peace that passeth all understanding and its joy that is ever rich and abiding is born at the Cross. The world is stripped of its charm at the Cross. Earthly glory fades at the Cross. Intellect is sanctified at the Cross. Sin dies at the Cross. Our condemnation is lifted at the Cross. Our ruin is removed at the Cross. Our death sentence is revoked at the Cross. Our slave chains are snapped at the Cross. The bitters of life are sweetened at the Cross. The shadows of death are dispelled at the Cross. The Heaven of the redeemed is built upon the Cross. The darkness of eternity is irradiated at the Cross! Hallelujah for the Cross!

And, while we live, we will never cease to praise Him, our God, that He who was "made flesh" and who was "made of a woman" and who was "made under the law" and who was "made a curse" and who was "made sin" is "made unto us wisdom, and righteousness, and sanctification, and redemption" (1 Cor. 1:30). Amen!

CHAPTER FIVE

The Triumphant Tense

But Mary stood without at the sepulchre weeping:
and as she wept, she stooped down, and looked into the sepulcher,
And seeth two angels in white sitting,
the one at the head and the other at the feet.
John 20:11–12

If you visit Mohammed's tomb, a tomb adorned with diamonds, you say: "Here is the mortal body of Mohammed."

If Mount Vernon you visit and see the tomb of George Washington, you say: "Here is the dust of George Washington who, when alive, was just, pious, humane, temperate, sincere, dignified, commanding."

If to Stratford-on-Avon you travel, and look upon the grave of Shakespeare, you say: "Here is the dust of Shakespeare, that myriad-minded genius."

If to Paris you journey and stand before that magnificent sarcophagus gilt and gold, you say: "Here is all that is left of Napolean's body."

If you linger in Westminster Abbey, you say: "Here is the body of Queen Victoria." Or, "Here is the body of Robert Burns." Or, "Here is the dust of once-mighty soldiers and once-influencial statesmen."

If to Lexington, Virginia, you go and stand by the tomb of the sweetest memory of the Southland, say: "Here is the body of that great military genius."

If to Northfield you wander and stand by the grave of Dwight L. Moody, the preacher who rocked two continents toward God, you say: "Here is the body of Moody," as you read on his tombstone: "He that doeth the will of God abideth forever."

If to Springfield, Illinois, you go, and, as you stand before the tomb of the railsplitter of Sangamon, you say: "Here are the remains of that master of men who belongs to the ages. Lincoln, who

> Held on through blame and faltered not at praise.
> And when he fell in whirlwind,
> He went down as when a kingly cedar green with boughs
> Goes down with a great shout upon the hills,
> And leaves a lonesome place against the sky.

Moreover, if you go to that tiny grave of the little dimpled darling who went away and left you with empty arms and an aching heart, you say: "Here is the baby that once nestled in my arms."

If you go, some of you, back to the old country graveyard where snows of many winters have fallen, you stand by some grave, and, looking down, say: "Here is where my mother sleeps."

If you go, some of you, to some city vault where slate roofs and marble slabs shelter your dead, you say: "Here is the body of my beloved."

On May 1, 1932, two million people in closely-packed ranks passed by Lenin's tomb in Moscow, a day-long parade. And everyone in that vast throng, whether he spoke it by word of mouth or not, had to acknowledge: "Here is the body of Lenin."

Where the Body Had Lain

But if all the millions of all the ages could be brought to life again, and could form a procession and march by the tomb of Joseph of Arimathea, not one could truthfully say: "Here *is* the body of Jesus." All of them, young and old, black and white, red and yellow, rich and poor, of low estate and high estate, could say: "Come see the place where the Lord *lay*." For when you walk into Joseph's garden, you walk off the *present* tense into and upon a glorious *past* tense. There you can assuredly say that His thorn-torn head *lay*, not *lies*, here. You can say: His scourge-cut back *rested*, not *rests*, here. His nail-pierced hands *were*, not *are*, folded here. His fist-beaten face *was*, not *is*, shrouded here. His compassionate eyes *slept*, not *sleep*, here. Here He *was*, not *is*. Mary saw "two angels in white sitting, the one at the head, and the other at the feet, where the body of Jesus HAD lain" (John 20:12, emphasis added). "Come see, the place where the Lord lay" (Matt. 28:6).

Why are most of our tombs dear to human hearts and sweet in human memories? Why, on some days, do I see people going their way to our cemeteries? Because there, "by the flow of an inland river," sleeps in a grave one whose voice was once the music of a home.

Why do I see when I go occasionally to cemeteries, somebody here and a group of people there by a great tomb and there by a lowly grave placing flowers? Because there, where they place these tributes are some "asleep under the sod and the dew waiting the judgment day," whose eyes, now closed, once held the light of love.

Why is every plat "where the blades of the grave grass quiver," where "asleep are the ranks of the dead," a sacred plot? Because of what they now contain, because of what they now have and now hold till "the trumpet of the Lord shall sound."

I go to the tomb of B. H. Carroll in Texas. I stand with head covered. Why? Because I stand by the grave of that theological juggernaut who left a trail of glory across a wide state.

I stand near the slab that marks the last resting place of Copernicus who gave the name to the system, who was called the mover of the earth and the establisher of the heavens, who asked to have written on his monument in the venerable church at Thun these words:

I crave not the favor which Paul received,
Nor the grace wherewith Thou didst pardon Peter.
I only pray for that which Thou
Didst bestow upon the thief upon the Cross.

And, as there I stand, I say: "Here is the testimony that Copernicus is dead."

I stand on the deck of a ship where Judson was buried. And my heart is moved. Why? Because there, somewhere down in the far-reaching, rolling waves, is the hero of many conquests.

I stand by the humble grave in a Virginia cemetery. And my eye is moist with tears while the sunshine of gratitude floods my heart. Why? Because that underneath the sod rests the bones of one of the greatest preachers of our Southland, John Broadus.

I Am He That Liveth, and Was Dead . . .

So it is with the burial place of father, whether it be a great marble vault or a spot of lowly soil in some obscure village. So it is with the grave of mother, whether she was placed there years ago or only yesterday. So it is with the grave of the little baby, whether the babe was buried in a corner of a country graveyard or marked with a tiny stone in the shadow of great tombs in a city's "city of the dead." So it is with the grave of the neighbor who shared generously of everything he had, except his troubles. So it is with the grave of the lover for whom some heart is still "just a-wearying." So it is with the friend who, when walking the dusty ways of earth with us, lost money but never lost faith in God. So it is with nearly all graves, "from Greenland's icy mountains to India's coral strand." The entombed dust and bones of kindred and friends and loved ones "hallows the place of their entombment." All these graves and tombs are valued because of what they contain, what they now have and now hold. And there is only one tomb that has imperishable glory. It is the tomb of Joseph of Arimathea "where never man before was laid" till therein was placed the body of Jesus, marred and scarred with the stigmata of the Cross, where for the first time in thirty-three years the cruel world left Him alone.

"Now there stood by the cross of Jesus his mother, and his mother's sister, Mary the wife of Cleophas, and Mary Magdalena" (John 19:25).

"I AM he that liveth, and WAS dead; and, behold I AM alive forevermore, Amen, and have the keys of hell and of death" (Rev. 1:18, emphasis added).

> Until the day in which he was taken up, after that he through the Holy Ghost had given commandments unto the apostles whom he had chosen: to whom also he showed himself alive after his passion by many infallible proofs, being seen of them forty days, and speaking of the things pertaining to the kingdom of God (Acts 1:2–3).

We rejoice in the triumphant tense of this Triumph of Scripture.

The Triumphant Tense

The triumphant tense justifies to the literal bodily resurrection of the Lord Jesus Christ as the distinguishing mark of Christianity. This sets it apart from all the man-made religions of the world. False religions must stop at the tomb. Christianity takes us to the throne.

The founders of Brahmanism died and are dead. The founders of Hinduism died and are dead. Buddha died and is dead. Laotse, founder of Taoism, died and is dead. Confucius died and is dead. Zoroaster died and is dead. The founders of Shintoism died and are dead. Mohammed died and is dead. Mary-Baker-Glover-Patterson-Eddy-Frye died and is dead. "Pastor" Charles Tate Russell died and is dead. Joseph Smith of Mormonism died and is dead. Madame Helena Petrova Blavatsky died and is dead. Bahaullah, founder of the Bahai movement, died and is dead.

Go to the tombs of Buddha, Lao-tse, Confucius, Zoroaster, Mohammed, and the other founders of false religions. The bodies of these leaders lie mouldering in the dust.

Go to the tomb of Jesus Christ. Men and angels shout "HE IS NOT HERE: FOR HE IS RISEN: COME, SEE THE PLACE WHERE THE LORD LAY!"

Blessed thought! Death cannot keep his prey! The One who was dead is no longer there. He is no longer dead. He is alive.

The whole earth is a cemetery. The sea is a tomb. The disintegrated bodies of millions have been swallowed up. But it will not always be so. At the shout of the Lord of Glory the dead will stand upon their feet. The righteous will be raised for their glorification. The unrighteous will be raised later for their damnation.

Our Lord said, "I am the resurrection." At His command this old earth emerged from its watery grave. At His command the saints will be raptured. At His command Israel will be nationally resurrected. At His command this earth will give up its dead, be renovated by fire, purified, made perfect. It will become the seat of the throne of the living God.

Death flees at His presence. He touched the bier of a young man "And he that was dead sat up, and began to speak" (Luke 7:15). "Maid, arise. And her spirit came again, and she arose straightway" (Luke 8:54–55). He stood before the disintegrating body of Lazarus "and cried with a loud voice, Lazarus, come forth. And he that was dead came forth" (John 11:43–44).

He embraces the lost son from the vineyard with His malodorous garments and shouts, "This my son was dead, and is alive again" (Luke 15:24).

John, the beloved, trembles in His presence. He lays His right hand upon him and says, "Fear not . . . I am he that liveth and was dead; and behold, I am alive forevermore, Amen; and have the keys of hell and of death" (Rev. 1:17–18).

Christianity Versus Man-made Religions

What is it that distinguishes Christianity from all man-made religions? It is the resurrection of Jesus Christ. Whatever He touches is transformed whether it be individuals or nations.

Accept the miracle of the literal bodily resurrection of Jesus Christ, and all other miracles are easily possible.

All the pages of history contain no event more wonderfully-interesting than the most tremendous and the most momentous fact of history: the resurrection of Jesus.

His resurrection is the foundation and pivotal point of Christianity.

His resurrection—the greatest evidence of Christianity, the greatest exhibition of God's power, the greatest truth of the gospel, the greatest reality of faith, the greatest assurance of coming glory, the greatest incentive to holiness—is marked with the fullest credibility.

His resurrection—a fact thrillingly touching the human heart—a truth powerfully influencing human character and human destiny—a fact mentioned directly more than one hundred times in the New Testament—is as fully attested as any other historical fact, remote or recent.

The resurrection of Jesus—the whole alphabet of human hope, the certificate of our Lord's mission from heaven, the heart of the gospel in all ages—completed Christ's substitutionary work on the Cross.

It was evident that God accepted the sinless Substitute. Without Christ's resurrection, His crucifixion and death would have been in vain. These two fundamental facts cannot be separated. Christ's Cross, purposed from all eternity, prophesied through ages, peered into by angels, found its complement in the empty tomb where Jesus wrestled from death's brow his black diadem—shivered at a single blow death's empire of skulls and skeletons, changed humanity's bleak winter into flowery summer, "brought life and immortality to light."

Accept the literal bodily resurrection of Jesus Christ as a fact and you will never doubt that He caused the earth to emerge from its watery grave; that He preserved Noah and his family in the ark; that He overthrew the tower of Babel; that He opened the Red Sea for the Israelites; that He held back the swelling tide of the Jordan; that He locked and unlocked the heavens; that He preserved the witness in the fiery furnace; that He padlocked the jaws of the lions; that He fed the multitudes; stilled the waves; walked on the waters; read the thoughts of the hearts of men; gave the blind their sight, the deaf their hearing, the mad their reason. He healed the sick. He raised the dead. He lived before He was born. He lived after He died. He always was. He is. He always will be. He is the eternal God. The Alpha and the Omega. The Beginning and the Ending. Best of all He is the Resurrection and the Life. None else can make or fulfill this claim. Because He lives, we shall live. If He comes today, we will escape death. But should He tarry until this earthly tabernacle be dissolved, it is comforting to know that HE COMES FIRST TO BREAK UP OUR TOMB, THEN TO SET UP HIS THRONE.

How we rejoice in the truth which John expresses:

> Beloved, now are we the sons of God, and it doth not yet appear what we shall be: But we know that, when he shall appear, we shall be like him For we shall see him as he is (1 John 3:2).

So, listen!

> If thou shalt confess with thy mouth the Lord Jesus, and shalt believe in thine heart that God hath raised him from the dead, Though shalt be saved. For with the heart man believeth unto righteousness; And with the mouth Confession is made unto salvation. (Rom. 10:9–10).

Be not hard to convince.
Be not slow of heart to believe.
Be not slow of faith.
Be not foolish of mind.

Let not your heart be so set upon this world that you have no eyes or ears for the world to come.

Come to Christ!
Christ your Physician. You shall have health.
Christ your Bread. You shall never hunger.
Christ your Light. You shall not walk in darkness.
Christ your Joy. You shall have comfort in sorrow.
Christ your Righteousness. You shall have no condemnation.
Christ, your Acquittal. You shall have no sentence.

Look unto Him on the Cross crucified for your sins. Look unto Him risen from the dead for your justification. I call you to accept this saving Christ, and to accept Him now. You will gain nothing by further delay. Today is the tomorrow you talked about yesterday. You said, "Tomorrow I will confess Christ." Do it NOW! "Tomorrow, being saved, I will join the church." Do it NOW! You said: "Tomorrow, I will let the world know that I am not ashamed nor afraid to accept Him before the world." Do that NOW!

CHAPTER SIX

Blood on Ears and Hands and Toes

And [Moses] . . . brought the ram of consecration. . .
and he slew it; and Moses took of the blood of it,
and put it on the tip of Aaron's right ear,
and upon the thumb of his right hand,
and upon the great toe of his right foot.
And he brought Aaron's sons, and Moses put of the blood
upon the tip of their right ear, and upon the thumbs
of their right hands, and upon the great toes of their right feet:
and Moses sprinkled the blood upon the altar round about.
Lev. 8:22–24

We have been taught and we believe that Leviticus stands in the same relation to Exodus that the Epistles do to the Gospels, that Exodus is the record of redemption and lays the foundation of the cleansing, worship, and service of a redeemed people. "Leviticus gives the detail of the walk, worship, and service of that people. In Exodus God speaks out of the mount to which approach was forbidden."

God said to Moses: "The Lord shall come down . . . upon Mount Sinai."

> And thou shalt set bounds unto the people round about, saying, Take heed to yourselves, that ye go not up into the mount, or touch the border of it: whosoever toucheth the mount shall be surely put to death (Exod. 19:12).

In Leviticus, God speaks out of the tabernacle in which God dwells in the midst of His people to tell them that which befits His holiness in their approach *to* and in communion *with* Himself. So says Scofield. Holiness is the keyword of Leviticus—and occurs eighty-seven times. The key verse of Leviticus is:

> Speak unto all the congregation of the children of Israel, and say unto them, Ye shall be holy: for I the LORD your God am holy (Lev. 19:2).

Consecration

The eighth chapter of Leviticus shows how Aaron and his sons were publicly set apart and inducted into the office of the priesthood.

Aaron is the only man about whom we have read whose garments were designed and designated by the omniscient God.

> And thou shalt make holy garments for Aaron thy brother for glory and for beauty. And thou shalt speak unto all that are wise-hearted, whom I have filled with the spirit of wisdom, that they may make Aaron's garments to consecrate him, that he may minister unto me in the priest's office. And these are the garments which they shall make; a breastplate, and an ephod, and a robe, and an embroidered coat, a miter, and a girdle: and they shall make holy garments for Aaron thy brother, and his sons, that he may minister unto me in the priest's office (Exod. 28:2–4).

Before the garments of glory and beauty were put on, Aaron and his sons were washed together.

"And Moses brought Aaron and his sons, and washed them with water" (Lev. 8:6). Water was a symbol of the Word of God. Washing means applying the Word—applying the truth. Applying the truth and setting apart for a particular service is sanctification.

Sanctification

The washing of Aaron and his sons *together* sets forth *unity* in sanctification—even as Christ and His church are a unit in sanctification before God.

> For both he that sanctifieth and they who are sanctified are all of one: for which cause he is not ashamed to call them brethren (Heb. 2:11).

For the sake of those cleansed and redeemed by His precious blood—the crimson cash He paid in crucifixion agonies and death, Christ Jesus sanctified Himself, devoted Himself to God, and sanctified the saved.

> And for their sakes I sanctify myself, that they also might be sanctified through the truth (John 17:19).

Truly, Aaron was a God-clothed man. And in this act of God-designed decoration, we behold our Lord Jesus Christ in typical prefiguration—as many truth lovers have taught us.

The Eight Garments

Moses, doing what God commanded, dressed Aaron in the eight garments of glory and beauty. He put them on piece by piece so that they could be seen in all the details of skilled workmanship and surpassing beauty.

On Aaron was put the embroidered linen coat with the linen breeches. He was girdled with the girdle which bound him in with its fineness of texture and perfection of color. Moses put on Aaron the blue robe with its ringing golden bells and pomegranates in their trinity of color. Moses put on the gold ephod, buttoned it on the shoulders with two onyx stones, set the breastplate, and put on the Urim and Thummin—two precious stones signifying light and perfections. Then this was bound to the shoulders with wreathen chains, underneath the ephod at the waist with the curious girdle or belt. Last of all, Moses took the snowy white linen, the costly bussus, wound it fold on fold around his head, making a turban of it. Then he put blue lace on the front of it, and on that fastened the golden plate with the graven words upon it: "*Holiness to the Lord.*"

In this manner of investiture, the people saw the intricate worth of these garments of glory and beauty. Thus they beheld Aaron set apart from all others, exalted above the people, yet *for* the people.

- The breastplate signifies the *loving* Christ.
- The ephod speaks of the *human* and *divine* Christ.
- The robe speaks of the *heavenly* and *gracious* Christ.
- The linen coat and breeches set forth the truth of the *sinless* Christ.
- The girdle speaks of the *serving* Christ.
- The shoulder pieces declare the truth of the *strengthening* and *sustaining* Christ.
- The miter is emblematic of the *obedient* Christ.
- The golden plate symbolizes the *holy* Christ.

Thinking of how Aaron, dressed by Moses in garments of glory and beauty, was exalted and set apart *from* all others, exalted *above* the people and yet *for* the people, we say that for two thousand years Jesus, whom God hath highly exalted and to whom God hath given a name which is above every name (see Phil. 2), has been set forth in His aloneness upon the consciousness of the world.

The more Jesus is studied, analyzed, the more His character is taken apart, the more His life is submitted to critical analysis, each element of it, like the separate pieces in the garments of glory and beauty, the more it will reveal Christ to be the perfect, the glorious, the beautiful, the wonder of all wonders, perfect man and very God—yea, the verity of God's truth, the beauty of God's holiness, the purity of God's nature, the surety of God's promise, the reality of God's love, the majesty of God's throne, the authority of God's power, the pity of God's heart, the legacy of God's will.

We must not forget, however, that oil was poured on Aaron's head.

> And Moses took the anointing oil, and anointed the tabernacle and all that was therein, and sanctified them. And he sprinkled thereof upon the altar seven times, and anointed the altar and all his vessels, both the laver and his foot, to sanctify them. And he poured of the anointing oil upon Aaron's head, and anointed him, to sanctify him (Lev. 8:10–12).

This oil was not only an anointing for service, but the seal of the redemption that came by the blood, the blood of Christ.

The centuries from Adam to Christ were crimson with the blood of innocent victims killed as types of the slain Lamb of God. The diversified, systematic sacrifices of the Jews, like finger posts along the highway of time, pointed worshipers to a sacrificial Savior. Significant shadows of redemptive entity still ahead, adumbrations of a substance yet to come, by the blood of a thousand altars, these sacrifices, elemental, preparatory, rudimentary, preliminary, introductory, pointed to Christ, the propellent center to which the faith of mankind before and since gravitated.

There is a theology that counts such truth too vulgar to be attributed to divine ordinances, but to be viewed as belonging to the grosser mind of man in his unrefined stages of development. But men label God and label the Bible a lie by believing anything contrary to the truth, or by preaching or by teaching anything contrary to the truth that the blood stream was ordained of God. The promise to fallen men in Eden means Christ. All the ceremonies of Judaism mean Christ. The music of Israel's sweetest harps means Christ. The light that burns in prophecy means Christ.

Now, let us think of

The Blood Applied

The blood of the sacrifice was applied to Aaron and his sons. The blood was put upon the tip of the right ear, upon the thumb of the right hand, and upon the big toe of the right foot. This was the three-fold consecration of the holy priesthood.

What was the meaning of all this? The meaning was simple enough. It meant the *hearing* had been ceremonially purchased by the blood and was now solemnly and individually consecrated to God. It meant the *service* had been ceremonially purchased by the blood and was now solemnly and individually dedicated and consecrated to God. It meant the *walk* of the priests had been ceremonially purchased by the blood and was now solemnly and individually consecrated to God. This old enactment exactly represents my own dedication, our own dedication, to the service of God and of our fellowmen.

The touch of sacrificial blood on the ear, and hand, and foot seemed to say, and did say: You have been redeemed for this one end that you may be holy servants of a holy God. You have been redeemed that you may surrender to Him every faculty, every organ, ever power. Your whole self from head to foot is to be your Lord's. If you have been redeemed by the "precious blood of Christ," it is only that you may serve in newness of spirit, both the God above you and your brethren at your side.

Our hearing, our service, our walk, all for Christ. For us who believe all these, even as all members of our mortal bodies, belong to Christ Jesus who has purchased us, has bought us from Satan's slave markets of sin and bondage by His own precious blood, and from whom we have this urging through the apostle Paul:

> I beseech you therefore, brethren, by the mercies of God, that ye present your bodies a living sacrifice, holy, acceptable unto God, which is your reasonable service (Rom. 12:1).

Yes, and from whom also, through the same great apostle, we have this exhortation:

> Let not sin therefore reign in your mortal body, that ye should obey it in the lusts thereof. Neither yield ye your members as instruments

of unrighteousness unto sin: but yield yourselves unto God, as those that are alive from the dead, and your members as instruments of righteousness unto God (Rom. 6:12–13).

Let us think of the application of the

Blood on the Ear

"Moses put of the blood on the tip of the right ear."

God, knowing that we know that the ear is the mysterious home of reverberations and echo, wants our ears to be instruments of righteousness.

The *ear* is the Grand Central depot of sound. The ear, the headquarters to which there come dispatches, part of the way by cartilage, part of the way by air, part of the way by bone, part of the way by nerve—the slowest dispatch coming into the ear at the speed of 1,100 feet per second.

The *ear*, small instrument of music on which is played all the music you ever hear—from the grandeurs of the summer thunderstorm to the softest breathings of a flute. Small instrument of hearing only one quarter of an inch of surface, with the thinness of one two-hundred-and-fiftieth part of an inch, and that thinness divided into three layers.

In the *ear* there is the musical staff: lines, spaces, bars, rest.

The *ear*, a delicate bridge leading from the outside *natural* world to the inside *spiritual* world. We see the abutment of this bridge at this end, but the fog of an uplifted mystery hiding the abutment at the other end of the bridge.

The *ear*, wonderful whispering gallery of the soul.

Oh, the *ear*, the God-honored ear, grooved with divine sculpture, poised with divine gracefulness, upholstered with curtains of divine embroidery, corridored with divine carpentry, pillared with divine architecture, chiseled in bone of divine masonry, conquered by processions of divine marshalling—as Talmadge taught.

The *ear*! None but God could plan it; none but God could build it; none but God could work it; none but God could understand it; none but God could keep it.

The *ear*, more wonderful than any arch man ever lifted. More wonderful than any transept window man ever illumined. More wonderful than any Corinthian column man ever crowned. More wonderful than any Gothic cloister man ever elaborated.

The *ear*, more mystifying than any circular stairway ever invented. More majestic than any stone gable ever put in place; more solemnizing than any ocean depth ever fathomed. Blood on the ear with its arches. Blood on the ear with its walls. Blood on the ear with its floors. Blood on the ear with its canals. Blood on the ear with its aqueducts, galleries, intricacies, convolutions, and divine machinery.

Because of the blood upon our ear, we are to recognize our hearing does not belong to ourselves. We have no right to listen as it may please us. These are things which, if we permit them to enter the ear, will pass into the mind, poison it, and paralyze all activities for Christ. There is even more peril in listening than in looking and seeing. We are to have the consecrated ear, ever open to the heavenly voice, but closed to the earthly ones that would call us away from truth and godliness. An ear sensitive to the quiet whispers of the spirit, which a dull ear will wholly miss. We are to have an ear gladly listening to the tale of sorrow or distress that comes from the lips of any sufferer or sinner at our side. We are, therefore, called upon to be careful not only as to how we hear but as to what we hear. "And he said unto them, Take heed *what* ye hear" (Mark 4:24, emphasis added). "Take heed therefore *how* ye hear" (Luke 8:18, emphasis added).

The blood upon the ear tells us He claims our ears that they may hear Him speak, listen to His words, give attention to His message.

Wherefore, it is written: "Who hath ears to hear, let him hear" (Matt. 13:9).

Blood on the tip of the right ear meant that the priest was to listen to only one voice, was to be keenly sensitive to God's voice only, no matter how many clamorous voices were speaking in whispers or in shouts. All believers are kings and priests unto God through Christ Jesus who loved them and washed or loosed them from their sins in His own blood (see Rev. 1:5–6).

And God says to believers what He said to the three disciples on the mountain of transfiguration glory: "This is my beloved Son in whom I am well-pleased; *hear* ye him" (Matt. 17:5, emphasis added).

A blood-anointed ear is required to hearken to divine communications. No other ear can hear divine communications. No other ear is familiar with God's divine communication. No other ear is familiar with the divine voice. No other ear is able to understand the language of heaven or the voice that speaks in Holy Scriptures.

God says:

> But the natural man receiveth not the things of the Spirit of God: for they are foolishness unto him: neither can he know them, because they are spiritually discerned (1 Cor. 2:14).

So, do not expect the natural man to find pleasure in the voices of the Scriptures. Do not expect the unregenerate scholar to know the simplest truths of divine revelation. There is no blood upon the ear. That is why some scholars do not see at the end of the microscope God's infinitesimal care. That is why many, with college diplomas, do not see at the end of the telescope God's infinite greatness.

If scholars do not see God's immutable ways in the sciences and mathematics; if scholars do not, in the flowers of botany and the sweetness of music, become acquainted with God's ineffable beauty; if scholars do not find in the rocks testimony of God's incomprehensible agelessness, it is because there is no blood on the ear. Unless there is blood on the ear, no man can obey these words:

> He that hath an ear, let him hear what the Spirit saith unto the churches; To him that overcometh will I give to eat of the tree of life, which is in the midst of the paradise of God (Rev. 2:7).

We read: "We have heard with our ears" (Ps. 44:1).

Workers with the deaf say that the child who is hard of hearing is the victim of more misunderstanding than any other child. Often he is ashamed to acknowledge that he cannot hear and he is thought to be stupid, when he simply cannot hear what is said to him. It is the same with those who are spiritually deaf; for there are those who are so framed that they have very little sense of spiritual things. The idea of God is vague in their minds. Christ means little to their soul. The Holy Spirit is a mere name to them. The ears of their souls are stopped up.

And the ear is first anointed because one must first hear the Word and through it become instructed in the things of Christ, before one can intelligently act in those things or walk worthy of them!

Now, we think of

Blood upon the Thumb of the Right Hand

"Moses put the blood upon the thumb of the right hand." Thus God bids us to use our hands in His service. This means that we should, with purposed consecration, pray: "Take my hands and let them move, At the impulse of thy love."

To handle holy things the blood-sprinkled hand alone is worthy. For the worship and service of the heavenly sanctuary, to which we belong, it only is competent. Other hands, however morally clean, would but defile. "The precious blood" upon our hands has set them apart to God to be occupied with His affairs, and it makes them both worthy and competent for whatever priestly service He may appoint for them.

A consecrated hand is a hand of ready help; a hand of generous compassion, a hand of strong uplifting for the fallen and the poor. It is a hand of strength "stretched out to wrestlers with the troubled sea!"

A consecrated hand means to give ourselves to Him for His service; to hand ourselves over to Him completely for His use of us. It means we must never come before Him with an empty hand; always and under all circumstances we must come with something in our hand for Him, some service accomplished and handed to Him or some gift presented to Him!

Hear what the Scripture saith: "For Moses said, Consecrate yourselves today to the LORD" (Exod. 32:29).

Literally rendered that means, "Fill your hands this day to the Lord." This is the actual meaning of the words used in these instances. It means "to fill the hand"! That is God's concept of consecration, coming into His presence with something in your hands.

David said: "Who then is willing to consecrate his service this day unto the LORD?" (1 Chron. 29:5). Meaning: "Who then is willing to *fill his hand* with service this day unto the Lord?" "And none shall appear before me empty" (Exod. 23:15; 34:20).

A noted journalist wrote: "The greatest word in the English language is service. This is true; and the hands are largely the means by which this service is rendered!"

The hands of the artist are skillful to serve mankind through the medium of beautiful pictures.

The hands of the musician are delicately sensitive that they may serve mankind through the medium of inspiring music.

The hands of the sculptor are triumphantly skillful to serve mankind by raising "from the sterile womb of stone children unto God."

The hands of the laborer are scarred and hard that they may serve mankind through the medium of manual labor.

The hands of the doctor and surgeon are wonderfully sensitive and accurate that they may serve mankind through the medium of medical and surgical treatment.

The hands of the mother are soiled and worn with the loving work of the household.

We would that the hands made into fists to strike others had the touch of blood upon them. We would that grasping hands, always open to get and never to give liberally, had the touch of blood upon them. We would that the cruel hands of the world, so careless and inconsiderate, had the touch of blood as did Aaron's thumb, and thus be blest with gentleness.

We would that the scornful hands of men the world over, so ready to throw stones of hate, were touched with blood as were the thumbs upon the right hands of Aaron and his sons.

We would that all the hands of all of us had the touch of blood upon them as had the thumb of the right hands of the priests.

Then all hands would be the servants of loving wills, the representatives of kindly thought, the tender ambassadors of great hearts, the messengers of God's love and God's grace.

A Glorious Day. . .

It was a glorious day in the land of Burma when John E. Clough and Lyman Jewett led down into the baptismal waters in a single day 2,222 believers to bury them with Christ in baptism; and surely that was a harvesting season when during the single year of 1878, ten thousand people were baptized on that mission field. But go back fifty years and get the picture of the lonely plowman and his suffering companion, the heroine of Ava. For seven years Adoniram Judson toiled on without seeing any fruitage of his labors, sustained only but sufficiently by the promises of God. And through what trials, hardships and sufferings he and his delicate companion passed in those years of plowing, harrowing, and seed-sowing which were to bring forth such a rich harvest in later years. Behold Judson, unjustly cast into a foul prison, languishing therein for months, chained to other prisoners, stripped of most of his clothing, forced to march bareheaded and barefooted under the heat of a torrid sun, his feet torn and blistered, driven by the lash of slaves, himself so exhausted that he would have fallen down and died but for the timely and kindly aid of a Bengalee servant; his wife with infant in arms trying to follow after, to minister, to help if she might, distracted and intrigued against, herself stricken with illness and her babe starving; Judson given a degree of freedom, going from hut to hut begging for his famishing babe a little nourishment from the breasts of native mothers, and you have a picture of the hardships, the labors, the sufferings, the sacrifices of those whose mission it is to go before and to prepare the way for the inheritance of a rich harvest of souls.

The point I am making is, the others who labored had the hard part, the difficult part. We who enter in, who reap the results of their tearful labors, while elated with joy to be reapers, should remember with gratitude, with deepest appreciation, with sincere humility of mind, that greatest praise and greatest honor belong to the toilers who went before.

All honor and gratitude to those, too, who had the touch of the blood upon their ears, so that they listened to the voice of God. There was the touch, too, of the blood upon the hands, so that they were found serving faithfully the Christ whose hands were nailed to Calvary's cross for them, even for us all.

Christ's Hands

And this brings us to see to it that the blood is upon our hands. Yea, by Christ's hands touching the eyes of the blind into sight, may our hands be yielded unto God as instruments of righteousness.

By Christ's hands touching deaf ears into hearing, touching the fevered brow into coolness, many our hands be hands serving in sympathy.

By Christ's hands reached out to sinking Peter on the water, let our hands be reached out to men and women who are down, even if they be in the gutter.

By Christ's hands placed with healing upon the loathesome leper, let not your hands draw back in revulsion from tasks that are not pleasant, even though essential.

By Christ's hands breaking bread for hungry multitudes, may we see to it that our hands are held out with food for the hungry, satisfying the poor with bread (Ps. 132:15), so that we will never be found guilty under the indictment contained in the words of Eliphaz: "Thou hast not given water to the weary to drink, and thou hast withheld bread from the hungry" (Job 22:7).

By Christ's hands placed blessingly upon little children (Matt. 19:15), let us minister helpfully to little children, remembering the words of Jesus: "Inasmuch as ye have done it unto one of the least of these . . . ye have done it unto me" and "Inasmuch as ye did it *not* to one of the least of these, ye did it not to me" (Matt. 25:40, 45).

By Christ's hands plying the scourge upon the hucksters and herds in the temple, let us see to it that we use our hands as pens that write against wicked forces, as cudgels that break down ramparts of evil, always working for what the devil is against, always active against what Satan is for.

Behold the hands of Christ spiked to Calvary's cross. His hands set the pillars of the earth in their sockets and drew the blue curtains of the night across the windows of heaven and pinned them together with clusters of stars. His hands put the planets in space, so that for ages they have been following their orbits with meticulous accuracy, not one second behind nor one second ahead of the Christ-appointed schedules. His hands laid the first foundations of the waters. Yes, take a look at Christ's hands, *holy* hands, black from the blows of the bruising hammers, hands broken with nails, stained with the sacred oozings of His precious blood. Look gratefully at His hands straining painfully under the weight of His body, while every breath He drew was a pang of pain, while every heartbeat was a throb of agony. May our looks at Christ's hands make us earnestly say:

Lord, Lord,
Take my hands and let them move
At the impulse of thy love.
Lord, when I am weary with toiling
And burdensome seem Thy commands;
If my load should lead to complaining,
Lord, show me Thy hands;
Thy nail-pierced hands,
Thy cross-torn hands,
My Saviour, show me Thy hands.

Now consider the

Blood upon the Great Toe

"Moses took of the blood and put it upon the great toe of the right foot."

The blood upon the great toe of the right foot was to make it fit for treading in the holiest and for walking before God in God's love and fear. No other can approach God's dwelling place. Blood answers blood. We read about what took place on the Day of Atonement. Blood was sprinkled seven times before God's throne inside the veil.

> And the priest that is anointed shall bring of the bullock's blood to the tabernacle of the congregation: and the priest shall dip his finger in some of the blood, and sprinkle it seven times before the LORD, even before the veil. And he shall put some of the blood upon the horns of the altar which is before the LORD, that is in the tabernacle of the congregation, and shall pour out all the blood at the bottom of the altar of the burnt offering, which is at the door of the tabernacle of the congregation (Lev. 4:16–18).

There we behold our perfect standing ground in His presence. There the blood-sprinkled foot may stand.

The blood on the toe means the consecration of the walk before God. The blood means we should be found walking before God, walking in integrity, walking uprightly, walking humbly with God, walking not after the flesh but after the Spirit, walking by faith, walking circumspectly, walking worthy of the Lord, as we are urged to do in God's Word.

Such is to be our walk as those who profess the name of the Lord and own His blood as having all purchasing rights upon us. As Christians we are to live and serve as those who have no initial claims upon ourselves. We strive earnestly to make our walk and conversation glorify Him who has all purchased and invested rights in us. We shall not hestitate to testify that His out-poured blood for us requires that we shall walk as those who seek to walk worthily before men and before God, remembering that we are not our own.

Blood on the *ear*. Blood on the *thumb*. Blood on the big *toe*. How perfect a picture this is of our great Lord Jesus Christ! His ear was ever listening for His Father's voice, ever keenly sensitized to the cry of the needy. His hands were ever busy in the gracious work of ministry to the blind, the deaf, the dumb, the leprous, the helpless, the starving, the devil-possessed, the diseased, and the crippled. His feet, carrying Him over the rough and rocky roads, wearied frequently. But He was never too weary to speak a saving word as He did at Jacob's Well.

Surely, it was this vision of Christ Jesus which the great apostle Paul had ever before him when, seeking zealously to magnify the name of Jesus, he wrote: "I magnify mine office" (Rom. 11:13).

> According to my earnest expectation and my hope, that in nothing I shall be ashamed, but that with all boldness, as always, so now also Christ shall be magnified in my body, whether it be by life, or by death (Phil. 1:20).

By life! By death! The second of these alternatives is sometimes easier than the first. To die a martyr's death is not so difficult as to live a consecrated, definitely-devoted, Christ-honoring life, to be "always bearing about in the body the dying of the Lord Jesus, that the life also of Jesus might be made manifest in our body" (2 Cor. 4:10).

Yes, there is quite a difference in dying in a few minutes with the head beneath the guillotine blade, or by rifle bullets before a firing squad, or on a bayonet's point than in living greatly day by day under boresome grind, under heavy burdens, under bitter experiences, under wearisome responsibilities, amid environments that are repulsive where sacrifices are necessary for the support of others and for the achievement of worthy goals.

Our ears. Our hands. Our feet. Our *ears* that gladly hear the blessed words: "I have redeemed thee"—and how can they listen with pleasure to any blasphemous utterances, slanderous words, ribald jests, or falsehoods? We should remember ever these words: "A wicked doer giveth heed to false lips; and a liar giveth ear to a naughty tongue" (Prov. 17:4).

And we should be warned by these words: "He that turneth away his ear from hearing the law, even his prayer shall be abomination" (Prov. 28:9).

And we should be obedient to these words: "Incline your ears to the words of my mouth" (Ps. 78:1).

His Voice

Kitty McKeever is the chief telephone operator at Kings Features Syndicate of New York City. Her friends say she never forgets a voice although she handles about two thousand calls a day. Such voice memory is exceptional. But there is one voice we should always "know" regardless of how many voices we are unable to recall. That is the voice of the Good Shepherd, the Lord Jesus Christ.

"His sheep . . . know his voice" (John 10:4). He speaks to them through His Word by His Spirit. What a grand thing to know His voice:

- In salvation, when He says, "Come unto me" (Matt. 11:28).
- In fellowship, when He says, "I will never leave thee" (Heb. 13:5).
- In guidance when He says, "Follow me" (Matt. 4:19).
- In tribulation when He says: "Be of good cheer" (Matt. 14:27).
- In communion, when He says, "In remembrance of me" (1 Cor. 11:24–25).
- In service, when He says, "Serve me" (John 12:26).
- In anticipation when He says: "I will come again" (John 14:3).

Our *hands* that take unto them the emblems of Christ's broken body and shed blood when we observe the Lord's Supper, how can they seize any sinful thing, or do things that hurt rather than help? How can we, knowing the usefulness of our hands, use them in careless ways, to receive bribes, to do evil with both hands earnestly (Mic. 7:3), to keep them idle when they should be diligent in work, to stretch them out with scorners (Hos. 7:5), to strengthen hands of evil doers? (Jer. 23:14).

Our *feet*. These feet that enable us to carry our bodies wheresoever we will, that carry us to the house of work. How can they carry us on other days to places where God is dishonored and His servants condemned, and His laws trampled under foot, with feet that run to evil? (Isa. 59:7). How we need to ponder the paths of our feet. Knowing that we speak with our feet (Prov.

6:13), we should never, as does the wicked woman, have feet that go down to death (Prov. 5:5), never believing that "he that hasteth with his feet sinneth" (Prov. 19:2).

As those who claim to love and follow Jesus who walked in blessed benediction among men, we should walk circumspectly, redeeming the time.

We need to pray:

Take my life and let it be
Consecrated, Lord, to Thee;
Take my hands and let them move
At the impulse of thy love.
Take my feet and let them be
Swift and beautiful for Thee.

CHAPTER SEVEN

The Tongue of the Human Body

For in many things we offend all. If any man offend not in word, the same is a perfect man, and able also to bridle the whole body.
James 3:2

If any man among you seem to be religious, and bridleth not his tongue, but deceiveth his own heart, this man's religion is vain.
James 1:26

Death and life are in the power of the tongue: and they that love it shall eat the fruit thereof.
Prov. 18:21

When we read the Bible—Book above and beyond all books as a river is beyond a rill in reach, Book beyond all books as the sun is beyond a tallow dip in brightness—we find that in commanding the obedience of mankind, it speaks much of the human body and its members. And not a few words but many words do we read within its sacred pages of the tongue. Lines wherein mention of the tongue and its usages are found are as plentiful as flowers in a spring garden, as various in description of the tongue as fishes found in seven seas, as strong as the devils in the Gadarene demoniac. Yes, often is the tongue the topic of the Bible—that Book which is divine in authorship, human in penmanship, universal in scope, infallible in authority, validated and confirmed by the Holy Spirit with a divine certainty that is incommunicable by reason and impervious to the assaults of doubt, the miracle Book of diversity in unity. While some topics are dealt with in comprehensive brevity, the loose tongue has a whole chapter given to it in the Epistle of James.

The human tongue is made up of many muscles turning and intertwining astonishingly. Paley writes:

> It is worth any man's while to watch the agility of his tongue; the wonderful promptitude with which it executes change of position, and the perfect exactness. Each syllable of articulated sound requires for its utterance a specific action of the tongue, and of the parts adjacent to it. The disposition and configuration of the mouth for every letter and word is not only peculiar, but if nicely and accurately attended to, perceptible to the sight!. How instantaneously are these positions assumed and dismissed! How numerous are the permutations, how various, yet how infallible!

Unless the tongue be yielded to God as an instrument of righteousness, it will be a

Terrible Tongue

The terror of an unrighteous tongue is shown in strikingly descriptive biblical words, is shown by the indictment passed upon the tongue by sacred writers. Note:

The tongue is a fire.

The tongue is full of deadly poison.

The tongue is a little member (of the body) and boasteth great things.

The tongue is an unruly evil.

The tongue is a world of iniquity.

The tongue defileth the whole body.

The tongue setteth on fire the course of nature.

The tongue can no man tame.

Job spoke of the tongue as a *scourge*. "Thou shalt be hid from the scourge of the tongue: neither shalt thou be afraid of destruction when it cometh" (Job 5:21).

The psalmist indicted the tongue as an instrument of unrighteousness in these words:

> For there is no faithfulness in their mouth; their inward part is very wickedness; their throat is an open sepulcher; they flatter with their tongue (Ps. 5:9). The LORD shall cut off all flattering lips, and the tongue that speaketh proud things (Ps. 12:3).

The apostle Peter, recalling some Old Testament wisdom, wrote:

> For he that will love life, and see good days, let him refrain his tongue from evil, and his lips that they speak no guile (1 Pet. 3:10).

The terror of an unrighteous tongue is set forth in words closely akin, written by the psalmist and the author of Proverbs:

> Thy tongue deviseth mischiefs; like a sharp razor, working deceitfully (Ps. 52:2). There is that speaketh like the piercings of a sword (Prov. 12:18).

And God in His holy hatred of evil finds equally guilty the liar's devilish tongue and the murderer's bloody hands.

> A proud look, a lying tongue, and hands that shed innocent blood (Prov. 6:17). Death and life are in the power of the tongue (Prov. 18:21).

The tongue is a trouble producer for the soul. This is shown in these words:

> Whoso keepeth his mouth and his tongue keepeth his soul from troubles (Prov. 21:23).

Paul, in the third chapter of Romans, is as a prosecutor giving a summary against man. Out of six counts having to do with man's body, four implicate and indict the tongue:

> Their throat is an open sepulcher; with their tongues they have used deceit; the poison of asps is under their lips: whose mouth is full of cursing and bitterness (Rom. 3:13–14).

The terror of the unruly tongue is set forth in these words, sober words which we should seriously and penitently, with humility and humiliation, ponder:

> His mouth is full of cursing and deceit and fraud: under his tongue is mischief and vanity (Ps. 10:7). The LORD shall cut off all flattering lips, and the tongue that speaketh proud things (Ps. 12:3).

And how great is God's goodness shown in these words: "Thou shalt keep them . . . from the strife of tongues" (Ps. 31:20). What a terror the tongue is when it transgresses the laws of God for the tongue. How we need to pray that God will keep our tongues from evil and our lips from speaking guile.

Now let us think of the

Tormenting Tongue

There are many things that torment us. The filthy fly, carrying disease, making the butter the landing place for his dirty feet or the glass of milk his swimming pool—and finding no place to land, when we seek sleep, except the tip of the nose or the bald place on our heads—is a great tormentor.

The rat, purveyor of plague, gnawing annoyingly in the still hours of the night, robbing us of sleep and destroying valuable treasures and using the velvet of the piano for the making of his bed, is a sly tormentor.

The drip of the leaky water faucet—"oft in the stilly night"—dropping our comfort into the chasm of its irritable persistence, is a tormentor indeed.

The bed bug, despicable in the way he makes his living, impudent in his uncultured invasion into our bed areas, together with the pillows thereof, is a great tormentor.

An aching tooth, pounding every nerve with the invisible fists of pain, is a tormentor indeed. The aching ear, acting as though it would fain remove its habitation from the head, gives torment which is not to be desired.

Cigarette smoke, blown north, south, east, west by those who care not whom it irritates, is, to all hay fever victims, a tormentor indeed.

The mosquito, with a solo flight that holds a hum that harasses like the whine of a Scotch bagpipe, as alien to melody as poison to health, filling his maw with man's blood and then, in base ingratitude, giving him a hypodermic of malaria, is a tormentor indeed. Writing of the malicious mosquito, someone has said that the rattlesnake strikes to defend himself, the skunk will not distribute his perfumery unless he is in danger, the lions kill for food, hunger and its young governs the predatory eagle, the fox robs the hen roost because he has a stomach to feed, even man—the most relentless and successful in sin and wrong—kills cattle for provender and to get leather for his shoes, and shoots quail ostensibly to adorn his table. The tornado may be the only way of restoring the equilibrium of the air. The volcanic eruption may be due to some sort of terrestrial indigestion (judging from the sulphuric belches it emits). But the mosquito makes us think of the purely malicious in life.

Then this same writer (I am sorry I cannot remember his name) says that it appears to be the unavoidable truth that some folks are just plain mean. In children we sometimes see it, because even the most angelic of them take pleasure at times in causing pain. Most of them happily get over this. Some do not. Some men take pleasure in tormenting their wives. Some folks are so full of petty spite that they go out of their way to do someone an evil turn. Some thugs there are who beat men for the pleasure of the exercise. Some teamsters there are who lash horses to see them suffer. Some boys there are who torment cats to hear their cries of agony. Some pranksters there are who tie strings across sidewalks and laugh to see people stumble and fall. Some people there are who like to put flies in someone's ointment.

People who say there is no personal devil should explain about the someone or the somewhat that gets into men and women and dehumanizes them, makes them hurt people and have little regret as to wounds made. What tormentors are people whose tongues know no more about putting down a period than a monkey knows about trigonometry? What tormentors can people be whose talkative tongues find no more rest than "old man river who jes' keeps rollin' along"—no more rest than the rasping jaws of the mouse disturbing more than occasional thunder. Surely there is no torment so ruinous, so mean, so malicious as the torment of the tongue which never observes the law of kindness.

I think Joseph was tormented more by the lying tongue of Potiphar's wife than by the depths of the dungeon and the jail bars. I am sure Moses was tormented more by the murmuring and complaining of the people than by the plagues of frogs and flies and lice and boils and blain and blood in Egypt, because we read:

> And they said unto Moses, Because there were no graves in Egypt, hast thou taken us away to die in the wilderness? wherefore hast thou dealt thus with us, to carry us forth out of Egypt? (Exod. 14:11).

> And the whole congregation of the children of Israel murmured against Moses and Aaron in the wilderness: and the children of Israel said unto them, Would to God we had died by the hand of the LORD in the land of Egypt, when we sat by the flesh pots, and when we did eat bread to the full; for ye have brought us forth into this wilderness, to kill this whole assembly with hunger (Exod. 16:2–3).

> And the people thirsted there for water; and the people murmured against Moses, and said, Wherefore is this that thou hast brought us up out of Egypt, to kill us and our children and our cattle with thirst? (Exod. 17:3).

More tormenting to Moses than the hardships of the wilderness wanderings were the tongues of Miriam and Aaron who spoke "against Moses because of the Ethiopian woman whom he had married" (Num. 12:1). When God's anger was kindled against the seditious two, then God asked, "Wherefore then were ye not afraid to speak against my servant Moses?" (Num.

12:8). And then, "Miriam became leprous, white as snow" (12:10).

More tormenting to Samson than the young lion who met him out of the vineyards of Timnath, the lion which "he rent as he would have rent a kid," was the tongue of Samson's wife, who wept before him, saying, "Thou dost but hate me, and lovest me not: thou hast put forth a riddle unto the children of my people, and hast not told it me" (Judg. 14:16). More tormenting than the Philistines to Samson was the tongue of Delilah who sought to find wherein his great strength lay:

> And she said unto him, How canst thou say, I love thee, when thine heart is not with me? thou hast mocked me these three times, and hast not told me wherein thy great strength lieth (Judg. 16:15).

More tormenting to David than Goliath's size and armor was the tongue of Goliath, for 'tis written: "And the Philistine cursed David by his gods" (1 Sam. 17:43).

More tormenting to David than the stones cast at him and at all the servants of King David by Shimei was the cursing tongue of Shimei (2 Sam. 16:6).

More tormenting to David than his hunger and thirst and weariness in the wilderness was the tongue of Absalom which stole the hearts of many from love and loyalty to the king.

More tormenting to Jesus than the pangs of hunger was the tongue of Satan in the wilderness, and the tongues of those who falsely accused Him.

More tormenting, too, to Paul than the many stripes laid on him in Philippi were the tongues of "certain philosophers of the Epicureans, and of the Stoics," who "encountered him. And some said, what will this babbler say?. . . And when they heard of the resurrection of the dead, some mocked" (Acts 17:18, 32).

What a tormentor the tongue has been in the world. It has been a dagger to stab the hearts of loved ones with its sharp thrust of pain. It has been a scourge to torture the lives of those who live nearest us. It has been a whetted sword. It has been a mortar out of which has sped the bomb that has exploded and rent asunder whole communities. It has been a razor wielded as by a madman on a children's playground. It has been a battering ram that drives its way through walls of communities and breaks down society. It has been a thunderbolt that crashes the organ with force into splinters and leaves it without shape or tone. It has been an instrument of giving all conceivable pain to men.

I read the other day that the Spanish in Cuba before the war between Spain and the United States were wont to put their pitiable Cuban victims to torture by pouring into the ear molten lead from the hot crucibles and thus give them excruciating pain. But how much more poignant anguish has been given by means of the tongue as it has poured into the ears of men the words red hot with malignant hatred and with ridicule and sacrilegious sarcasm and with folly and shameful wrong. I think the tongue may be indicted as the worse criminal in the world with all the guilt of the devil, since by blasphemy of God and by blasting human life with its devastating power, it is a satanic mischief.

Better for the welfare of mankind, the tongue should be torpid as a toad in marble than the tormenting tongue which, like the dark of death, spares neither sex nor age.

But I would have us think now of the

Tongue as a Torch

> Even so the tongue is a little member, and boasteth great things. Behold, how great a matter a little fire kindleth! And the tongue is a fire, a world of iniquity: so is the tongue among our members, that it defileth the whole body, and setteth on fire the course of nature; and is set on fire of hell (James 3:5–6).

How sobering these words! Hell has more to do in promoting the fire of the tongue than men believe. An uncontrolled tongue, set on fire of hell, is mischievous beyond words. It produces hatred, anger, rage, contentions and those evil things which serve the purpose of the devil. We should dread the evils of the careless and evil tongue as we dread fire, because "a careless word may kindle strife; a cruel word may wreck a life; a bitter word may hate instill, a brutal word may smite and kill."

The tongue can be a fagot of hell. The tongue is as dangerous as fire when fire is the master. As a spark can set a forest on fire, as one little lighted match can start a conflagration in a city, so the tongue kindles the whole nature into flame.

Recently the Associated Press reported that an Air Force officer said that the atomic bomb is the size of a golf ball and is equal to 5,400,000 pounds of TNT. Lt. Col. William R. Stark, member of a five-man team from the Industrial College of the Armed Forces, puts it this way: "The atomic bomb, the size of one golf ball, would be the equivalent of 270 ten-ton TNT bombs. The damage of such a bomb comes from three sources: blast, flash heat and radioactivity." But the tongue itself, set on fire in hell, is more of a devilish torch than the atomic bomb.

Sometimes Death chooses pestilence or flames,
Hot avalanches of the molten sand,
Or lightning bolts hurled recklessly thro' space,
Or famine stalking hungrily the land.
Sometimes titantic mounds of glacial ice
The instruments come to blot out life,
The mighty earth may quiver—break apart,
Or nation slaughter nation in war's strife.
A cloud of vapor, poisonous and rank,
Makes shrouds for thousands, checking life and breath.
All these and more gigantic forces serve
As the command of the destroyer Death.
But the warmest love may die perchance
From bitter word or hostile glance.

Thus we are made to think of the tongue, a deadly evil, which does more hurt than catastrophes of earth, because it "setteth on fire the whole course of nature."

Better, for mankind—for young, for old, for all—the talkless tongue than the tongue which is a torch—like the incendiary's flambeau.

Better—for others—for folks to be "speechless as a mummy" than to have tongues such as Joseph Hale spoke of who said: "His tongue, like the tails of Samson's foxes, carried firebrands, and is enough to set the whole field of the world on a flame."

I think, too, I prefer the mouth that has a speechless tongue to the mouth with a tongue thus described: "His tongue is like a bagpipe drone, that has no stop, but makes a continual noise, as long as he can squeeze any wind out of himself."

"If any man offend not in word, the same is a perfect man, and able also to bridle the whole body" (James 3:2).

But think with me of the

Traducing Tongue

To traduce means to misrepresent willfully the character or conduct of someone. It means to defame, to slander, to calumniate. Roger Williams said: "The weak and peaceable are traduced as rivals."

The traducing tongue is indeed "a world of iniquity." The tongue that slanders is a traducing tongue. It is like a hidden assassin who shoots his arrows in the dark. No wonder Plautus said: "Those who carry about, and those who listen to slander, should, if I could have my way, all be hanged—the tattlers by the tongue, the listeners by their ears."

"A wicked doer giveth heed to false lips; and a liar giveth ear to a naughty tongue" (Prov. 17:4).

"He that hath a froward heart findeth no good: and he that hath a perverse tongue falleth into mischief" (Prov. 17:20).

Tennyson said of Vivien, who contributed not a little to the breaking up of King Arthur's Round Table:

> She let her tongue
> Rage like a fire among the noblest names,
> Polluting and imputing the whole self,
> Defaming and defacing till she left
> Not even Lancelot brave nor Gallahad clean.
> And Shakespeare said:
> "Tis slander
> Whose edge is sharper than the sword; whose tongue
> Outvenoms all the worms of Nile, whose breath
> Rides on the posting winds, and doth belie
> All corners of the world; kings, queens and states,

Maids, matrons—nay, the secrets of the grave
This viperous slander enters."

The traducing tongue steals a good name which is rather to be chosen than great riches. A man's name is himself. To rob him of his good name is fundamentally to violate the eight commandment. Truly did Shakespeare write:

Who steals my purse, steals trash,
But he who filches from me my good name
Robs me of that which enriches not him
And makes me poor indeed.

To traduce one's good name is like stealing bread from the hungry with no better purpose than to throw it in the sewer. The traducing tongue of slander and gossip is yet the cancer of the social body, the leprosy of the community, the pestilence that walketh at noonday, the destruction that wasteth at midnight, the hailstorm beating with icy hammers, the flood sweeping away sacred things, the fire that burns to ashes, and the cold that freezes to the marrow.

A traducing tongue is an assassinator of character, a purveyor of moral poison, a viper that stings to death the reputation of others, a vulture that lives off the carrion of lives, a hyena that digs into the graves of the departed that it may drag forth the corpse of some wrong act, a scavenger that drives its car through every community.

The traducing tongue is the climax of meanness, the apotheosis of the absurd, sackcloth at a wedding, bones at a banquet, sarcastic laughter at a funeral. And gossip, another product of the traducing tongue, is a humming bird with eagle wings and a voice like a foghorn. It can be heard from Dan to Beersheba, and has caused more trouble and heartache than the world will know until the universe shuts up and begins the final invoice.

George Meredith said: "Gossip is a beast of prey that does not wait for the death of the creature it devours."

In the words of another, "a bitter word dropped from our lips against a brother is like a pistol fired amongst mountains. The sharp report is caught up and intensified and echoed by rocks and caves, till it emulates the thunder. So a thoughtless, unkind word in passing from mouth to mouth receives progressive exaggerations, and, snowball-like, increases as it rolls."

Gossip mongers are persons who tear the bandages from social wounds, and prevent their healing. They are persons who bring flint and steel, and acid and alkali together, and are justly chargeable with all the fire and ebullition. A whispered word of slander is like that fox with a fire brand tied to its tail that Samson sent among the standing scorn of the Philistines. A gossip in a village, or anywhere, is like a viper in a bed.

At the close of a talkative ladies aid session at which the ladies had over-indulged in gossiping comments about various members of the community, a young woman who had attended for the first time proceeded to call the group the "Ladies Raid Society." Nor would she stand correction. "Raid Society!" she exploded. "You have raided homes and good names and reputations plenty this afternoon. Good day!" The society at once underwent a radical change.

The lying tongue that traduces, God lists along with the most evil of evildoers:

> But the fearful, and unbelieving, and the abominable, and murderers, and whoremongers, and sorcerers, and idolaters, and all liars, shall have their part in the lake which burneth with fire and brimstone: which is the second death (Rev. 21:8).

The lying tongue has caused wars between nations, separations of husbands and wives, barriers between brothers and sisters, father and son, mother and daughter, friends and neighbors. Lying tongues have produced feuds that have lasted for decades, even centuries. Lying tongues have blackened the reputations of young girls, beardless boys, happy ambitious matrons who are rearing families, and old men whose lives are almost spent. Lying tongues have split churches, hindered Christian progress, and planted the germ of bitterness and hatred in the hearts of millions of people, and this germ has passed on from generation to generation.

If all the tears that lying and unruly tongues have caused to be shed were put in one place, they would make a river. The traducing tongue has caused enough sighs to create the moan of a perpetual storm—and has been the source of enough misery and despondency to wipe every smile from every pair of human lips. Satanic the traducing tongue that is a trader in scandal and evil gossip.

I would think now of the

Tar Tongue

I mean by that the tongue which, in several ways, gives people a coat of tar and feathers. The backbiter has a tongue of tar. In Psalm 15, the citizen of Zion is described as one who "backbiteth not with his tongue." He says nothing that might hurt his neighbor in his character, person, property. He is the author of no slander. He insinuates nothing by which his neighbor may be injured.

Dr. Adam Clarke said: "The word 'backbite' was intended to convey the treble sense of knavishness, cowardice and brutality. He is a knave who would rob you of your good name, a coward who would speak of you in your absence what he dared not do in your presence—and only an ill-conditioned dog would fly at and bite your back when your face was turned. Hence, the backbiter's tongue is the tongue of a knave, a coward, a dog."

Backbiters are classed in the Bible with an awful crowd. They are classed with those who do not like to retain God in their knowledge: "Being filled with all unrighteousness, fornication, wickedness, covetousness, maliciousness; full of envy, murder, debate, deceit, malignity; whisperers, backbiters, haters of God, despiteful, proud, boasters, inventors of evil things, disobedient to parents, without understanding, covenant breakers, without natural affection, implacable, unmerciful: who knowing the judgment of God, that they which commit such things are worthy of death, not only do the same but have pleasure in them that do them" (Rom. 1:29-32).

The tongue that smears with tar is a talebearing tongue. The talebearer is a slanderer, a busybody; one who takes up a reproach against his neighbor and spreads it abroad. There is a "shalt not" with respect to this matter, and it is just as binding on us from the Divine point of view as "Thou shalt not kill." "Thou shalt not go up and down as a talebearer among thy people" (Lev. 19:16). In the name of God and holy religion, let everyone who reads these lines covenant with God, and with one another, that we will forever quit such business.

Well, you say, "But it is the truth; and the truth hurts no one." That may be true, but the repeating of it is *evil speaking* and God condemns evil speaking. The wisest of men, Solomon, has said in Proverbs: "A talebearer revealeth secrets" (11:13). "He that covereth a transgression seeketh love; but he that repeateth a matter separateth very friends" (17:9). "The words of a talebearer are as wounds, and they go down into the innermost parts of the belly" (18:8). "He that goeth about as a talebearer revealeth secrets: therefore meddle not with him that flattereth with his lips" (20:19). "Where no wood is, there the fire goeth out: so where there is no talebearer, the strife ceaseth" (26:20).

The tongue that spreads tar is a faultfinding tongue. It takes no brains to find fault. A buzzard can always find a carcass. A fly can always find a sore. A hog can always find a place to wallow. A butcher bird can always find a thorn or a spike on which to impale its victim. Tennyson spoke of those

> Who hate each other for a song,
> And do their little best to bite
> And pinch their brethren in the throng,
> And scratch the very dead for spite.

We tell, we are told. And mythology tells us that when Jupiter—years and years and years ago—made man, he, impelled by his generosity and wisdom, gave man two bags, a large one and a small one, for man to carry about with him wherever he should go or should not go. One of these bags was for man's neighbor's faults. And the other was for the man's own faults. What did man do? Which bag did he select for his neighbor's faults? Which for his own faults? And how did he carry the bags? Listen!

The man took one bag, the larger one, and fastened it securely to one end of a cord. He took the other bag, the small one, and tied it tightly to the other end of the same cord. Then, no one to compel him or to ask him to do otherwise, he flung the cord joining the bags over his shoulder in such a manner and with such dexterity that the larger bag rested on his chest and the smaller bag between his shoulders. The larger bag, the one for his neighbor's faults, was in front of the man, right before his eyes, never out of sight, never forgotten. And, holding a neighbor's faults, it was always full and overflowing.

The smaller bag, the one for the man's own faults, was behind him, right between his shoulder blades, seldom seen, usually forgotten. And this bag, this wee small bag, was always empty. All the wrong his neighbor did was always before this man. All the wrong he himself did went unnoticed and was unremembered.

There are many folks today who are, by inclination and practice and training, like this man with whom Jupiter had to do. Living in glass houses, they throw stones. Imperfect themselves, they see and bitterly condemn the imperfection of others. Themselves carnal-minded, they deplore and censure the lack of spirituality in others. Humped themselves, they ridicule the humped. Crooked themselves, they laugh at the crooked. Mockers themselves, they mock the mockers. Wrong themselves, they condemn others who are wrong. Feed them meat, they want bread. Give them bread, they want meat. Give them tea, they want coffee; give them coffee, they want ale; give them ale, they prefer wine. Offer praise, and praise is improper. Render rebuke, and rebuke is not necessary. If they do a thing that is praiseworthy, they praise themselves. If others do the same thing, it is, according to these pick-a-faults, all wrong. Picking fault with those they see on the street, picking fault with the neighbors whom they meet, picking fault at work, picking fault at play, picking fault because they cannot have their own way, picking fault with the preacher, picking fault with the pew, picking fault with as many as differ in view, picking fault with foe, picking fault with friend, until we all wish their picking fault would end. And this they do, the pick-a-faults!

They are always finding something bad in all good, something ugly in the beautiful, something false in the true.

How we need to pray: "Keep thy tongue from evil, and thy lips from speaking guile" (Ps. 34:13). God keeps us from having the tongue that "speaketh proud things," that "frameth deceit," and "deviseth mischiefs like a razor," that is "bent like a bow for lies," that is as "an arrow shot out," that "boasteth great things."

In connection with the tongue we have the

Task Transcendent

What is that task? It is the task of taming the tongue. The writer of the Epistle of James says the task is a most difficult one.

> For every kind of beasts, and of birds, and of serpents, and of things in the sea, is tamed, and hath been tamed of mankind: but the tongue can no man tame; it is an unruly evil, full of deadly poison. Therewith bless we God, even the Father; and therewith curse we men, which are made after the similitude of God. Out of the same mouth proceedeth blessing and cursing. My brethren, these things ought not so to be (Jas. 3:7-10).

We can, with the help of God, tame the tongue so that it will speak in tenderness and not in anger, not speaking "grievous words that stir up anger," but giving the "soft answer that turneth away wrath."

The tongue can be tamed to give forth "golden gossip" that blesses rather than gossip that wreaks havoc and brings blight. The tongue can be helpful rather than hurtful, can bring balm rather than blisters, can enrich rather than impoverish, can be pure rather than putrid, can be restraining rather than ruinous, can be faithful rather than flatterous, can be truthful rather than false, can place smiles rather than frowns on human faces, can bless God rather than blaspheme God, can be prayerful rather than promiscuous, can be as health rather than pestilence.

The tongue is the greatest power for good in the world. It electrifies the mind by its declarations of truth. It creates enthusiasm with its eloquent words of love. It rouses the whole nature by its appeal to the conscience. It is the most stirring musical instrument in the world. It is the bugle, ringing out its clarion call to duty; it is the lute, with its soft, sweet melodies of love.

The tongue is the compass needle swinging truly between the two poles, and pointing out the pathway of eternal hope.

Wonderful blessing the tamed tongue can bring to many, speaking words that God approves. The tamed tongue has the power of life rather than death in it. It will bless God and not curse men. While the man with an unbridled tongue is a agent of misery and confusion, he can so tame his tongue as to be a blessing to the community, the church, the home. Such a man will know how to be silent, too, when others are hectic and frantic, having a virtuous tongue rather than a vicious tongue.

The tongue can be filled with honey, rather than being full of deadly poison. These truths are authenticated by these words:

"The tongue of the just is as choice silver: the heart of the wicked is little worth" (Prov. 10:20).

"The tongue of the wise is health" (Prov. 12:18).

"The Lord God hath given me the tongue of the learned, that I should know how to speak a word in season to him that is weary: he wakeneth morning by morning, he wakeneth mine ear to hear as the learned" (Isa. 50:4).

"The tongue of the wise useth knowledge aright; but the mouth of fools poureth out foolishness. . . . A wholesome tongue is a tree of life: but perverseness therein is a breach in the spirit" (Prov. 15:2, 4).

"In her tongue is the law of kindness" (Prov. 31:26).

Peter had a tongue that once spoke foolishly and cursed and denied Jesus. But that tongue was so tamed and empowered by the Holy Spirit that, at Pentecost, it was God's agent in help to bring three thousand to their knees.

Paul had a vitrolic tongue, malicious and murderous, which spoke against Christ and commented with pleasure, no doubt, upon the death of Stephen. But, tamed by the Holy Ghost, it spoke so as to make Felix tremble.

John Knox had a tongue that was once out of God's keeping, but God so tamed it and empowered it that, in prayer, it became more alarming to a wicked queen than the bayonets of ten thousand men.

Mel Trotter once had a tongue foul, filthy, wicked, and wild, which spewed out vile epithets. But this same tongue, losing half its vocabulary in conversion, because a tongue of holy fire for God.

While the untamed tongue is a world in iniquity and a deadly poison and a fagot of hell, the tamed tongue will be a tongue that prays for a soul beset by sin, that speaks peace when tempests rage, that praises God. While there is the untamed tongue that twists truths into abominable exaggerations, there is the tame tongue that is always truthful. While there is the raucous tongue that speaks evil of others and besmirches fair names with its innuendoes of wrong and rancor, there is the tongue which, to use Milton's words, drops manna. There is the lecherous tongue with its suggestions of sensuality and its delight in foul stories, but there is also the tongue described in the words:

> Adding once more the music of the tongue
> To the sweet speech of her alluring eyes.

Though there is the untamed tongue which spreads firebrands that set the whole community ablaze, there is the tongue, tamed of God, which is a tongue of infinite graciousness. Though there is the stammering tongue, there is also the eloquent tongue.

Hutchings tells us how the power of the eloquent tongue guided by a sincere heart has given the world immeasurable blessings.

The tongue of Abraham Lincoln spoke three minutes at Gettysburg with such logical and emotional power that not a single cheer arose from the massive audience. His words, like a silver bell, will ring in the hearts of men to the end of time.

The tongue of Henry Grady, stilled by untimely death when he was yet young and vigorous with ambition and hope, spoke words that brought the North and South closer together than any words that have come from human lips, before or since. So eloquent was the tongue of this young statesman that John Temple Graves said at Grady's funeral, "He sprang from a banquet hall into national fame and died, literally loving the nation back together."

The tongue of Cordell Hull helped to turn the tide of suspicion in South America to truth, confidence and friendly relations toward North America.

The tongue of Winston Churchill inspired patriotism, courage, and fortitude in all the allied nations of the world in the darkness of the darkest days of World War II.

What shall I more say? Nothing more say I except to beg you by the tongue of Jesus that spake words of tenderness, of righteousness, of holy and scathing denunciation, of praise, of commendation of right and condemnation of wrong, of comfort, of purity, of truth—by the use He made of His tongue, I beg you to yield your tongue to God as an instrument of righteousness.

"If any man among you seem to be religious, and bridleth not his tongue, but deceiveth his own heart, this man's religion is vain" (James 1:26).

CHAPTER EIGHT

Bed of Pearls: Constraint

For the love of Christ constraineth us . . . he died for all, that they which live should not henceforth live unto themselves, but unto him who died for them, and rose again.
2 Cor. 5:14–15

We go not from a highway to a bypath when we speak of the constraint of Calvary.

We go not from a parlor to a cellar when we speak now of the constraint—the constraint of the Cross.

The Cross constraint, only that, can compass our necessities.

Truth on the altar will more adequately and more quickly triumph than truth in the controversial arena, or on the billboard, or on the adding machine.

Subterfuges, stop-gap performances, argumentative appeals with subtle suggestions of self-pity in them, will fail.

Run these roads how we will, we seek power and victory by ways that never lead to it.

The Constraint of the Cross

But, under the constraint of the Cross, which "bids us not stand nor sit but go," we shall avoid being "bound who should conquer," shall avoid being "slaves who should be kings," shall avoid "hearing our one hope with an empty wonder," shall keep ourselves from being "sadly contented with a show of things."

Not only so.

We shall be kept from a passive acquiescence in small attainments, from slothful timidity in daring, from careless indifference to great stretches of the unattained, from tepid supineness in the face of unscaled peaks that await the pilgrim feet of spiritual pioneers.

What urged early Christians along life's highway?

What gave them joy in hardships, hazards, sufferings?

What drove them toward mobbings, scourgings, prisons, unto death itself?

The words "The love of Christ constraineth me" hold the secret.

They found unflustered sufficiency in the Cross.

So shall we.

Duties God-sent, opportunities God-arranged, privileges heaven-born are ours. Therefore, heroism we must manifest—a heroism eclipsing the heroism born of the bloody ministry of war.

The Atrophy of Heroism

So, in words vivid as lightning, Jesus warns against the atrophy of heroism!

A vast Vanity-Fair is in our country, of artificial beauty parlors, jazz orchestras, comic strips, shrieking posters, night clubs, cocktail-crusaders, bathing reviews, bootleggers, flippant marathons, tom-tom dances, idle parties playing bridge, itching ears, folks giving heed to "raucous cheapjacks shouting palpable lies"—jaded folks seeking thrills, dancing to the music of self-indulgence, chasing short-lived butterflies of pleasure, pottering with shabby nothings in cheap shams of deception.

But how revoltingly cheap and worthless and unheroic this way of life looks as people remember Jesus on the Cross.

By His Cross He shows us how poor many things we count great, how shoddy our splendor, how tawdry our luxury, how worthless many things about which we boast.

Fearsomely easy it is to take the Cross for granted, to be no different because of that tremendous fact.

But there is no possibility of following Christ except by living the crucified life!

The Cross that Stands Between. . .

The Cross stands between us and God's wrath—so that now the community between Jesus and sinners is real, the community of their debt on one side and His merit on the other.

But let us not forget that the Cross should also stand between us and the great world system of sin and pleasure.

We need to think in terms of the Cross, in all things applying it as our standard, carrying it daily through life's multitudinous details, meeting our tasks in its spirit.

Today, men, slaves of wrong values, bound to the world's view of success, love the rewards, not the risks, of the Christian life.

Ornamental cross *wearing* is more popular than sacrificial cross *bearing*.

But to follow Christ is to get His Cross so in our minds that it becomes the standard by which we judge everything, a watershed which shows through all we think and are and do, the solemn background before which our whole life is enacted.

Shall we extol the bleeding sacrifice of Calvary? Shall we

- praise the martyrs whose blood stained the mouths of lions?
- eulogize the saints who went to the stake or dungeon, and then, when our turn comes to sacrifice, ask for ether?

- act as though the symbols of our faith were silken slippers or downy chairs?

Shall we continue to exhibit the weakness of modern Christianity in its deceptive views as to the cost of spiritual power?

Shall we have no suggestion of the thorn crown and the nail prints about us?

Shall we be easy, untroubled, satisfied, facing the world's need and wreck?

Do we know Christ in any real way if we remain unconcerned, have not His sorrow for sin, having not His passion for souls?

Challenged by the world's great need, holding in our hands limitless resources—what will we do?

Has not Christ waited long enough for us to crown Him Lord of all?

Has He not waited all too long already for us to take from His brow, scarred for us, the crown of thorns set there by scoffing men and place thereon the crown of the kingdoms of the earth?

Have Christians Disgraced Christ?

A Jewish Rabbi recently said: "The Jews have rejected Christ, and Christians have disgraced Him." He charges that by our worldliness we misrepresent Christ's spiritual teachings. He says that we, by our pride, misrepresent Christ's humility. He accuses us of being guilty of the lack of heroism and loyalty, by which we misrepresent Christ's Cross!

Speaks the Rabbi truth?

Robert Speer recently speared us when he said: "After thirty years of leadership in missionary work it is my conclusion and conviction that the greatest missionary problem is just the failure of Christian people to live up to their professions."

Is Speer right?

Another, a Mr. Johnston, a soldier of the Cross of Jesus, has, with regret, dared to say this: "The chief obstacle to the spread of Christianity is not Hinduism, not Buddhism, not even paganism, but the rotten behavior of people who call themselves Christians."

Has this good man spoken words of truth and soberness?

Applying the Principles of the Cross

Such things could never be *true* of us if we apply the principles of His Cross to our conduct—make its spirit regnant in politics, in business, in Kingdom battles, in the tasks of God! Such things could never be *thought* of us, even momentarily, if we test our convictions, our inheritances, by the tests of the Cross—subdue every region of our lives to its imperial concern.

The only marks of victory Christ bears are the wounds of Calvary.

Have we forgotten what a claim these scars constitute upon every life they have redeemed and their tenderly mighty appeal as they bid us share His crucifixion?

Hath He marks to lead me to Him
  If He be my Guide?
In His feet and hands are woundprints
  And His side.
Is there diadem, as monarch,
That His brow adorns?
Yes, a crown in very surety,
  But of thorns.

Much it will mean if we can meet Him, arm in arm with Paul, able to match Paul's statement, "I bear in my body the marks of the Lord Jesus,"—able to match Bunyan's testimony, "My marks and scars I carry with me to show I have fought His battles well."

Life and progress are inspiration, not mechanical.

So, the necessity and value of the Cross, the dynamic of personal life.

Warm Wonder Versus Cool Analysis

Our unregenerate humanity is set in the midst of palaces, art, philosophies, scientific wonders, but remains a bedraggled beggar still, while many Christians are frostbitten in realms of luxury.

So the Cross is our superlative, our supreme inspiration.

As Christians, in danger of making a show before the world, doing too little in demonstrating the power and the message of the Holy Spirit, our hope is the proclamation and practice of the Calvary gospel.

In this unreconciled, alienated, dislocated, sin-troubled, sin-saddened world, cluttered up with conceits, with things inchoate, with things inordinate, multitudes from all nations turn to us.

- From Europe: Peoples burdened, peoples bitter, in the near shadow of a quadrennium of blood and tears and the nearer shadow of atheistic orgies.
- From the Philippines: Folks physically freed by Dewey's guns, intellectually freed by educational missionaries from America, some already freed from bondage to relics and friars because of the gospel's liberating.
- From Japan: Peoples with their shrew eyes that see everything, with their polite eyes that stare at nothing, agile seekers for the world's trade and oriental rulership. Perils, they, if they get the coarse power of our civilization without knowing its redeeming Author, possibilities if their leadership of the yellow races comes itself under the leadership of the Lord, who, being national, is still universal.
- From Korea: Multitudes bearing the pathetic despair of their own nationality, and the curse of sin.
- From Africa: Black millions from the land where Livingstone died, where heroes who saw clearly and dared valiantly in their obedience to the heavenly vision, left white tombstones to mark the highway over which Ethiopia stumbles with hands stretched out to God.
- From China: Millions who are waking from the sleep that made them slaves of a long and drowsy past, their eyes still on ancestral tombs, their hands clumsily feeling the levers that may mean danger for the world, until such time as they see Christ's Cross, yellow hordes if captured by the milita-

ristic devil, golden throngs if marshaled by the Prince of Peace, who alone can be trusted with their awful power.

- From India: Her lines of cruel caste waiting for erasure by the pierced hand of the impartial Christ.
- From all nations: Multitudes unled and misled, multitudes knowing not our God, multitudes whose hearts within them are desolate.

Our Commission

Our commission is: "Go and disciple all nations."

Our assurance is: "I am with you."

Knowing this, we must conceive a providence which encircles the world.

We must proclaim the vastness of the divine orbit.

We must acknowledge the tremendous sweep of the divine decrees.

Our Southland, with its imperial advantages, resources, opportunities, has imperial responsibility. And that responsibility, in these hours big with destiny, is for the world's lost millions. Nothing—neither poverty nor pestilence nor famine nor any other creation—exempts us from this responsibility.

Our circumstances do not offer soldiers of the Cross an easy parade ground, where we can loll and sing our lilting songs; they rather offer hard, broken fields which demand as heroic and chivalrous virtues as ever clothed a child of God.

May the Cross, therefore, claim us.

May the Cross haunt us!

May the Cross lay compulsion upon us.

Behind paltry revenues, behind frail instruments, behind erring agents, the Cross works with irresistible efficiency.

Having big conventions will not suffice.

Brooding on blunders will not suffice.

Mustering big numbers will not suffice.

Having only abstract recognition of the claims of Jesus will not suffice.

Not one of these things.

Not *all* of these things.

But laying down our lives.

Any cheaper process is doomed to failure.

Facing our most compelling hour, our biggest opportunity, since Calvary, we wake to the challenge with vast plans, with machinery, with publicity, with executive ability.

But we must do more than maintain great organizations and project worldwide plans. Anything an asset we must use.

Laying Down Our Lives

But our lives we must lay down. Else we shall limp on in a lame old way.

Nothing is won without sacrifice, nothing held without blood.

Can we—will we?—lay down our lives?

This, under God, will lift us from mediocrity to genius!

This, only this, will lift us from provincialism into world citizenship!

This, just this, will lift us from defeat to victory.

With the Cross our experience, not a mere historical statement, we will be lifted from pride to humility, from passion to poise, from selfishness to renunciation, from rolling marbles to removing mountains, from contentment with corners to conquest of continents.

So long as Southern Baptists have a passion for the salvation of sinners everywhere, there is little danger of our drifting into materialism—little danger of our frittering away our energies in "the ethical development of the world."

But, if we give up our position as an evangelistic storm center and court riches and court fashion and court the friendships of self-elected scholars with bloodless gospels, we shall not be found following in Christ's train.

If we seek the approval of religious bodies with spiritual latitudes wide as the Sahara Desert and correspondingly dry, we do err greatly—even foolishly.

In these days of molluscous liberalism, of self-satisfied complacency, if we emphasize little the old familiar notes of Calvary, of hell, of sin, and take up the merely tender note of humanitarian philosophy, we sound our death knell, dig our grave, write our epitaph.

At Christ's Cross is the solution for our indebtedness problem, the sufficient stimulus for our lowered morale, the adequate replenishing for empty treasuries.

By prayer and heroic struggles our Southland has been consecrated beyond all power of priestly hands.

Our fathers whose flame burned steadily in wildest winds, passed through perils, making field stakes, whipping posts, prison bars, to blossom like Aaron's rod.

Shall we, with the such ancestry blessed, hand down our blood-bequeathed legacies reduced in quality and in quantity?

Pigmies be where our fathers were giants in mind and conscience?

Shall we make the superstructure less than the foundations they laid?

Shall we let rot in ignoble anchorage the ships whose keels they laid and set with ribs of steel?

Our Baptist fathers, fearing not the wrath of man in the consciousness of God's presence, believing that all people have a right to approach God without any ecclesiastical or state interference, wrote history in blood before they wrote it in ink.

Shall we write history in ink only?

As Baptists, we believe, as did our fathers, in the rights of the individual, not ecclesiastical rights; in personal faith, not proxy faith; in the priesthood of all believers,, not the priesthood of a class; in free grace, not sacramental grace; in the direct approach to God, not the indirect; in believer's baptism, not infant baptism; in the voluntary principle in religion, not the coercive.

And we must, without apology, without fear, without ceasing, preach and practice our beliefs, carrying them out to the point of suffering.

Down all highways, down all bypaths, we must shout the truth that in religion we have no priest but Christ, in sin no sacrifice but Calvary, in all things no authority but the Bible, and—always, everywhere—no confessional but the throne of grace!

Believing all this, shall we claim fellowship with and give obedient ear to men who, bearing the university brand, claiming the authority of a self-elected scholarship, substitute a "Thus saith the mind of man" for a "Thus said the Lord"—men who see no virgin birth in Bethlehem, men who read no deeper meaning in the Cross than heroic martyrdom, men who cannot find in Joseph's garden an empty tomb? God forbid.

The World, in Desperate Need

The world speaks in desperate need to us.

Guilty we shall be of giving it a scorpion when it asks an egg, a serpent when it needs fish, if we point it not to Calvary.

Our one hope, in all things, is to deal with the tragic terms of the Cross, whereby callous hearts warm in gratitude to Him who came to earth, enduring the indifference which drove Him to the manger and the malice which nailed Him to the Cross.

When the Roman General Pompey, was warned against the danger of his return from Egypt to Italy, he said:

"It is a small matter that I should move forward and *die*, it is too great a matter that I should take one step backward and *live*."

It was said of Napoleon: "He never lost sight of his way onward in the dazzle and uproar of present circumstances." He was never blinded by the glare of victory or by the cloud of defeat.

So let it be with us—in thought, in word, in deed.

As soldiers of the Cross, no right have we to take one step backward—no right to make today's encampment the place of permanent habitation.

No victory have we won with which we have a right for a moment to be content.

No defeat that ever disheartened us ought permanently to discourage us.

No army of occupation we.

An army of conquest.

At the Cross, standing there beside the gift of His whole life for us, can we stand unmoved?

At the Cross, seeing Him who knew no sin bleeding His sweet life away for sinner, can we hug our lives close, withholding ourselves from the altar and, when the bugles of duty call, from the arena?

"He died for all!"

Why?

The answer is, "that they which live should not henceforth live unto themselves, but unto Him who died for them and rose again!"

"Rose again!"

Consider those two words—and the realities to which they point.

"*Rose again*!"

Follow, follow now, while we consider the house of many wonders to which these two words are the key.

CHAPTER NINE

The Whirlwinds of God

Behold, the whirlwind of the LORD goeth forth with fury,
a continuing whirlwind.
Jer. 30:23

All the prophecies in the Book of Nahum pertain to Nineveh. Nahum lived and prophesied from 664 B.C. to 607 B.C., approximately. I mean by the expression "Before Christ" so many years before Christ was made flesh. For "He before all things" (Col. 1:17). And He had glory with the Father before the world was (John 17:5).

The Book of Nahum is chiefly a sequel to the Book of Jonah. Both Nahum and Jonah had their minds and hearts stirred in thoughts of, and in giving God's message to Nineveh—"Nineveh, that great city" (Jon. 1:2); Nineveh; "an exceeding great city of three days' journey" (Jon. 3:3); Nineveh, "wherein are more than six score thousand persons that can not discern between their right hand and their left" (Jon. 4:11); Nineveh, with walls one hundred feet high surrounding, the walls themselves having two hundred towers of commanding height.

Jonah, with pungent and fiery repetition, had already warned Nineveh concerning her wickedness and of the impending punishments of God, punishments which God remitted when Nineveh repented. Nahum now repeats these denunciations. The one theme of his prophecy is the destruction of Nineveh—Nineveh then at the height of its power, then in the noonday of her pride, then in the midnight of her sin, then in the depths of her degradation.

In the chapter wherein we find mentioned, in beautiful language, the majesty of God in goodness to His people and the severity of God against His adversaries, we find our text gleaming like a pearl amid pearls. "The Lord hath His way in the whirlwind." Much truth of God we can learn by thinking upon what the Bible reveals in connection with its mention of whirlwinds. May the truth we learn help us to serve Him who "hath made the earth by his power . . . [who] causeth the vapors to ascend from the ends of the earth: [who] maketh lightnings with rain, and [who] bringeth forth the wind out of his treasures" (Jer. 51:15–16).

The Whirlwinds of God Speak of His Eternity

A *continuing* whirlwind!

A whirlwind *ceaseless*.

A whirlwind ever active.

A whirlwind active when the flowers and fruits of summer are in the land.

A continuing whirlwind when the fires of autumn are burning over hill and vale.

A continuing whirlwind when the snows of winter cover the earth in snow and ice.

A continuing whirlwind in spring, when God weaves a mystic skein over cragmoor, hill, and plain.

A *continuing* whirlwind, showing forth the eternity of God, testifying to His ceaseless activity in the universe.

"Now unto the King eternal, immortal, invisible, the only wise God, be honor and glory for ever and ever" (1 Tim. 1:17).

"Before the mountains were brought forth, or ever thou hadst formed the earth and the world, even from everlasting to everlasting, thou *art* God" (Ps. 90:2).

"But thou, O LORD, shalt endure for ever, and thy remembrance unto all generations" (Ps. 102:12).

"Hast thou not known? hast thou not heard, that the *everlasting* God, the LORD, the Creator of the ends of the earth, fainteth not, neither is weary?" (Isa. 40:28)

"Blessed be the LORD God of Israel from everlasting, and to everlasting" (Ps. 41:13).

To this, the eternity of God, the *continuing* whirlwind of the Lord gives testimony in symbol significant.

The eternity of God is duration without beginning or end, a *continuing* fact.

The eternity of God is existence without bound or dimension, a *continuing* existence.

The eternity of God is present, without past or future, a *continuing* present.

God's eternity is youth without infancy, youth without old age.

God's eternity, His *continuing* existence, is life without birth, life without death.

God's eternity is today, today without yesterday, today without tomorrow.

He is the unchangeable God. Nations go. But not God. Above the graves and tombs of all nations God reigns. God, "the same yesterday, and today, and for ever" (Heb. 13:8). God, "with whom is no variableness, neither shadow of turning" (James 1:17). There is no wrinkle ever on the brow of God. Forever He is the God who fainteth not, neither is weary. God is where He was at first. He continues forever a God of eternal and infinite power. He is able, willing, mighty to save those who trust in Him, powerful to prompt us in our perplexities, His goodness failing never to guide us in our gloom, His hand held out to help us in our hazards.

> And God is the first Cause, absolutely.
> God is the first Cause, universally.
> God is the first Cause, everlastingly.

If we take the back track on science, we assuredly will arrive at the mind of God. If we face the past and trace back moral principles, we will certainly arrive at God's character. If we count all the years that lie in the tomb of time and trace back existence, we arrive at God's existence. What He was, He is. What He is, He will be. What He will be, He ever has been. He changes not. We cannot say that too often. Essentially immutable is God. His essence asserts so much. His laws assert so much. His government asserts so much. Christianity asserts so much. That is something of what Jeremiah meant when he spoke of "the whirlwind of the Lord . . . a *continuing* whirlwind."

And God's immutability and eternity are pledged for the perpetuity of His church. God's immutability and eternity are pledged for the immutability of His church. Originally was the church built upon Christ. Never has it been shifted from its foundation. Never can it be. Never will it be. Never.

Somebody gave us volumes of truth in a few lines, gave us acres of truth in inches of language, gave us rivers of religious reality in a rill of speech, who said:

> See that huge granite boulder heaved by volcanic power from some mountain's side, lying upon the ocean's shore amid the accumulated debris of the centuries, exhibiting the abrasions of tides and drifts, worn by winds and driving rains, and scarred and cracked by the heavy tramp of ages? Even its indurated structure has not been able to resist the power of change. But the church of God, uncorroded by the teeth of flying years, unmarked by the fragments of thrones and republics continually drifting by on the roaring current of time, and unbattered by the infringement and concussion of hell's infernal

> thunderbolts, lifts its walls and turrets in unscathed and imperishable strength to heaven, as impregnable as the throne of God!

Which is just another way to emphasize what Jesus said in Matthew 16:18—that the gates of hell should never prevail against His church.

Such truth gives us the assurance that drives away our fears.

Such assurance delivers our hands from weariness in well-doing.

Such assurance gives our feet faithfulness in following where He leads.

Such assurance delivers our hearts from fainting.

Such assurance gives our shoulders strength for burden-bearing.

Such assurance keeps us from thinking that *all* is lost when *one* battle is lost.

Such assurance comforts us and strengthens us, not only concerning the work and mission of the church, but such assurance comforts us and strengthens us concerning each individual life.

And this comfort and strength gives us victory over the fear that often comes when we think of eternity, and for the hour when we face eternity. "Eternity whose incalculable and incomprehensible value no subtraction can diminish, whose incalculable and incomprehensible value no addition can increase."

I think one of our recent-day poets has expressed this with beauty in "FEAR," a poem which presents Youth speaking and Age speaking.

And Youth says:

> "The night is dark; the wind is still;
> A hound bays on a distant hill;
> The world is large! and I am small;
> My path is veiled, ah, I shall fall!
> O Mother, let me have your hand!"

And Age speaks, saying:

> "The night is black; the wind is shrill;
> The hounds bay on a closer hill;

Oh, larger world! and I so small!
Eternity, one long, last call
My God, my God, give me Thy hand!"

With the hand of the eternal God upon ours, fearlessly can we face eternity, eternity in whose awful shadow all worlds, all men, all angels, all devils perform their parts. Yes, with the hand of Him who hath His way in the whirlwind—a *continuing* whirlwind—we can face eternity with the joy of a little child who goes out to play, with the dignity of a king who goes forth to coronation.

The Whirlwinds of God Testify That God Has Answers for Man's Questions

"Then the LORD answered Job out of the whirlwind" (Job 38:1).

Only God has an answer for every question of man. Man says: "I have life, what shall I do with it?" And God answers: "In all thy ways acknowledge him, and he shall direct thy paths" (Prov. 3:6). "The LORD is the strength of my life; of whom shall I be afraid?" (Ps. 27:1).

Give your life to God. God is the fashioner of royal character, and in His hand the reed which is shaken by the wind is transformed into an iron pillar which cannot be moved. Give your life to God. Put it on His altar. Put it to His ploughshare. Then your mind will be established in the truth of God. Your heart will be confirmed in the purpose of God. Your will will be possessed by the holy strength of God. You will confront all hostilities without breaking, bending, or yielding—invincible before the onslaughts of the world, the flesh, the devil. Against all enervating airs from the South you will be able to stand. Against all fierce blasts from the icy North you will be able to stand. That is part of the answer God gives to the one who says, "What shall I do with my life?"

But man asks a harder question: "What shall I do with my sins?" God, God alone, has the only answer for that tragic question. And as I turn the pages of Holy Writ, I find that question asked again and again, echoed again and again, sobbed out again and again, uttered with lamentation again and again, wailed out with intonations of misery over and over. Generation after generation asks that question. Age after age after age asks that question. The stoic asks it. The philosopher asks it. The scholar asks it. The saint asks it. The savage asks it—in one way and another. Yet, aside from God, never once has it received the slightest hint of an answer, never once in all the ages the least suggestion of an answer, aside from God. And, depend on it, verily, if Jesus, Son of man and Son of God, had never come into the world, that sad question would have echoed around the world, up and down the corridors of all the centuries, unanswered and unanswerable until this very day.

"O Plato!" cried Socrates, "it may be that the gods can forgive sins, but alas! I do not see how!" No. Nor anybody else. Job's question fell back upon his face. The universe could give him no reply. Philosophy could find no reply. Nature could give him no reply. Only God.

"I have sinned. What shall I do?"

"I have sinned!" Pharaoh said it.

"I have sinned!" Balaam said it.

"I have sinned!" King Saul said it.

"I have sinned!" Achan said it.

"I have sinned!" David said it.

"I have sinned!" Judas said it.

"I have sinned!" The prodigal said it.

"I have sinned!" Millions, in chorus of confirmation, have said it.

"I have sinned!" Millions are saying it now. "I have sinned!" *I* have said it. *You* have said it. *All* of us have said it.

"I have sinned!" What shall I do? We may scour sea and land for some answer to that sad question of the soul. We may search earth and sky for some answer to that wild question of the soul. We may climb the lofty summits of the mountains seeking to find some answer to that question. We may tread the labyrinthine mine, hoping to find some answer to that question. We may call to the heights of the heavens. We may call to the depths of the sea. But there will be no answering voice. And we are left to nurse a piteous despair until we come to

A green hill far away,
Without a city wall,
Where our dear Lord was crucified,
Who died to save us all!

No man knows of any other fount in all the wide universe of God, which has cleansing efficacy for sin, except the fountain which was opened in the riven side of our Lord Jesus, our Redeemer, that fountain "filled with blood drawn from Immanuel's veins," that fountain beneath which sinners are plunged and "lose all their guilty stains." That is the only sufficient and efficient fountain for sin and uncleanness. Where else can men discharge that crimson stain of sin? Nowhere else.

Can the pool of Siloam do it? No.

Can the snows of Hermon wash us whiter than the snow? No.

Has the Jordan in full spate power to cleanse us from the foulness of our human guilt? No.

Can Abanar and Pharpar, rivers of Damascus, rid us of our leprosy? No.

Can all the multitudinous seas wash us and make us clean? No. Never.

None other Lamb, none other Name,
None other hope in heaven or earth or sea;
None other hiding place from guilt and shame,
None beside Thee!

There is no other hiding place. Roofless and wall-less the refuge of morality. A *veil* for armor man has when he wraps the righteous robe of his respectability about him. A roofless ruin for a house of abode man has who trusts in his self-righteousness—thanking God in his pharisaic complacency that he is not as other men are, "extortioners, thieves, adulterers, unjust," or "even as this publican." Flimsy finds man any fence of ethical superiority within which he shuts himself. A refuge of lies which will go down in ruin when the blast of the terrible One is as a storm is anything aside from Jesus Christ. Other refuge have we none!

In the day of accusation, when conscience rises as a strong man armed, we shall need a defense far more substantial than a man-made refuge. In that day of discrimination, when God makes searching inquisition for sin, all our fine-spun philosophies will prove unavailing. When the foundations of the earth are being removed, and the heavens roll up as a scroll, and the firmament melts in the heat of the final conflagration, and the judgment flames like into paths of dust all the waterways, we shall come to that refuge eternal, the Rock of Ages. And then we shall make, even as now we do, a fervent prayer the old hymn:

> Rock of Ages, cleft for me,
> Let me hide myself in Thee;
> Let the water and the blood,
> From Thy wounded side which flowed,
> Be of sin the double cure,
> Save from wrath and make me pure.
> Could my tears forever flow,
> Could my zeal no languor know,
> These for sin could not atone;
> Thou must save, and Thou alone:
> In my hand no price I bring,
> Simply to Thy cross I cling.
> While I draw this fleeting breath,
> When my eyes shall close in death,
> When I rise to worlds unknown,
> And behold Thee on Thy throne,
> Rock of Ages, cleft for me,
> Let me hide myself in Thee.

That question, "What shall I do with my sins?" God answers out of the whirlwind of man's remorse.

That question, "If a man die, shall he live again?" God answers out of the storm of human sorrow. And He answers it in such a way as to give a divine hope to the travail of the ages. By the empty tomb in Joseph's garden, He answers it in such a way as to give a note of gladness in a world of sorrow, a note of hope in a world of despair, a note of assurance in a world of doubt, a note of victory in a world of defeat. In many ways, but chiefly and with entire sufficiency in Jesus who hath brought life and immortality to light through the gospel (2 Tim. 1:10), He answered that question. God, the eternal God, who answered Job out of the whirlwind, is not baffled by any question that man lifts up before Him. Our profoundest questions are not puzzles to Him. God, the eternal God, who hath His way in the whirlwind, is not perplexed by our perplexities. God, whose whirlwind goeth forth with fury, a *continuing* whirlwind, is not baffled by what baffles us, is not wearied by what wearies us, is not discouraged by what discourages us, is not mystified by what mystifies us. "God answered Job out of the whirlwind!" And God has an answer for all our questions concerning pain, concerning our cares, concerning our all—through Christ His greatest revelation who Himself once asked, in painful questioning of soul suffering, "Why hast Thou forsaken me?"

The Whirlwinds of God Speak of the Harvest Day

For they have sown the wind, and they shall reap the whirlwind
Hosea 8:7

Thus saith Hosea, speaking of how, for impiety and idolatry, destruction shall come against the house of the Lord, because God's people had trespassed God's covenant and trespassed against God's laws! Hosea summed up the punishment that would come to them because of their numerous transgressions in one sentence, saying, "They have sown the wind, and they shall reap the whirlwind."

We have the mystery of life. We have the mystery of death. Upon both these men often think. Moreover, we have the mystery of growth. From the chamber of life God hath never drawn the curtains. From the chamber of death God hath never drawn the curtains.

But the chamber of growth is another most holy place in which God alone doth stand. Deeply impressed by the fact and the mystery of growth, we have marveled at the principle that controls the harvest.

"Whatsoever a man soweth, that shall he also reap."

For he that soweth to his flesh shall of the flesh reap corruption;" but he that soweth to the Spirit shall of the Spirit reap life everlasting" (Gal. 6:7–8).

In other words, like produces like.

He who sows wheat reaps wheat, not pepper.

He who plants a grape reaps a purple cluster, not a bunch of thorns or a sprig of thistles.

He who sows honor, reaps confidence and honor.

He who plants figs gathers figs, not berries.

He who sows grass, reaps grass, not moss.

He who plants cotton, gathers cotton, not pumpkins.

Nature's law, all men know, is universal and inexorable. Like produces like. The sheaf is simply the seed enlarged. The bale of cotton is simply the seed enlarged and multiplied through the mystery of growth. The sowing contains the germ of all harvests to be reaped.

If a man sows the wind, he shall reap the whirlwind.

If a home sows the wind, it shall reap the whirlwind.

If a nation sows the wind, it shall reap the whirlwind.

If a woman sows the wind, she shall reap the whirlwind.

That has been true through all the years gone forever into the tomb of time. That will be true of all the years that may come from the womb of time. If a man sows the wind, he will reap the whirlwind. If a man sows tares, he will reap them. It may not be today. It may not be tomorrow. It may not be this week. It may not be next week. It may not be this year. It may not be next year. But the time of reaping will surely come, just as surely as night follows day. And when the reaping time comes, sad will the harvest be. Then those who have sown bad seed and reap the harvest thereof would gladly exchange places with the Christians whom they despised, or shunned, or believed to be foolish.

When the whirlwind harvest day comes, I think no murderous Cain would need an argument to get him to exchange places with any spiritual Abel.

I am sure no cowardly Pilate would need any persuasion to induce him to exchange places with Elijah, the prophet of God, and with Obadiah "who feared the Lord in Ahab's house."

I think, were John the Baptist's place offered him, Herod would quickly accept it.

I think, had she the chance to have it, Jezebel would gladly take Dorcas' place.

I don't think any delegation would be necessary to go to Nero and argue with him to get him to exchange places with Paul. I don't think the most blundering man in matters of speech would have a hard time persuading Potiphar's wife to exchange places with Joseph.

I don't think there would be any delay on Dives' part accepting Lazarus' place were it offered him.

And I should not be at all surprised if the day is not near when Clarence Darrow would swap and give lots of "boot" between his death-bed and that of William Jennings Bryan.

I think it was Mr. Moody who, in his own matchless way under God's Spirit, kept saying to the hearts of men and women the truth that though the worldling may look with contempt upon Christians, the time is coming when the worldlings will give anything to exchange places with the meanest Christian that walks the streets.

Bear in mind and be no doubters concerning the truth that those who sow the wind will reap the whirlwind. Be not doubters of this truth even though the harvest is slow, ever though it comes on leaden heels. Let me give you this passage from God's eternal Book:

> Because sentence against an evil work is not executed speedily, therefore the heart of the sons of men is fully set in them to do evil.
>
> Though a sinner do evil a hundred times, and his days be prolonged, yet surely I know that it shall be well with them that fear God, which fear before him: but it shall not be well with the wicked, neither shall

> he prolong his days, which are as a shadow; because he feareth not before God (Eccles. 8:11–13).

Years ago, years too far gone for some of us to remember so well, a man and a woman killed the child of their sin, killed the fruit of their bodies, the child in sin begotten and illegitimately born. Then they buried it. And years went by. But the harvest day came, though it seemed to come slowly, as snails crawl. The day of the whirlwind came—the terrible harvest day, when their deeds came back upon their heads, when they gathered into their bosoms the sheaves of their sowing. Out in the far Northwest they had gone. The man was found one day frozen, standing upright in a huge snowdrift, where the blizzard had overtaken them. At his back gaped the portal of a mountain defile, a wintry chaos of glacier-riven rock and snow-laden firs. In the gorge, around its first turn, in a sheltered nook, the woman was found. On her, too, the ice king had breathed. The woman was crouched before the ashes of an extinct fire. Around her lay scattered widely the contents of a treasure box which held all their belongings. Clutched close to her breast by her rigid fingers, as though she would shield it from storm, lay a strange bundle—a faded shawl rolled into the semblance of the muffled form of a child. Upon the frozen whiteness of the icy wall behind her were traced with a blackened ember, in a woman's uncertain handwriting, these words: "The Wages of Sin Is Death." The wind they sowed. Terrible the whirlwind they reaped.

There are a great many things in this world we are not sure of. We are not sure we shall reach the end of the voyage which we start at the wharf, or the end of a railroad journey we start at the depot. We are not sure we will finish the book we begin to read. We are not sure we will plow to the end of the furrow in the field. We are not sure when we go to sleep that we shall wake again in this world. We are not sure when we greet the sunrise that we shall be here to greet the sunset. But there is one thing we are sure of, that all nations are sure of, that all peoples are sure of, that every individual is sure of, for God has said it: "Whatsoever a man soweth, that shall he also reap."

"They have sown the wind, and they shall reap the whirlwind." There is not a "probably" attached to that statement. There is no "perhaps" before or behind it. There is no uncertainty dwelling in it. There is no "maybe-so" found in it anywhere. The idea of uncertainty is nowhere to be found in it. "They that have sown the wind shall reap the whirlwind." What harvest awaits you?

Sowing the seed by the daylight fair,
Sowing the seed by the noonday glare,
Sowing the seed by the fading light,
Sowing the seed in the solemn night;
Oh, what shall the harvest be?
Oh, what shall the harvest be?
Sowing the seed by the wayside high,
Sowing the seed on the rocks to die,
Sowing the seed where the thorns will spoil,
Sowing the seed in the fertile soil;
Oh, what shall the harvest be?
Oh, what shall the harvest be?
Sowing the seed of a lingering pain,
Sowing the seed of a maddened brain,
Sowing the seed of a tarnished name,
Sowing the seed of eternal shame;
Oh, what shall the harvest be?
Oh, what shall the harvest be?
Sowing the seed of an aching heart,
Sowing the seed while the teardrops start,
Sowing in hope till the reapers come,
Gladly to gather the harvest home;
Oh, what shall the harvest be?
Oh, what shall the harvest be?

The Whirlwinds of God Speak of Retribution

Because I have called, and ye refused; I have stretched out my hand, and no man regarded; but ye have set at naught all my council, and

> would none of my reproof: I also will laugh at your calamity; I will mock when your fear cometh; when your fear cometh as desolation, and your destruction cometh as a whirlwind; when distress and anguish cometh upon you. Then shall they call upon me, but I will not answer; they shall seek Me early, but they shall not find Me (Prov. 1:24-28).

"I will laugh . . . I will mock . . . when your destruction cometh *as a whirlwind*!" This is no philosophical aphorism. This is no empty threatening. This is no catchy quip. This is no linguistic twist of words. This is no limerick of levity. It is the language of divine inspiration—language clothed with the eternal truth of Him who cannot lie, and backed by the arm of inexorable justice, which will sooner or later verify it. Apply it where you will. Apply it to the churches. Apply it to the minister. Apply it to the sinner reveling in his midnight debaucheries. Apply it to the woman who hires herself out as a harlot. Apply it to the man who holds women's virtue of little worth. Apply it to the nations that have forgotten God. Apply it to the man who maketh money without regard to man or God. Wherever there is sin collectively or individually, it has a retribution day, a day of finding out the sinner.

Knowing this, know also that it is dangerous to do wrong. Sin's road may seem to be soft and smooth, but sin's road grows rough toward the end, and ends in black night.

Sin plants its flowers and puts underneath each one of them a tarantula.

Sin spreads its silken and downy couch of indulgence which outwardly appears beautiful, but at the same time sin puts a nest of brooding serpents underneath that silken couch.

Sin opens sparkling pleasure fountains, but every one who drinketh thereat and therefrom drinks water which is bitterer by far than the bitter waters of Marah.

Sin, with opaline lights, lures us out to sea, and then, in the horror of the night, strangles our cry in the deep.

Sin promises us substance and store if we will but walk its deceptive streets, and then, having pierced our feet with thorns, it leaves us to stumble on to the dungeons of hell.

The stag pursued by hungry hounds with open mouths is not more miserable than the man who is pursued by his sins.

The bird taken in the fowler's net and laboring vainly to escape is less wretched than the woman who, yielding to sin's enticement, has woven about herself a web of deception.

An eagle, once used to the sunlight heights, but now beating his wings out against the brass bars of his cage, is less unhappy than the man who has a skeleton in his house of life.

A swimmer in storm-stirred sea, harassed by the sight of a shark's fin and jaws near by, is not more tormented than the man who goes on to meet the retributive hour of his sinning.

The fish in the talons of a fish hawk has more comfort than the man whose conscience scourges him down the last lap of life's road to meet just retribution.

The serpent writhing and hissing in a bed of hot coals is not more to be pitied than the man, the woman, who has come to sin's retributive payday.

The judge may seem to be unobservant. The watchman may seem to be asleep. But God never slumbers. Law never sleeps.

The Memphis *Commercial Appeal* carried a news despatch in April 1931 which told of a man across the river in Arkansas who had a pet rattlesnake. The man found the snake as a baby snake. He took it and fed it and made quite a pet of it. The reptile would come when he whistled. It would eat from his fingers. It would coil around his arm and let him stroke its head with the palm of his hand or with the tips of his fingers. One day he took it to town to exhibit it among his friends. They marveled at its gentleness; marveled at the way it coiled itself with apparent gentleness around his arm; marveled how it would come when he whistled; marveled that it would eat from his hand. He went back home with his pet. When he got home, suddenly, with only the slightest provocation, the reptile became angry. Quicker than the zig-zag lightning flashes from the bosom of a dark cloud, that pet rattler buried its fangs in the man's arm. In a few hours the man was dead. In one quick instant, with poisonous fangs, the serpent had written his death in his own blood. Two nights after that, the man who should have been sitting with his family in their humble but happy home was sleeping in the mud of an Arkansas grave.

With such dread cometh such an hour to every man and woman who makes a pet of sin. So cometh such a horror and death to every man who refuses when God calls. An hour of kindred terror awaits the man or the woman who regards not when God stretches out His hand. A day of dreaded despair like unto that the man met when he pulled the pet snake's fangs from his arm and hurled it to the ground, is out yonder somewhere to all who set at naught God's counsel and will none of His reproof. "Be not deceived; God is not mocked." Turn you at God's reproof. Turn now. There's danger and death in delay. Let go that sin. Drop it—now.

Dr. Lee Rutland Scarborough, burden-bearer for God, tells how one day he got a message fraught with sadness and woe.

"Mr. So-and So has shot himself through the heart and he is calling for you!"

The man of God, ready and willing to help, was soon by the man's side. It was a home of poverty, a home of neglect, a home of sin. For two weeks the man had been on a drunken spree. Recovering from the wild time, he found himself sick and discouraged. Finding himself so, he took his own pistol and shot himself. And here is what Dr. L. R. Scarborough said:

> He took my hand at seven in the morning, and I was not able to get free from his grip until eleven, when his hand fell pulseless at his side. I begged him for hours to give his heart to Christ. Just before he died I called in his family. His oldest boy, fourteen years of age, came and hugged and kissed his father goodbye. I will never forget what that father said to that son. And then the children came one after another until the sixth one, the baby, came. And then he came to say goodbye to his wife who was a Christian woman. He took her by the hand, still holding on to mine.
>
> "Molly," he said, "you have been a good wife. For these sixteen years you have had to do all the praying. You have had to do all the Bible study, all the teaching of the Word of God to our children. You have had to do all the church-going and all the godly living. I have not helped you at all, Molly. For sixteen years you have stood for me in

> religion. Now, I am dying and I want to know if you are going to stand for me at the judgment bar of God?"
>
> The pale, sad-faced woman, with tears covering her face, turned to me for an answer. I said, "Old fellow, your faithful wife has done everything she could for you, but at the judgment bar of God you will have to stand in your own shoes."
>
> And he died, and went out to meet God, unprepared.

Retribution! Destruction coming as the whirlwind.

There is a question *I* cannot answer. There is a question *you* cannot answer. There is a question which *all the knowledge of all the scholars* of the world cannot answer. There is a question all our *scientists* cannot answer. A question the *angels* cannot answer. A question all the *intelligences in earth and heaven* cannot answer. A question *God* in heaven cannot answer. The question is: How can we escape if we neglect the salvation which delivers us from sin's dread penalty? How, if men keep on sinning, if men keep on refusing when God calls, if men keep on regarding not when God stretches out His hand, how can they escape the dread day of retribution when God will laugh at their calamity, when God will mock at their desolation? If men keep on in sin's road, their fear will come as desolation and their destruction will come as a whirlwind.

The Whirlwinds of God Speak of the Hour of Farewell

> And it came to pass, when the LORD would take up Elijah into heaven by a whirlwind, that Elijah went with Elisha from Gilgal. And Elijah said unto Elisha, Tarry here, I pray thee; for the LORD hath sent me to Bethel. And Elisha said unto him, As the LORD liveth, and as thy soul liveth, I will not leave thee. So they went down to Bethel.
>
> And the sons of the prophets that were at Bethel came forth to Elisha, and said unto him, Knowest thou that the LORD will take away thy master from thy head today? And he said, Yea, I know it; hold ye your peace. And Elijah said unto him, Elisha, tarry here, I pray thee; for the LORD hath sent me to Jericho. And he said, As the LORD liveth, and as thy soul liveth, I will not leave thee. So they

> came to Jericho. And the sons of the prophets that were at Jericho came to Elisha, and said unto him, Knowest thou that the LORD will take away thy master from thy head today? And he answered, Yea, I know it; hold ye your peace. And Elijah said unto him, Tarry, I pray thee, here; for the LORD hath sent me to Jordan. And he said, As the Lord liveth, and as thy soul liveth, I will not leave thee. And they two went on. And fifty men of the sons of the prophets went, and stood to view afar off: and they two stood by Jordan. And Elijah took his mantle, and wrapped it together, and smote the waters, and they were divided hither and thither, so that they two went over on dry ground. And it came to pass, when they were gone over, that Elijah said unto Elisha, Ask what I shall do for thee, before I be taken away from thee. And Elisha said, I pray thee, let a double portion of thy spirit be upon me. And he said, Thou hast asked a hard thing: nevertheless, if you see me when I am taken from thee, it shall be so unto thee; but if not, it shall not be so. And it came to pass, as they still went on, and talked, that, behold, there appeared a chariot of fire, and horses of fire, and parted them both asunder; and *Elijah went up by a whirlwind into heaven*. (2 Kings 2:1–11)

"Up by a whirlwind!" It was goodbye. Here is a lesson for us. It is this. There is a time of going for us. And another lesson. The time of our going is in the Lord's hands, and the way of our going is of the Lord's determination. One says, "I want to go on my birthday." But God wills that it shall not be so. One says, "I want to die a lingering death." But God says: "No, suddenly thou shalt go. Suddenly a bolt shall strike thee. Thou shalt go to bed well, and with the morning shalt be in heaven, without one pain, without a spasm, without a notice given anyone!" Another say, "I want to go with my friends around me, their hands holding mine, their ears hearing my last voice." But God may will it that thou shalt die in loneliness, away from friends, among strangers. Another says, "I should like to go as a shock of corn fully ripe." But God may will that thou shalt be cut down in the greenness of thy youth! All of which is to say that the farewells concerning which the whirlwinds that took up Elijah speak are realities awaiting us—down a nearby road, down a distant road, across a nearby Jordan, across a faraway Jordan.

Goodbye—separation—some day. Of this God's whirlwind speaks.

Goodbye—separation—the ships sailing out from the harbor say so.

Goodbye—separation—the trains, massive juggernauts of steel and steam, puffing out of terminal stations and puffing away from village depots and speeding across the lands, say so.

Goodbye—separation—the airplanes, arousing the lands with roaring noise and mounting on steel wings to the eagle's domain and swooping across continents and seas, say so.

Goodbye—separation—to this testify the automobiles as they speed over our highways, a moment seen and in a moment gone.

Goodbye—separation—to this the loud voice of Mars testifies as he walks with bloody boots across the gardens of the world, with bloody fingers tying crepe on the door knob of millions of homes.

Goodbye—separation—in the court room when a mother, struggling like a Spartan to keep the tears, says "Goodbye" to her boy being taken off to prison, or to the death house.

Goodbye—separation—of this the mother kissing her child as it goes off to school for the first time gives evidence.

Goodbye—separation—this is the reality that shadows the heart of the mother sitting with a dead baby in her lap.

Goodbye—separation—this is the inevitable result as the bride, with the one upon whom her heart's love has been fastened, leaves the old home nest.

Goodbye—separation—in childhood. In youth. In old age. All the time. Among all peoples. Everywhere!

"Parted . . . asunder" (2 Kings 2:11).

"And Elisha . . . saw him no more" (2 Kings 2:12).

Yes, that is the way it is. "Parted asunder!" We all know what that means.

"And Elisha saw him no more!" We all know what that means.

Mothers taken away from little children, and the children see them no more. Parted asunder.

Fathers taken from the household, and the families see them no more. Parted asunder.

Husbands taken from the arms of wives, and the wives see them no more. Parted asunder.

Sons marching off to war, choosing the garments of flame and blood as their garments of glory, parted asunder from loved ones who see them no more. Parted asunder.

Little children, whose laughter was the sweetest music of the household, whose smiles made sunshine for the home, taken from the arms of mothers. And mothers, longing for them all the while, see them no more. Parted asunder.

Youth turning from the old home gate to seek his fortune in the great city, leaving the old homestead, and he sees the old home no more. Oft 'tis so. Parted asunder.

Multitudes in the city and multitudes in the country scattering flowers on tomb-marked graves. Multitudes down by desolate seashores that reach in ragged lines around the world, flowers on the ocean, which is a tomb of tombs, a vast mausoleum, all hoping, with the blue light of the ageless morning, to see those from whom they are parted asunder. And here we learn that the pain of love is parting.

Youth comes on a pace. Parted asunder from childhood. And we see our childhood no more. And old age, insidious and lethal, comes before we want it and before we hardly know it. And we are parted asunder from our youth, and we see youth again no more.

And the money for which we toiled is lost in the bank crash or in some foolish investment. Parted asunder from our money. And we see it no more.

And fame comes and crowns us with a withering crown. And then, by some misstep or by means of the brighter shining of the crown of one who has outdone us, fame leaves us. Parted asunder from feeble candles of fame which were blown out by the same crowd that applauded us, applauding another. And fame we see no more.

And the accumulation of property comes, but, before we hardly knew it, the time comes to go and leave it in the hand of another and all our needs then require is a small area that, by measurement, is about six feet long and two feet wide. The same a beggar requires. Parted asunder. And none of our accumulations we take with us.

But why proceed in this strain any longer? "Parted . . . asunder!" "And Elisha . . . saw him no more." These words put before us experiences familiar to everyone of us, experiences our forefathers back in the dim past knew about, experiences we ourselves are familiarly familiar with, experiences which our children's child shall come to understand. But what matters it all—all this parting asunder—as when Elijah went up by a whirlwind into heaven—if for a little while we do *not* see them, and in a little while we *shall* see them? What victory hath this parting asunder with our accumulations here if our going is but to see the treasures we have laid up in heaven? What sadness hath our being parted asunder from our loved ones here if it is to greet other redeemed loved ones in the other world? What sting hath our going if it is God's whirlwind that comes for us? What sorrow to us in our staying behind when others go—if we have the Lord God of Elijah with us still? What sadness the walking the way alone—if, at our word, the Lord God parteth still the Jordan waters? Why bitter tears when one of God's days we shall have them forever, if God sent for them to be with Him?

Darling baby of the heart, I shall have you and love you forever. Think of that, when the chariot and the whirlwind goeth up.

Mother, you whose going up was like a soldier from hard warfare, I shall love you and have you forever.

Father, you whose leaving was, to you, like a sailor home from a stormy sea, I shall have you forever.

Friend of mine, you whose leaving me stopped the singing of the birds, I shall have you forever.

Lover, you whose going plucked the sun out of life's sky, I shall have you forever.

Comrade, comrade, you who refused my invitation to stay awhile longer, you who denied my heart's yearning to stay a little longer, I shall have you forever. And it shall be when the chariot comes for me, even as it came for you.

And, in this thought, in this belief, we shall face the farewell of our friends and the goodbye from our loved ones in the spirit of old Elijah as he went from Gilgal with Elisha, as he came to

Bethel with Elisha, as he came to Jericho with Elisha, as he came to Jordan with Elisha, as he stood by Jordan with Elisha, as he crossed over Jordan with Elisha in calmness and dignity and unspeakable tenderness.

As it was with Elijah when the whirlwind from heaven sent brought him home, so shall our farewells here be changed into greetings yonder. And we, as Stanton standing in the shadows sang, can say:

Adieu, sweet friends—I have waited long
    To hear the message that calls me home,
And now it comes like a low sweet song
    Of welcome over the river's foam;
And my heart shall ache and my feet shall roam
    No more—no more: I am going home!
Home! where no storm—where no tempest raves,
    In the light of the calm, eternal days;
Where no willows weep over lonely graves
    And the tears from our eyelids are kissed away.
And my soul shall sigh, and my feet shall roam
    No more—no more: I am going home!

CHAPTER TEN

God in History

And, Thou, Lord, in the beginning hast laid the foundation of the earth; and the heavens are the works of thine hands! They shall perish; but thou remainest . . . they shall be changed: but thou art the same, and thy years shall not fail.
Heb. 1:10–12

A picture these words present of the perishable and the permanent, the transient and the eternal. And, in view of these truths, we would speak of God in history.

Carlyle says: “History is the essence of innumerable biographies.”

Voltaire says: “History is little else than a picture of human crimes and misfortune!”

Kaufman says: “History is making a collection of autopsy reports!”

Kossuth: "History is but the development and revelation of providence!"

Napoleon: "History is a fable agreed upon!"

Bancroft: "Each generation gathers together the imperishable children of the past, and increases them by new sons of light alike radiant with immortality!"

But Lanahan came nearer the real truth when he said: "God is in the facts of history as truly as He is in the march of the seasons, the revolutions of the planets, or the architecture of the worlds!"

And Cromwell, doubtless wiser than they, said: "All histories are but God manifesting Himself, shaking down and trampling underfoot whatsoever He hath not planted!"

Anyway, we are now ready to agree with him who said: "It is when the hour of conflict is over that history comes to a right understanding of the strife, and is ready to exclaim, 'Lo, God is here, and we knew it not.' "

But no matter what may be the definitions men give as to the meaning of history, we know that what Cromwell said is true. And we know that

Before the World Is God

> Thou, Lord, in the beginning hast laid the foundation of the earth (Heb. 1:10).

> Before the mountains were brought forth, or ever thou hadst formed the earth and the world, even from everlasting to everlasting, thou art God (Ps. 90:2).

God made and set the pillars of the earth in their sockets, and hung the world on nothing (see Job 26:7). He made and drew across the windows of heaven the blue curtains of the night and pinned them together with star clusters. He set the lakes like huge crystals among the green velvet pockets of the hills. He kindled the first fires. He set the sun in His tabernacle in the heavens. He shut up the sea with doors. He commanded the morning. He sent forth the first ray of light across the uncharted dark, like some flaming archangel with garments afire. He started the sweet influences of the Pleiades and put the bands about Orion. He brought forth Mazzaroth in his season. He guided Arcturus with his sons. He sent for the lightnings, even as now He doth hold the lightning in His fists. He lifted up the mountains and wrapped them in robes of clouds and crowned them with diadems of snow. This is what Paul, the great Aristotle and Demosthenes of the Jewish race, tells us in the first chapter of Colossians:

> For by him were all things created, that are in heaven, and that are in earth, visible and invisible, whether they be thrones, or dominions, or principalities, or powers: all things were created by him, and for him: and he is before all things, and by him all things consist (Col. 1:16–17).

Not only is God before all things, but we have evidence irrefutable on every hand of

God's Presence in the World

God's presence in the world has always been a fundamental truth of Christianity. He is not far away in the heavens, seated upon a white throne—an absentee God, a God detached from the lives which men and women are living here.

The present world is the workshop of the Almighty God! Full of noise, yes. Full of dust, yes. Full of confusion, yes. Full of snarling clamours of those who loose wild tongues that hold not God in awe? Yes. Full of evils that would lead our greatest graces to the grave and leave the world no copy? Yes. Full of the intellectual conceit of men who are unaware of the rattle of the dry bones of their conceit? Yes. This we do not deny. With much superficial mental illumination that lacks the urge of sacrificial passion? Yes. The whole ground littered with the splinters of fallen greatness—frustrated ambitions, broken health, blighted hopes? Yes. Suffering saints and flourishing sinners? Yes.

Yes. But there is a scheme of divine government, even though it is too vast for me to comprehend, its methods too intricate for me to follow. Yes, even though we are often staggered by what this divine government ordains or permits. Yet, through all the trying years, nothing can make us doubt the power of His guiding hand in history.

God is everywhere in the world. Our eyes may be holden that we cannot see Him. But the fault is in our eyes and not in His presence. God crowds upon us on every side—in the street, in our homes, in the office, in the store, in the shop, on the hills, in the country lanes, in the festering alley, on the shores of the sea. Everywhere! We cannot get away from God. When Paul preached to the Athenians he said that they should seek the Lord if haply they might feel after Him and find Him, though He be not far from everyone of us; for "in him we live, and move, and have our being" (Acts 17:28).

In the dawn of creation the morning stars sang together and the sons of God shouted for joy because of the recognition of the presence and activity of God in the universe. Take God from nature, and this universe would indeed be "a fortuitous concourse of atoms"—and worse. But we have all been conscious, at times, that there is something in nature which we cannot see—an invisible presence and power that breathes through it all and impresses itself upon our minds. God is stamped on everything in nature. There is purpose, mind, design—the presence and activity of God. God is active in all things in the realm of nature. God is manifest in all things. He is in the blowing of the winds and in the light of the setting sun and in the glory of the rising sun. He makes the lightning, for "The God of glory thundereth!" through all the processes of nature the divine plan is being wrought out. God is at the center of it all.

Yes! The moulding hand of God is in the infinite constellations which seem to crowd the very amplitude of infinity. And God is not a prisoner, pale and emaciated, in the universe He made, sitting when and where the universe says sit, standing when and where the universe says stand—the lackey boy of His own house. He is no law-limited God, no mere superannuated butler in the world house He conceived by His omniscience and created by His omnipotence. Is not this universe a vast autograph album? Are not the covers of this album wrought of matter bound up in myriads of forms, its pages molecules and atoms and constellations and planets and electrons and mountains and motes? And has not God written His signature upon every page, every single page, whether gigantically large or microscopically small? Yes, verily.

God did not create the universe, make all things beautiful in their season, and set His spirit in man, then turn His back and vanish into silence. This world is not a piece of clockwork finished once and for all and set agoing by an almighty mechanic. The one door to all of it is God. God *in* His world means God *throughout* His world. And by this we mean that God is not only present everywhere, but that He inheres in all things and is the immediate and active cause of all the operations of nature. The forces of nature are not forces which He has merely set in operation, but they are God's powers actively at work, producing results—various results. The force of gravity is God' s presence and power working in our direction. The force of chemical affinity is God's presence and power working in another direction. The centripetal and centrifugal forces are but God's presence and power working by a direction and guidance not of man. So all the forces of nature are simply manifestations of God's power; and they represent the life of God, as your manual labor or as your intellectual labor is something which you are actually putting forth yourself! Truly, in the realm of nature, even as elsewhere, He is the inescapable God.

> Whither shall I go from thy spirit? or whither shall I flee from thy presence? If I take the wings of the morning, and dwell in the uttermost parts of the sea; even there shall thy hand lead me, and thy right hand shall hold me. If I say, surely the darkness shall cover me; even the night shall be light about me. Yea, the darkness hideth not from thee; but the night shineth as the day: the darkness and the light are both alike to thee. (Ps. 139:7–12).

Paul's declaration to the Athenians that "in him we live, and move, and have our being" so proclaims Him. And so does His statement to the Colossians which saith: "By him all things consist."

The essential thing is that we recognize God's presence in the world, and that we remember that He is not far from everyone of us!

I would have you think with me of

God in Human Experience

Everyone who has named the name of Jesus by faith, and to whom God is a reality, can look back along the pathway of his experience and trace the Divine Presence at work in his life. It may not have been apparent in our lives in the past, but, in the light of the larger experiences of life, we discover that it has been so. For us it has been taken out of the realm of the accidental, and we can see now the divine leading.

Countless thousands of Christians during the centuries have been equally confident that, in one way or another, and at one time or another, God has manifested Himself to them. The hymns of Christianity are full of these expressions of Christian experience. Such as "Amazing grace, how sweet the sound, that saved a wretch like me."

From ten thousand times ten thousand we get testimony of the experience that ended in drunkards being made sober, in debauches made pure, in liars made truthful, in thieves made honest, in harlots made to wear the white flower of a beautifully pure life, in crooks made straight, in men in bondage to sin made free, in men dead in trespasses and sins quickened unto real life and blessedness.

But the main thing we are to speak about in this message is

God in Human History

God has always been present in history. It is because His ways are not as our ways and His thoughts are not as our thoughts that men have sometimes said, "There is no God anymore." But we may be sure that God is always with us and always active. Oft we may not see His mighty arm nor hear the still, small voice. But it is impossible to think of a loving God, divine, all-powerful, intelligent, sitting off somewhere in space remote from His world, doing nothing, thinking nothing, caring nothing for them.

Often man has made history and left God out. Yes, left Him out as those who shut out the night and shut in the day. But really God has never been left out, no matter how much nor how often man has tried to leave Him out! God was there. All history contains God, whether the human historian gives Him a place or not in its annals.

And if God is with the world at all times, most certainly shall we not believe He is with it during its *crises* of history? During calamities? And during great financial disasters? And during unparalleled trouble? And widespread unrest? Or vast changes in affairs? God allows men to govern themselves. He does not step in and do everything for them, anymore than He feeds the sparrow by throwing its food in its nest. But through and in all experiments of nations, God is present and ready to help. He certainly does not banish Himself from the world just when the world is most in need of His wisdom and love. God has never abdicated. He still rules. He has "prepared his throne in the heavens; and his kingdom ruleth over all" (Ps. 103:19). This truth answers the plausibility of the doctrinaire, the perplexities of the scholar, the riddle of life.

Therefore, we shall not be discouraged, if, perchance, a sudden blast of the noisy winds of anarchy should occasionally demolish a small portion of our edifice.

Whatever may be the terror of the earthquake, it does not finally destroy confidence in the stability of the earth. Whatever may be the terror of the storm that hides momentarily the sun, it cannot make us believe that the sun is gone!

> Whatever may be the darkness of the night, it does not cause us to believe that no other day will come from the womb of time.

> And I heard as it were the voice of a great multitude, and as the voice of many waters, and as the voice of mighty thunderings, saying, Alleluia: for the Lord God omnipotent reigneth (Rev. 19:6).

From the days of the Exile and the deliverance of the Hebrew nation until the present hour, has there not been evidence that

God is in human history? Is it difficult for us to trace, sometimes, the footsteps of God in the ebbing and flowing of human progress? Yes. But the footsteps are there. No darker days Israel ever knew than the days of exile. Driven from their land, their sacred city in ruins, their temple deserted, they hanged their harps upon the willows and said they could not sing the Lord's song in a strange land! But God was present with them, for "in all their affliction he was afflicted" (Isa. 63:9). And, in this exile experience, they came to a new recognition of God.

Historians are conscious that something goes into the making of history beyond the policy and power of statesmen and soldiers. They are constantly stumbling upon unknown factors. One historian refers us to the "anonymous powers" which shape the lives of people.

Anonymous powers! Power to whom or to which they can ascribe no position, assign no name, and whose actions they cannot comprehend, but of whose presence they are conscious. The ages and the history of the ages are more than flesh, more than mechanism, more than kings, more than diplomats, more than dragons, more than millionaires. All unseen and all unheard are hosts of mighty workers, who, in defiance of men and evils, by night and by day, build, making even the wrath of men to praise God.

So the divine forces which control the world of humanity are subtle, invisible, inscrutable.

> Now the Egyptians are men, and not God; and their horses flesh, and not spirit. When the LORD shall stretch out his hand, both he that helpeth shall fall, and he that is helped shall fall down, and they shall all fail together (Isa. 31:3).

The spiritual power of God shall prevail against every hostile force. Marvelous warriors are God's invisible cavalry. Never taken prisoner. Never returned missing. Never wounded. Never for them sounds the last blast. They fight, but never taste death. They fight with noiseless artillery, with smokeless powder, with ethereal weapons, but are mighty through God. However much the carnal regimental array may impose upon our imagination, the decisive battles of the world are decided by His secret working who is infinite in wisdom and strength, who is the sum total of all immensity, of all intelligence, of all energy.

We must choose between a world *with* God and a world *without* God. Yes, between a world in whatever comes to pass does so with the knowledge and permission of God, and in some way finds a place in His purpose and plan, and a world where everything just happens so—happens so with no governing will or plan or purpose back of it all. Do we not have to choose between freedom and fate, between a personal God and blind chance? Between faith in prayer and trust to luck? We are bound to choose. Only the short-sighted and the superficial mind can find a resting place between these two opinions.

But if we believe in God as a moral being, as the moral governor of the universe, then it follows that we must believe that He rules and governs and that His plan is beneficent and just. At first glance the history of the world seems to be just a rush and roar and clatter and clash of wheels within wheels, getting nowhere, guided by no intelligence, accomplishing no end. But if we look at history in the light of our faith in God, we shall have little difficulty in discovering that, as Ezekiel shows, the spirit of the living creature is in the wheel, that the wheels are full of the eyes of purpose and intelligence, and that the general movement of the chariot of Providence is straight on. The whole course of history seems to have been the voluntary effort of man, the ambitions of this world empire or of that world empire, the evil designs of this adventurer or king, the pressure of economic forces, the conflict of race antipathies, the collision of plans of dominion. But all the movements of history are with God's permission and do not fail to register His will.

Take America, for example. If ever a nation could point to the hand of God in its history, we are that nation. God's hand is as clearly seen in our history as in Hebrew history. It is as clearly manifest in our history as when God led His people of old through the Red Sea, through the wilderness ways, feeding them with angels' food from heaven, making flinty rocks gush forth crystal waters, guiding them with a pillar of fire by night and a pillar of cloud by day.

If ever the hand of God guided the destinies of a nation, molded and fashioned its very life, shaped its purposes, inspired its ideals, and intervened in its behalf in crisis times, then this is true of this republic. Never since the days of the Hebrew theocracy has this been so true as it is today. Who, knowing the facts of our history, can doubt that the United States of America has been a thought in the mind of God from all eternity? Not in arrogance, but in deep humility, and not without a measure of fear and trembling, we believe that the United States of America is the chosen nation of the later dispensation. We cannot regard the American Revolution, the Spanish-American War, the World War for the curbing of autocracy, as mere accidents. The great men of the Revolutionary period were not there when needed by mere chance. Ethan Allen crowded American history into a single sentence when he demanded the surrender of Ticonderoga in the name of the Great Jehovah and the Continental Congress.

And have we forgotten that the first Continental Congress, with the assembling of which the Revolution morally began, was opened with prayer? On the second day, as Sheppard tells us, the distinguished body met under the disturbing influence of a rumored bombardment of Boston. Indignation was on every brow, sympathy in every heart! Psalm 35, wherein David recites his wrongs and cries out for the shield and buckler of the Lord, was read by the chaplain with such fervor and such effect that John Adams afterward expressed the belief that heaven had ordained this passage to be read that morning. Patrick Henry expressed a similar sentiment when, in his memorable address before the Virginia revolutionary convention, he said that there was a just God who would raise up friends to fight the battles of the colonists. Can we question the especial aid of the Ruler of all world when we see the fog refuse to rise that August morning in 1776 until our army had retreated from almost certain annihilation on Long Island, and then some five years later observe the dawning daylight drive the escaping Cornwallis back to Yorktown and surrender? Can we deny the interposition of God, when in the gloomiest hours of the conflict, we see the tattered continentals retreat barefooted over frozen roads, crossing, when also overtaken, the Catawba and the Yadkin, whose waters successively rose to delay their pursuers?

And think of this. The western world was kept unknown to the world until the era of Reformation. Its discovery and the beginning of the great religious Reformation were almost contemporaneous. While the discovery of the continent was made under the prevalence of the papacy, the great papal powers of Europe all failed in every attempt to colonize that portion which afterwards became the United States of America. The nations which succeeded in colonizing and building up states were those which the Reformation leavened and made great. Nor did they succeed until Protestantism had been securely established in them. Every one of the thirteen colonies which fought the battles of independence and formed the federal government was founded by Christian men. The fathers of this republic "invoked God in their civil assemblies, called upon their chosen teachers of religion for counsel from the Bible, and recognized its precepts as the law of their public conduct." From the time when the first blood was spilled on the field of Lexington and the power of Jehovah, King of the kingless land, gave victory in the surrender of Cornwallis—from beyond those times until the times when our young men chose the garments of flame and blood for their garments of glory, knights of the right of the weak against the strong—from those times far back yonder until these recent times, times whose heroic deeds will be perpetuated in every temple dedicated to liberty, God's hand has been in our history!

Back of all events we believe the hand of God can be seen in our history. We date our history from the coming of Columbus. But let us not forget, as others have said, that, beyond doubt, America was discovered and attempts made at settlement long before Columbus was born. According to the researches of not a few students of history, the Mohammedans, in an early day, came very near the American coast. They would have effected a settlement if their boats had not been destroyed. Their fleet crossed and sailed far beyond the straits of Gibraltar, but was wrecked in a tempest. This occurred centuries before the coming of Columbus. But the expedition failed. Not to the Mohammedans was America to be given. God, in His providence, had another use for this country.

The Chinese made a direct claim to having discovered this continent many centuries ago. Charles G. Leland has written a work entitled *Fu Sang, or the Discovery of Amerca by Chinese Buddhist Priests in the Fifth Century*. Here the claim is made that a Buddhist monk visited New Mexico in A.D. 499, or nearly one thousand years before Columbus came to these shores. But for some reason no permanent settlement was effected, and the knowledge of the discovery was lost. Not to the Chinese, the followers of Confucius, was this country to be given. The God of nations had another use for America.

The claim seems well-founded that the Norsemen discovered this continent about the year A.D. 1000, or nearly 500 years before the time of Columbus. In the old Norse records is related that 150 of their number made a voyage to a distant land. In Bristol County, Massachusetts, is an inscription on the solid rock which is thought by scholars, by *many* scholars, to agree with the Norse records and to lead to the conclusion that this was the "distant land" visited by these hardy seamen. But for some reason this people did not effect a permanent settlement here, and the knowledge of the discovery of America was again lost. Not to the Norseman with his ancient hero worship and mythology was this country to be given. The great Controller of history had another use for America.

From the Mohammedans with their false prophet, from the Chinese with their Confucianism, from the Norsemen with their mythology, from the Aztecs and the Mound Builders and the earlier inhabitants of the country the land was withheld. Why? For what purpose? To whom is the country to be given?

Remember it was in 1517 that Martin Luther nailed his immortal theses to the Castle Church in Wittenberg. Soon the bitter persecution of the Reformers began. Just twenty-five years before Luther nailed his theses in Germany, Columbus discovered America. About that time, therefore, the Protestant Reformation had reached full headway and persecution began in earnest, the fact of America's existence became known to the world. Is there no philosophy in this? Is there no logic in such events? Religious persecution in England, and the Puritans came. And then the Quakers. Religious persecution in France, and more than half a million Huguenots came. Religious persecution in Austria, and the earnest-hearted, consecrated Moravians came. Pressing the point further, we can plainly see that both in earlier and later times there has been the hand of God in our history.

> [He] hath made of one blood all nations of men for to dwell on all the face of the earth, and hath determined the times before appointed, and the bounds of their habitation (Acts 17:26).

God is either determining the movements and bounds of men and nations, or He is just sitting aside and watching the performance! I cannot but believe the former!

One of the magnificent failures of the ages was the Crusades. In these crusades five million lost their lives. In sickening and nauseating measure followed unspeakable moral corruption. But Europe woke up from moral stupor with an arousal and intellectual uplift that would not be denied, and escaped its chains. The march of Mohammedanism was checked. Feudalism was underminded, until Europe grew strong enough to meet the issue as the issue was met before Lepanto. Who can say God's hand was absent from all those events?

Some say that the fall of Constantinople in 1453 seemed, at that time, to be the greatest disaster of history. Many thought the end of the world was looming darkly and immediately ahead. The thought prevailed that the Mohammedan shadow would crush the earth. Scholars fled before the possible event. The same scholars, with a fervor more than fright, went into the bypaths and the highways of Europe. As they went they took with them something of more value than rubies, manuscripts that were of great value, even priceless. They were met by the printing press. The printing press with its movable type profoundly aroused civilization. The Bible was given to the people.

And then mankind leaped over the antique walls of civilization, destroyed prejudices deeply-rooted in the immemorial past, and winded the blind alley of ignorance into endless highways of wisdom. The union of pen and press culminated in the Reformation of the sixteenth century. The possession of Constantinople gave the forces of Islam the pathway of commerce to India and the East. This meant, as many dared say, as many feared to say, as many who neither dared nor feared acknowledged, the bankruptcy of Europe.

The passion of the hour became the discovery of a new route to the wealth of the East. Here and there schools of navigation were founded. One result, one portentous result, was the discovery of America. Another result, weighted and freighted with significance, was the finding of two new roads to the East—one around Cape Horn, another around the Cape of Good Hope. Great Britain which, up till this momentous time, had been in the backyard of the wide world, was brought around to the front door and the front yard. Anchored there like a ship at the very spot where a nation ought to be in order to assume the leadership of the future civilization, she became the organ beneath God's fingers pressed. She became the ship whose sails the breath of God filled. For God made the Anglo-Saxon the pioneer of the future. Yes, and just as significantly, God gave the Anglo-Saxon the strategic position of the front yard. Who would say, who knows history, that this was of man and not of God?

Who would say that the Thirty Years' War was not the most terrible conflict of history, notwithstanding the recent bloody struggle when the brains and blood and bones of slaughtered sons of men covered the fair face of God's weeping world as with offal? Thirty thousand villages and towns were destroyed in that thirty-year struggle. Germany alone lost twelve million people. But, God forgive us if we should forget, that war saved Protestantism. Had it been otherwise, Europe would now be the terrible battleground of Roman despotism and Russian barbarism. Who would say that God did not plant His footsteps on that turbulent trouble of thirty bloody years? Who can say He did not ride upon its storms?

The oppression of the thirteen colonies by Great Britain was unreasonable and unjust—how unreasonable and how unjust we will not now try to say. We leave that to the historian. But out of it, out of this squeezed orange, came the sweet, healthful juices of our national independence. But why say more? Have we not seen, have we not heard that the everlasting God, the Creator, does employ the wrath of God to praise Him? Who would say, knowing the facts and studying the evidences, that God's hand is absent from the affairs of the universe?

The unrest of the fifteenth century was a bad unrest. The fifteenth century was a century of turmoil. It was a century of persecution. But this century of turmoil and persecution and bitterness, have you noticed how much it produced? Did it not produce Luther who walked out of a miner's hut and lit a lamp in the darkness? Did it not produce a Calvin who told the libertines of Geneva that they could shoot him in his pulpit if they wanted, but when they did he would fall on the open Bible? Did it not produce a John Knox who made queens turn pale? Did it not produce the Huguenots of France? Did it not bring forth the great old Covenanters of Scotland? Did it not produce the liberty-loving folk, the Dutch of Holland? Did not that most turbulent period of English history produce Hampden and Cromwell with his Ironsides and the Puritans? Was not God's hand in that turbulent and stormy century? Yes. And may such knowledge cause us to see beyond the fever and the pain of the present day, with its changing thought and emphasis, to that far-off divine event toward which the purposes of God lead and to which the plans of God point! God in history. Just as much in history as the sun is in His tabernacle in the heavens! Let His name be praised!

Not only so.

We get evidence of God's hand in history in noticing

God's Use of Little Things in History

Great issues have turned upon little happenings that *seemed* to be altogether fortuitous. So far as man's efforts and designs are concerned, the working out of the divine plan *seemed* to be the result of chance. But not so, this *seeming happening.*

Pharaoh happened, it seemed, to dream one night; and the chief butler happened, it seemed, to remember Joseph. And the result was the getting in motion of the events which led to the Egyptian captivity.

The daughter of Pharaoh happened, it seemed, to go down to bathe at the place where Moses, the baby, lay hidden in the reeds in the Nile. Out of that came the preservation and the preparation of Moses for the leadership of his people. Truly, in the tears on a baby's cheeks, God floated into Egypt all His mighty navies of deliverance. And the footsteps of a woman going to bathe were the prelusive footsteps to the footsteps made by a nation going from bondage to liberty, a nation born in a night.

Ruth happened, it seemed, to go into the field of Boaz. And thus she became not only the wife of Boaz but the ancestress of our Lord. This visit she made to the fields of Boaz has great relation to Bethlehem's barn where Jesus of the Virgin Mary was born.

King Ahasuerus, king of Persia, was unable to sleep one night, and so his secretary entertained him by reading the royal records. And thus the king learned how Mordecai had saved his life. And that event had its part in the saving of the life of the whole Jewish people.

When Columbus was feeling his way over the unknown ocean, it was the flight of birds that made him turn his ship to the south and to the southern continent. And thus the great continent to the north was reserved, in greater part, at least, to *English* civilization and Protestantism.

It rained the night before Waterloo, making the ground so soft that Napoleon could not get his guns in position until eleven o'clock. And thus "a cloud traversing the heavens out of season sufficed to make a world crumble!"

These are but a few of those strange events which, so insignificant in themselves, yet under God, who "Views with equal eye, as God of all, /A hero perish or a sparrow fall," are fateful to decide the issue of nations. "As fragments fit themselves into the finished mosaic, so what to *us* are *chance* and *trivial* events, fit themselves into the Divine plan!"

So nothing really happens by chance. Did I say "happen"? God forgive me. There are no chance meetings after all. As well said by someone, it was not by chance . . .

that David and Jonathan met in the field,

that Elijah and Ahab met on the grassy slopes of Carmel,

that Herod and John met on the highways of Galilee,

that Pilate and Jesus met in the judgment hall at Jerusalem,

that Philip and the Ethiopian eunuch met on the sandy road to Gaza.

No. It was not by chance . . .

that Nero and Paul met amid the antique splendors of ancient Rome,

that Savonarola met Lorenzo,

that John Knox met Queen Mary,

that Hugh Latimer met Henry the Eighth,

that John Bunyan met the three poor women sitting in the sun.

Not by chance that, in the crisis of spiritual anguish, Martin Luther met John Staupitz. Not by chance that Spurgeon met the local preacher that snowy morning in Artillery Street chapel at Colchester. Nor is it by chance that men and women who truly love meet. If 'tis by chance, then children and homes are products of chance.

Why did Jesus die? Was His death an accident? Was it one of those chance dark happenings of which there *seem* to be so many in this bewildering world? Was it due to the fact that Caiaphas *happened* to be the High Priest? Or that Pilate *happened* to be governor? Or that Jesus *happened* to speak a few phrases which the crowd *happened* to be in a mood to resent and to distort?

In the whirlwind of the wheels of circumstance, did Golgotha just happen to fall out? In the turning of the big world kaleidoscope, did the black bead smeared with blood suddenly and by chance appear? This is a conceivable explanation, but such an explanation will never satisfy the human mind and will never bring comfort to the human heart.

The only interpretation which has in it an abiding satisfaction is that which the apostles accepted two thousand years ago, namely, that the death of Jesus fell in with heaven's plan and that it forwarded God's purpose for mankind—and that Jesus was the Lamb slain from the foundation of the world! In the words of Peter in the first recorded apostolic sermon,

> Him being delivered by the determinate counsel and foreknowledge of God, ye did crucify and slay, whom God hath raised up, having loosed the pangs of death: because it was not possible that he should be holden of it. Acts 2:23–24

God is not then absent or asleep when Jesus dies on the cross. He knows what is going on. Jesus is not left to die by chance, or in vain. The world being what it is, it became necessary for the Son of God to die. Men being what they are, the death of Christ became inevitable. With His death, the power of sin cannot be broken.

And this brings us, in conclusion, to consider God's hand in history as seen in

God's Judgment upon the Nations

In God's judgment upon the nations, we see evidence of God's plan and of God's reign. He doeth "terrible things in righteousness" (Ps. 65:5). What is the history of the world but the judgment of the world? "I will dig thy grave because thou art vile," was the sentence which God through His prophet delivered to Nineveh.

Look at the past history of nations. What do we see? We see the fact of sin in the life of each nation, of all nations. We see also that all nations have been vile. We see, too, that the fact of brevity attaches itself to the life of all nations. Moreover, we see that the kingdoms and empires of the world have followed one another in quick succession to the grave. The conqueror from without and the internal strife along with corruption within—these have brought every kingdom low.

Where are the eagle empires of Babylon and Egypt, wheeling and screaming over the carcasses of nations that have been conquered and dismembered? Where are the winged lions of Nineveh? Where are the chariots of the Hittites? Where are the navies of Phoenicia? Where are the triremes of Carthage? Where are the phalanxes of Thebes? Where are the hoplites of Greece? Where are the legions of Rome? Where are the treasures of Spain? There is but one answer. This:

In outline dim and vast,
Their mighty shadows cast,
The giant forms of empires on their way
To ruin, one by one
They tower and are gone.

Where did they go? Was it only a question of time? Of age? Of national decrepitude? Or did the matter of sin and judgment enter into their fall? Consider Cromwell's conclusions:

What are all histories but God manifesting Himself, shaking down and trampling underfoot whatsoever He hath not planted?

God's sentences are sometimes long. It may be one thousand years between the subject and the predicate. But there is no doubt that God will finish every sentence. This truth has been shouted down a thousand highways of history! It is folly to try to cheat God, or in any way to thwart or stay His divine purpose! God's judgments may have leaden heels but they have iron hands! Which makes us to make this our prayer:

God of our father, known of old,
    Lord of our far-flung battle line,
Beneath whose awful Hand we hold
    Dominion over palm and pine—
Lord God of Hosts, be with us yet,
Lest we forget—lest we forget!
The tumult and the shouting dies;
    The Captains and the Kings depart:
Still stands Thine ancient sacrifice,
    An humble and a contrite heart.
Lord God of Hosts, be with us yet,
Lest we forget—lest we forget!
Far-called, our navies melt away;

On dune and headland sinks the fire.
Lo, all our pomp of yesterday
Is one with Nineveh and Tyre!
Judge of the Nations, spare us yet,
Lest we forget—lest we forget!
If, drunk with sight of power, we loose
Wild tongues that have not Thee in awe,
Such boastings as the Gentiles use,
Or lesser breeds with the Law—
Lord God of Hosts, be with us yet,
Lest we forget—lest we forget!
For heathen heart that puts her trust
In reeking tube and iron shard,
All valiant dust that builds on dust,
And guarding, calls not Thee to guard,
For frantic boast and foolish word—
Thy mercy on Thy People, Lord! Amen![1]

I think it is McArtney who has told us, even as we ourselves believe, that in the fulness of time God will bring history to its climax, and set up the everlasting kingdom of Jesus Christ. When that is done the whole earth shall know that "I the Lord have brought down every green tree and have exalted the low"—and we shall see that all the confused movements of time have been controlled by eternal purpose. If you and I had gone to Mount Lebanon where the laborers were felling the trees, sawing lumber for the temple, or if we had gone to the quarries where they cut the stone for walls and foundations, we should have seen only a tumult and we should have heard only a confused murmur of industry. But if we had stood on Mount Moriah at Jerusalem, we should have seen the meaning of it all. We should have seen the massive timbers and the great blocks of stone, in holy silence, without the sound of hammer or axe or any tool of iron, each fitted into its place in the temple of God.

Today we see the tumult and the noise and the crashing of stately cedars, the sound of hammer and chisel and warlike tool

1. Copyright, 1903, by Rudyard Kipling. All rights reserved.

of iron, lifted by godly or ungodly arm. God hides His temple and treasures up in His designs in the unfathomable mines of His sovereign will. But at last the meaning and plan and purpose of it all, for the world, for your life, for my life, will be made clear. Silently and majestically all the timbers and all the stones that have been prepared through time shall fit themselves into the finished Temple, the Holy City of God, the everlasting Kingdom of Jesus Christ!

McArtney the truth hath spoken.

"Thy years shall not fail!"

CHAPTER ELEVEN

This Critical Hour

And who knoweth whether thou art come
to the kingdom for such a time as this?
Esther 4:14

I am no photographer of sordid spots, no driver of a garbage wagon, no prober of abscesses, no seeker after carrion. One does not have to be these to say that we have come upon bewildering times—when nations have tobogganed into chaos, with billions sought for government vaults and millions in want, multitudinous churches and multitudes translating the blood-bequeathed privilege of freedom *of* worship into freedom *from* worship, innumerable laws on statute books and much criminal lawlessness, much gratitude for America yet the subtle infiltration of ideas which, if they found wide acceptance, would sound the death knell of liberty.

In 1840, when Queen Victoria married Albert the Good, people died of starvation in East London the morning she was married, and the unemployed burned a large part of the city of Birmingham. The Duke of Wellington, who still remembered the battle of Waterloo, said he had never seen anything worse in war.

At the close of the first year of the Civil War, Lincoln said: "I have no word of encouragement to give." And away back yonder, old Elijah, God's prophet of fire in an apostate day, the spiritual whirlwind whelped by the desert, said: "The children of Israel have forsaken thy covenant, thrown down thine altars, and slain thy prophets . . . and I, even I only, am left; and they seek my life, to take it." (1 Kings 19:14). And Isaiah said once: "They are out of the way through strong drink, they err in vision, they stumble in judgment." (Isa. 28:7). And the psalmist said of Ephraim, the tribe to whom Joshua and Samuel belonged: "The children of Ephraim, being armed, and carrying bows, turned back in the day of battle. They kept not the covenant of God, and refused to walk in his law" (Ps. 78:9–10).

When Jesus was born in Bethlehem, the scepter was frozen with the tyranny of impeached civilizations, old Athens the intellectual center of the world was drunk with the wine of skepticism, the Coliseum typed the cruelty of the heart of the Roman Empire, and religion and idolatry were holding hands. In the memory of many here is the quadrennium of blood, sweat and tears of World War I. But those days, gone forever into the tomb of time, were not as critical, I think, as is this present critical hour—in a world of storm and shipwreck.

Everywhere we look in this world today we are faced by upheaval, war, revolution, failure. The human race is bankrupt. Monarchy and republicanism, dictatorship and democracy, have failed. We are faced by bankruptcy—national, international, economic. This is a day of daring defiance, when by supercilious pose, when by an attitude of intellectual superiority, when by a critical and skeptical attitude toward the supernatural, there has been the substitution of out-worn, man-made philosophies and pseudo-science for the living Word of God's revelation—a parroting of the skepticism of free-thinkers. Impending crises! Mars walking with bloody boots—tying crepe to millions of doorknobs. All the sighs and sobs born of war if put in one sob would sweep the earth with the noise of a hurricane. Unreasonable devotions to sensual satisfactions, insane scrambles after gain, unmitigated villainies of multitudes of men and the unblushing vulgarities of multitudes of women abound, along with an undisciplined liberalism that goes nowhere so fast it arrives out of breath. The Bible is summoned to appear at the bar of human reason. Spiritual mercury falls low. Black snow falls. Faith's wings are clipped by reason's scissors.

There is the administration of laughing gas for painless extraction of sin. Philistines of transcendent cleverness submit the warm wonder of Christianity to cool and merciless analysis. Evils that would lead our greatest graces to the grave and leave no copy abound. Many fat deformities ask us to substitute for Christianity's vital bread a chunk of cloud bank buttered with the night wind. This is a day of invertebrate theology, of jellyfish morality, of India-rubber convictions, of see-saw religion, of somersault philosophy. There are spiritual latitudes as wide as the Sahara Desert and correspondingly dry. Civilization seems to be undergoing the frightful processes of self-burial. We are in danger of handing down our blood-bequeathed legacies reduced in quality and in quantity.

For Moloch, the spirit of unjust power, and Belial, the spirit of unholy pleasure, and Mammon, the spirit of unrighteous gain, are present in full force to corrupt and debase. In this critical hour there is the tendency to idolize science so that thousands of people undertake to interpret everything in terms of natural phenomena—reducing the supernatural to ignorance. There is the notion that ethics, religion, soul, and God are only concepts—having their origin in man's experience with shadows, dreams, trances, storms, seasons, and other natural forces.

There is intellectual recoil against emotional expression, and the obvious inadequacy of rationalism as a substitute. There is widespread agnosticism toward religion and religious organizations, and their consequent loss of wholesome authority are abroad. There is increasing widespread disregard for the Sabbath, and the growing tendency of society, business, and government to secularize the Sabbath, as well as the tendency to omit Christian standards from business, from professions, from education.

Amid the endless struggle for military supremacy, there is the reduction of Christianity to the status of humanism, social service, and national or individual therapy, with the resulting tendency to undermine faith and destroy the passion for souls.

But our consideration should be not to look long and pessimistically at such dark things, but to look to ourselves that we may be men and women doing God's will—weighing sixteen ounces to the pound and measuring thirty-six inches to the yard for God. While black snow is falling, the fever of life's fierce heat burning divine dew off the grass, and with so many epicures in philosophies, with so many feeders of inflamed popular appetite for amusements, with so many dealers in fine-spun metaphysical disquisitions, with so many experts in speculative cleverness dealing in the airy abstractions of an "up-to-date" gospel, God still asks: "Who will rise up for me against the evildoers? or who will stand up for me against the workers of iniquity?" (Ps. 94:16). May it be ours to say, "I will rise up for You against evildoers. I will stand up for You against the workers of iniquity."

Let us ask, what is wisdom and strength for us in this hour, which some have described in these words: "We are facing red ruin, and our citizens are as blind to it as Samson was after the Philistines punched out his eyes." What road shall we take when "civilization is undergoing the frightful processes of self-burial"? At a time when "as the fishes that are taken in an evil net, as the birds that are caught in the snare, so are the sons of men snared in an evil time." What shall those of us who are positioned as counselors, as watchmen on the walls, say to people in this poor, head-dizzy, heart-saddened, sin-smitten, war-blooded, hate-blackened, hell-bound world?

We must manifest

Christlike Conduct

We must register the unconquerable purpose to contend by lip and life for truth and right in our own generation. We must manifest the spirit of intense spirituality in any modern Babylon. We must make real the surprise of white robes in the streets of Sodom. This critical hour furnishes magnificent opportunities for the display of those virtues which made Jesus' life the greatest of mankind. Without those virtues our lives will be like painted fire to the cold, salt water to the thirsty, umbrellas rather than roofs in a storm. If the pure gospel is to be preached, spiritual religion preserved, "the macadamized bigotry of modern Phariseeism" pulverized, soul-destroying infidelity smitten with paralysis and death, all the "isms" that need to be "wasisms" uprooted from American soil, the infamous laws which are golden girdles to one class and galling shackles to another repealed, the power of the whisky ring broken, the church of the living God cleansed of her defilements and made worthy to be called the "Virgin Bride of Christ"—they must be accomplished by men and women who possess the same virtues which Christ illustrated in His conflict with evildoers when, day by day, in the midst of a crooked and perverse generation, He wore the white flower of a blameless life.

Is it not true that if the virtues productive of good citizenship are lost by the people, free government may give place to despotism without conquest by a foreign foe, and even without any change of political structure? Has not corruption, as often as conquest, caused the loss of human rights and liberties? History tells but one story about the downfall of the world's great nations. Strong at first because of the virility of its people, a nation rises to world power, then by its power acquires wealth, and through wealth sinks into luxury, by luxury becomes soft and spiritually-decadent, and then falls an easy victim to a strong aggressor. Therefore, cannot we see that our first line of defense is a spiritual one? Can we be strong if we fail to recognize and practice the virtue requisite to the building of noble character?

Living the Christlike life, we must abhor that which is evil and cleave to that which is good. We must be

> always bearing about in the body the dying of the Lord Jesus, that the life also of Jesus might be made manifest in our mortal flesh, for we who live are always delivered unto death for Jesus' sake that the life also of Jesus might be made manifest in our mortal bodies.

Jesus taught us to live by dying. And when our Lord speaks, the universities of the world may becomingly stop, look, and listen!

For if men are not in the path of truth and righteousness, they are in peril. If they see not with His eyes, they are blind. If they hear not His soulful sympathies, they are deaf indeed. If their ears are not keenly sensitized to His voice—a voice which never dies into feeble incompetence amid the cajoleries and clamors of today—they are foolish indeed.

In chemistry, men listen to Levoisier.

In pottery, they listen to Wedgewood.

In astronomy, they listen to Hershel.

In poetry and drama, they listen to Shakespeare.

In philosophy, they listen to Plato.

In invention, they listen to Edison.

In sculpture, they listen to Angelo who, "from the sterile womb of stone, raised children unto God."

In painting, they listen to Millet who held a thousand landscapes in a single brush.

In music, they listen to Beethoven who made "surging seas of tone subservient to his rod."

But in all matters of life and death, of duty and destiny, of time and eternity, men should listen to Jesus, look to Jesus, follow Jesus.

Christ is the way; men without Him are Cains; wanderers, vagabonds. Christ is the truth; without Him men are liars like the devil of old. Christ is the life; without Him men are dead in trespasses and sin. Christ is the light; without Him men are in darkness and go they know not whither. Christ is the vine; without Him men are withered branches prepared for the fire. Christ is the rock; without Him men are carried away with the flood. In Him our lives come to the fullness of their possibilities.

Men and women must have the spirit of Christ. Give people this spirit of Christ, and they will follow in His train, clothe themselves in vigorous realities, reach forth to larger ambition, have no passive acquiescence in small achievements, possess no careless indifference to great stretches of the unattained, roll no marbles when mountains should be removed, paddle not in the surf's edge when God calls for a launching out into the deep.

The apostle said: "Christ in you the hope of glory!" Not the glory of the future, but the glory and victorious conquest of character here and now, the glory of success after failure, the glory of well-rounded and developed manhood and womanhood with Christ enunciating Himself through precincts of personality!

Freed by Christ's truth, man's soul transmutes the flames of hell into perfume. But, are we too busy at ship docks and threading continents with a patchwork of steel rails and throwing skyscrapers at the stars to learn the lessons Jesus assigns? It is great to dream; greater to do; greatest of all to be!

Therefore, let this be our canticle of character: "Great are the symbols of being, but that which is symboled is greater." What else can we do in this day when "conscienceless profiteers inflame the emotions of fear and hate in the name of patriotism"? What else, when the literary camp followers of the new psychology flatter the passions in the name of science? What else, when the hucksters of finance tear our acquisitions with their ballyhoo in the name of security? We must witness a good confession. Where Mammon is worshiped, let us testify that a man's life does not consist in the abundance of things which he possesseth.

In Vanity Fair we must earnestly proclaim the seriousness of life. We must charm Sodom with the beauty of holiness. We must show those who have fallen the deepest that there is a way to heaven from the gates of hell, a way to high thrones from deep dungeons. We must set up God's altar by the side of Satan's seat, and pluck brands from the burning.

Though the spheres in which, as Christians, we must serve are painfully forbidding, starkly irreligious, defiantly impious, let us be faithful as Joseph was in the house of Pharaoh, as Obadiah in the court of Ahab, as Daniel in the palace of Babylon, as Elijah, God's prophet of fire, in an apostate age. Milton sings of Moloch:

> Nor content with such
> Audacious neighborhood, the moist heart
> Of Solomon he led by fraud to build
> His temple right against the temple of God.

Be it ours to reverse this process, and build the temple of God right against the idol shrine wherever it may be found—bringing our knowledge, influence, talents, to bear boldly and directly upon all that is evil—overcoming evil with good.

Spurgeon said:

> We shall not see any great change until we have some men in our ranks who are willing to be martyrs. That deep ditch can never be crossed till the bodies of a few of us shall fill it up.

We need to preach and live so that there shall be some mocking and scoffing, instead of perfumy plaudits. George Whitefield preached on the Kensington Commons. They threw dead cats and rotten eggs at him. He said: "This is only the manure of Methodism, the best thing in the world to make it grow; throw away as fast as you please." And when a stone cut him on the forehead, he seemed to preach better for a little bloodletting.

I wonder if we aren't puny because we are so precise, so placid, so unperturbed, so pleased with praise, forgetting that we who live are always delivered unto death for Jesus' sake.

We need a

Christlike Character Manifesting Itself in Compassion

Jesus, seeing the multitudes, misled and unled, was filled with compassion. One of the dangers of the present time is the paralysis of compassion. We get so used to horrors, to slaughter, to crippling of men and women, to war's crimson terrors, our peril is that we should cease to *feel* these things at all. We need all our compassion if the wounds of war are to be healed and we are not to live in the jungle. The secret of compassion is very simple. It means suffering with people. It will help us to be compassionate if we remember that our only hope is the compassion of God. "It is of the LORD's mercies that we are not consumed, because his compassions fail not." (Lam. 3:22).

Compassion keeps hospitals at work, gives to the service of the sick its healing qualities. The good Samaritan was moved with compassion. This compassion found expression in action. Whatever progress has been made toward a better world has come through the awaking of compassion.

Compassion forced into law the act which forbade the use of children in coal mines.

Compassion took General Booth into the slums.

Compassion sent Elizabeth Fry into the horrible jails of London.

Compassion kept Dr. Grenfell in Labrador.

Compassion kept Livingstone in a land where he opened the highway, marked now by the tombstones of martyr missionaries over which Ethiopia stumbles with outstretched hands toward God.

Compassion caused Jesus to weep over Jerusalem; and His compassion found an outlet in the Cross.

There is the story of an old saint who felt so strongly about the evil of the world that he prayed to God to send the fire of His judgment. He held out his hand in protest against it and declared he would continue to do so until God made an end of this evil world. As he stood with outstretched hand a little bird came, built a nest in it and hatched her young. Bit by bit the saint became interested. Then his tenderness was awakened until the hand held out in anger was kept stretched out in love. God's patience with us is rooted in His compassion. In that compassion of God is the hope of a better world. In the compassion which His love can awaken lies our power to make that hope come true.

Christlike Compassion Must Not Stop Short of the Cross

Christ's compassion and love kept His face set like a flint down the road environed with the horror of false accusation and blocked down yonder by a bloody cross. Christlike compassion will help us to see that crucifixion is the price of consecration, and that we bless when we bleed.

What are we profited if, singing "Onward Christian Soldiers," we go through perfunctory services, parroting prayers, yawning over watches, acting as excursionists on a pleasure expedition? What are we profited if gracious ladies and cultured men thank us for our sermons, but do not surrender their souls to the will of God?—open not their purses to the cause of Christ, while our institutions languish and our mission lines are near the breaking point? What hope, if, absorbed in the delights of scholarship, we let the fires go out on evangelistic altars? What hope, if, citizens of a civilization that makes ice in the tropics, we know not how, by the Cross, to attack frigid conventionalities with holy, spirit-impetuosity? Or, if adding telescopes to our eyes, viewing landscapes millions of miles away, we get in scientific fog banks and lose sight of Christ? Or, if, adding radios to our ears, hearing whispers from all corners of the universe, we have dull ears, deaf ears, or disobedient ears to the voice of Him who "soundeth forth the trumpet that shall never call retreat"? Or, if, installing and listening to a big pipe organ in great church buildings, we miss life's central melody and become victims of dawdling ditties. Or, if, adding the telephone to our tongues, talking across continents, expediting business, bringing friends within the sound of our voice, we preach a cultural, not a crucified Christ? Or know not how to talk to the boy in the elevator about Jesus? Or, if, building big buildings, we forget that "other foundation can no man lay than that is laid, which is Jesus Christ" (2 Cor. 3:11)? Or, if, adding the telegraph to our fingers, writing around the world, we are inefficient and blundering in writing the literature of godliness upon the fleshly tablets of human hearts? Or, if, adding the airplane to our bodies, flying swifter and mounting higher than eagles, we are slow in service to God, to "mount up with wings as eagles"? Or, if, adding the automobile to our feet, we follow after Christ limpingly and complainingly, taking His Name on in an easy fashion with loud professions and feeble possessions, afraid to walk to lockstep with Him who plants His footsteps upon the seas and rides upon the storm, who is "trampling out the vintage where the grapes of wrath are stored"? Or, if, following the violet road of the X-ray, studying the marrow in the bones of living men, we miss the secret of the Lord? Or, if, compressing a Caruso into a microscopic point of a needle, hearing dead men sing, we fail to sing the white song of purity into the souls of our youth?

Here is heroism! To venture the use of the spirit of Jesus in industry, in diplomacy, in the practical situations in which men find themselves in our complex relation. Our highest Americanism is our confidence that the Cross of Christ is the wisest and strongest force in existence—that to be led by its eternal Spirit is to be in possession of the only omniscience and omnipotence of God's command—that employing its strength only can we hope to weld the forces of our civilization, bind men's hearts in devotion to our country, and secure that measure of peace and happiness and joy among our citizenship and fidelity and loyalty to the Master.

Let us not forget

The Christlike Compassion That Goes to Calvary Must Have a Closet

By this I mean we must be a *praying* people. Surely, we profess to be God's people. And if we possess what we profess, we have as our weapon in the combat of life and facing the problems and opportunities of life, *prayer*—prayer which, in the days of Abraham, held back for a while God's hands from scattering fire over Sodom and Gomorrah.

Prayer, which, in the days of Joshua, reached up and caught hold of the red bit of the sun and stopped it in mid-heaven.

Prayer, which, in the days of Elijah, blew every cloud from the skies.

Prayer, which, in the days of Daniel, walked the earth as a lion tamer.

Prayer, which, in the days of the apostles, opened prison bars.

Prayer, which, in the days of many adversaries, enabled Paul, when put in jail, to come out of the prison with a jail door under one arm and a convert under the other.

Occasionally, amid the confusions of this day when civilization is undergoing the frightful processes of self-burial, somebody is wise enough and courageous enough to urge us to believe that the world needs God more than it needs guns; Christ more than it needs cannons; the Bible more than the bombs; the truth more than tanks; the gospel more than grenades; prayer more than powder; the New Testament more than TNT; tens of thousands of godly Christians more than tons of gun cotton. Forever is it true that the wooden Cross represents more power than the iron cross—that the hope of the world lies not in shedding the blood of man, but in the blood of Christ, which has already been shed—that we have more to fear from future hell than from a present Hitler—that we will have more hurt from tabooed truth than from totalitarian temporary triumphs.

Our greatest need is prayer that is strong, prevailing, believing—prayer that takes all we have and are to offer it to God, as it took all Jesus had on Calvary to give us the right to pray.

We need the kind of praying that Daniel did, that shook from stem to stem the Babylonian Empire: the kind that Nehemiah did that had rulers running after him with men, money, and material to help rebuild the walls of Jerusalem: the never-give-in kind of prayer that the man in the Gospel offered at the doorstep or under the bedroom window of his friend after a hungry man had come along with a need that had to be met without delay: or the kind of prayer that widow woman went in for until the judge had to arise from the bench, postpone business for the time being, and attend to her urgent pleadings.

It is only the prayer born in the very heart of God, shot through with the very blood and passion of the Son of God, filled with the power and persistence of the Holy Ghost and loaded with a deep and heavy sense of the Church's plight and the world's appalling need that sets the wheels of revival in motion. God save us from trying to turn these wheels by our own efforts!

You can pray for any need, for lengthened life, as Hezekiah did; for help, as Daniel did; for light, as Bartimaeus did; for mercy, as David did; for rain, as Elijah did; for a son, as Hannah did; for grace, as Paul did. You can pray, too, anywhere—in the deep, like Jonah; on the sea or housetop, like Peter; on your bed, like Hezekiah; in the mountains, like Jesus; in the wilderness like Hagar; in the street, like Jairus; in a cave, like David; on the cross, like the dying thief.

You can pray, too, any how—short, as Peter and the publican did; long, like Moses at the consecration of the tabernacle, or Solomon at the dedication of the temple. You can pray in silence as Hannah did in the temple. You can pray in your secret thoughts, as Nehemiah did before Darius; or aloud, as did the Syro-Phoenician woman; in tears, as Magdalene did; in groans or songs as David did.

You can pray any time—in the morning as David did; at noon, as Daniel did; at midnight, as Silas did; in childhood, as Samuel did; in youth, as Timothy did; in manhood, as the centurion did; in age, as Simeon did; in sickness, as Job did; or in death, as did Jacob and the dying Christ.

We must remember, going to and from the closet of prayer,

Our Commission

Our commission is still to engage in the greatest work that ever moved an angel's wing in flight, that ever stirred the heart of God in compassion, that ever moved the arm of God in power. Still our supreme business is to be fishers of men—to see that many who may be blown to bits by bombs, that many who may gasp their last amid blood bubbles on the high seas, that many who may die in the poisonous ditches of war shall have their names written not only in the service records of navies and armies, but written also in the Lamb's book of life.

In the *Christian Index*, I read of what Stephan Zweig tells of "The Fishermen on the Seine." It was based on an impressive historical incident that occurred during the French Revolution. After four eventful years the day arrived when Louis XVI was to be executed. Early in the morning, to the accompaniment of muffled drums, the condemned monarch began the fateful journey through the streets of Paris to the place where, high above the surrounding crowd, there stood the scaffold. When he arrived his arms were tied to his sides and he was led up the steps to the platform. The blade of the guillotine descended, and the crowd roared its exultant approval as the head of the anointed king of France rolled into the basket. In a sense it was the supreme event of the century for France. It climaxed a long and costly struggle for liberty.

A short distance from the guillotine, in plain view of the proceedings, there stood on the bank of the Seine River a row of fishermen with their lines in the stream. Their backs were turned to the scaffold and they paid absolutely no attention to the historic spectacle. Even when the thunderous roar of the crowd announced that the tremendous deed had been consummated, they did not even turn their heads. They continued to watch their corks bobbing on the water. It seems incredible that any Frenchman could have been so indifferent to such a momentous occurrence as to have ignored it by concentrating attention on a trifling business like fishing. Just why those fishermen were so apathetic can only be conjectured. One plausible explanation is that having passed through one crisis after another, having experienced so much tragedy, having witnessed so much cruelty and suffering, they were unwilling to subject their nerves and emotions to additional strain. For sanity's sake, they concentrated on fishing.

Commenting on this, the editor of the *Christian Index* tells us that properly interpreted, the conduct of those fishermen on the Seine contains a vital message for Christians just now. In this modern day momentous events are happening hourly. Each newspaper and each radio bulletin brings reports of sinking ships, crashing planes, bombed and burning cities, mammoth armies locked in mortal combat, statesmen negotiating stupendous affairs. Of course, all of this is of vital interest to us. It should be. But there is grave danger we will allow it so to distract our attention that we shall become completely diverted from the supreme business in which we should be engaged as Christians—serving as fishers of men in the name of Christ. For no matter what colossal events are happening, still the most crucial of all issues is that between the individual soul and God.

During the Civil War, Senator Charles Sumner became so engrossed in great plans for the abolition of slavery that when Julia Ward Howe invited him to meet some of her friends he answered in lofty fashion: "Really, Julia, I have lost all my interest in individuals." "Why, Charles," she answered, "God hasn't got as far as that yet." Nor will God ever get that far. Christ came to inaugurate stupendous changes in the world, to revolutionize human affairs. He did it. He lifted empires off their hinges and turned the stream of the centuries out of its course. But He did it primarily by changing individuals one by one. So, while tremendous events are happening in the world, and while vast plans and programs for national defense are being promoted in our own country, let us, in principle, emulate the example of those French anglers and continue to concentrate on fishing in the name of Christ. It will be a tragic hour, no matter what the emergency, when we declare a moratorium on personal evangelism. Still our greatest obligation and opportunity is to respond to that stirring challenge: "Follow me, and I will make you fishers of men" (Matt. 4:19).

Our Consolation

> These shall make war with the Lamb, and the Lamb shall overcome them: for he is Lord of lords, and King of kings: and they that are with him are called, and chosen, and faithful (Rev. 17:14).

This is God's world. Though Hitler and his hordes are having a succession of victories, this is God's world. Though this is admittedly one of the most tragic eras in history, this is God's world. Many may fall in battle, many may die on both land and sea, many may be blown to bits by bombs from the air, many may perish from the hardships, hunger, and ravages of disease always incident to war. Countless homes will be destroyed, millions of hearts broken, property destroyed that can never be replaced, our priceless shrines may be reduced to blackened ruins, and a loss of blood and treasure beyond estimate may face us. But this will still be God's world! And, no matter how often it may be assailed, the rule of right *must* triumph over the rule of might. Apart from the salvation that is in Christ Jesus, the most comforting doctrine in our day and generation is the absolute sovereignty of our omniscient, omnipotent, omnipresent God. It is still true that in spite of all that may seem to the contrary, "The Lord God Omnipotent reigneth," that God is over all blessed forever, and "worketh all things after the counsel of his own will" (Eph. 1:11). Since God is supreme, it must necessarily follow that He will compel all apparently contradictory conditions and conflicting circumstances to contribute to His causes. All apparently adverse plans and powers will be used to perfect His plans. This is what the Bible teaches—and whether we go to Paul, prophet, or psalmist, we find affirmation of this truth. Paul said that God "worketh all things according to the counsel of his own will," while the psalmist says: "Surely the wrath of man shall praise thee: the remainder of wrath shall thou restrain" (Ps. 76:10).

I woke in the night,
The wind was pawing at my shutters,
With his wild prancing hoofs.
The swishing of his tail lashed the trees into fury,
The flowing of his mane rattled the shingles on my roof.
The shriek of his neighing was as a siren,
Announcing all the fires of hell.
This sound of his going was all the engines
Of earth rushing to extinguish them.
I cowered under the covers with wildly beating heart,
Then—the truth came to my mind.
God rides that wind.

He holds the reins by arms of His might,
He guides those curveting hoofs aright;
The flying black Pegasus of the night,
Obeys God's voice in his untamed flight,
I am safe in God's care!

Let no man think, in these blood-dripping days, that our planet has broken away from the control of Almighty God. True, we are having brought home to us the terrible indictment of Gladstone's words:

> The history of nations is a melancholy chapter; that is, the history of governments is one of the most immoral parts of human history.

But the God of righteousness was never so much alive, never so wisely superintending affairs, as during this period of indescribable agony.

> Drunk with power and swollen with prosperity, Napoleonized nations insist on throwing themselves upon the international operating table. And once upon that table, for a long time they may resist the Surgeon's keen, steady knife. Yet the Surgeon cuts on and on, as grim as Death and clean as Truth. In due time, the offending eye of militarism shall be plucked out, the grasping hand of plunder shall be cut off, and the steel foot of invasion shall stumble over the abyss of world empire to its certain downfall.

Then shall men learn once again that right and not might, that character and not efficiency, that Christ and not Caesar, speak the final word by which both individuals and nations live. For Jesus Christ is the same yesterday and today, yea, and unto all the ages. And He has the last word. He will make things "come out right."

When I read the Book of Revelation, I love to pitch my mental tent a long time on that seventeenth chapter. I do not claim to be as wise as anybody who writes or speaks of the marvelous truths so mysteriously expressed therein. Sometimes I get scared of these horns—remembering some foolish things said about them. And if I talked at length of the meaning of all those horns I might sound as foolish as the boy who was asked, "What is the

Matterhorn?" To which the boy replied, "It was a horn the ancients blew when something was the matter."

But that great Book of the Revelation of Jesus Christ tells me that there is a time coming when God shall "wipe away all tears from their eyes"—and there shall be no more sorrow, no more poverty, no more sickness, no more death, no more war, no more sin, no more bloodshed.

I have sometimes recalled with comfort and joy what God's servant, Dr. McGinley, says in giving an experience which is identical with mine, an experience no doubt similar to the experiences of many who read fiction.

Like McGinley, I sometimes read the Book of Revelation as I used to read story books. I used to get a good fiction book and go to bed and read the thing. First I got the hero and studied him to see if he were really a hero. Then I got the heroine and examined her deeds and words to see if she were a full-fledged heroine. Then I got the villain. Then I got the plot. As I read, the plot thickened and then it got thicker—while the villain got more treacherous. By midnight, I would be halfway through the book. But, I'll let McGinley tell my own experience in his own words:

> And the heroine would be away off in an old deserted farmhouse, strapped to a table. And the hero would be in an old mill pond, chained to the wheel, and the water up to his chin. And the villain was in the saddle. About midnight, I'd have to go to sleep. My nerves were so shot to pieces, I couldn't sleep. Then, you know what I would do? I used to turn the page down where things went bad—and I would go away over to the last chapter, and I would find that the hero was no longer chained to the old mill wheel and the heroine was no longer in the old deserted farmhouse and the villain had fallen over a precipice and had broken his neck—and the hero and the heroine were happily married and sitting on the veranda of their cottage—and wee Johnny and Billy and May and Annie and Susan and the twins were playing out on the front lawn. And you know I would close the book and sleep like I was exhausted. Then the next time, I would go back to where things were bad and I would say to the hero: "Don't worry about the water up to the chin; everything is going to be all right."

> And I would say to the heroine: "Don't shriek and cry so, little lady! You'll get off that table and get those ropes untied someday!" Then I'd say to the villain, "You rascal! If you know what I know you would not be so triumphant, so exultant! You are riding for a fall!

Jesus is coming back again. We view this world of sorrow surrounding us in this dark and evil hour. And no one has even faintly imagined the appalling aftermath that must inevitably follow the present appalling upheaval. Viewing the terrible scenes of war and famine and pestilence and the tragedies and sufferings they occasion, well may we ask, in the words of the afflicted saints: "How long, O Lord, holy and true, dost thou not judge and avenge our blood on them that dwell on the earth?" (Rev. 6:10)

How long, O Lord, how long? That is the question on the lips of thousands today. Surely this long dark lane has a turning somewhere. Surely this awful night must sometime have a dawn. It will. It was to this day the apostle Peter looked forward hopefully when he said:

> And he shall send Jesus Christ, which before was preached unto you: whom the heaven must receive until the times of restitution of all things, which God hath spoken by the mouth of all his holy prophets since the world began (Acts 3:20–21).

> I wait for the LORD, my soul doth wait, and in his word do I hope. My soul waiteth for the LORD more than they that watch for the morning: I say, more than they that watch for the morning (Ps. 130:5–6).

The priest in the temple. The invalid on his couch. The prisoner at his window. The sentinel in the tower. The sailor, the soldier, all watch for the morning. Do they watch and hope without a promise? Does the sun disappoint them? Never. At a certain hour the black zenith grows blue again. The gray east grows amber and flushes with rose. Innumerable scintillant splendors shoot through the rose and amber, and spread abroad in the upper blue, and at the moment—there it flashes! The sun! The startled stars veil their faces and retire. The sky shows but one light. The mountains put on their purple and gold, and pay princely obeisance. The living torrents catch the living luster and leap with it into thousand welcoming valleys. From coast to coast the billowing seas uplift their jewelled arms and clap their hands with joy.

And what now? "I wait," not for the *sun*, but for the Lord. More intensely, more confidently, with infinitely more glorious expectations. And shall He who made the sun be less punctual than the sun itself? Is the coming of the Lord less certain than the sunrise? No. The day, the hour, the moment, is appointed and nothing can delay it. He who in Eternity rested on the bosom of the Father came once. He shall come again. He who is "the brightness of the Father's glory" is detained at the right hand of God "in the heavenly places, far above all principality, and power, and might, and dominion, and every name that is named, not only in this world but also in that which is to come" (Eph. 1:20–21)—who, as He is beloved of the Father, and adored and worshiped by saints and angels in heaven, is still "the desire of all nations" on earth—will appear, the second time without sin, unto salvation—not tinting the earth and seas and skies with the transient beauty of the sunrise, but raising the dead, changing the living, judging the world, glorifying His people, and establishing His everlasting kingdom of "righteousness, peace, and joy in the Holy Ghost."

What our science could not do, He will do.
What our theology and preaching could not do, He will do.
What our parliaments and senates could not do, He will do.
What our educational systems could not do, He will do.
What our fretting and furies could not do, He will do.
What our armies and navies could not do, He will do.

And that day will be the watcher's looked-for day, the purchaser's redemption day, the builder's completion day, the husbandman's harvest day, the servant's reckoning day, the master's payday, the Son's manifestation day, the Bride's wedding day, the King's coronation day. And in that glad day

> God shall wipe away all tears from their eyes; and there shall be no more death, neither sorrow, nor crying, neither shall there be any more pain: for the former things are passed away (Rev. 21:4).

"Amen! Even so, come quickly, Lord Jesus!"

> He which testifieth these things saith, Surely I come quickly. Amen. Even so, come, Lord Jesus. The grace of our Lord Jesus Christ be with you all. Amen (Rev. 22:20–21).

Until He comes—or until the close of life's little day, let us be known as those who are "with Him"—"Called and chosen and faithful." Dwelling long in thought and praise upon our consolations—saying to the world that we are "with Him, called and chosen and faithful," let us say "Behold, God is my salvation; I will trust and not be afraid: for the Lord Jehovah is my strength and my song; He also is become my salvation."

Plead your interest in Him, in all your dangers, troubles, and necessities. Envy none their worldly distinctions. Remember your preeminence: "You are the sons and daughters of the Lord Almighty." Do not complain because they may possess things of which you are deprived. You have God; they are destitute: you can sustain a loss uninjured; they would be undone. If your taper be extinguished, you have a sun: but when "the candle of the wicked is put out," they are involved in darkness—"darkness that may be felt." Honor your God by living upon His fullness, and endeavoring by faith to realize in Him, everything you seek for, in vain, in yourselves, or in creatures. Observe the address of Moses to the Israelites—"What nation is there so *great*, who hath God so nigh unto them, as the LORD our God is in all things that we call upon him for" (Deut. 4:7).

They were an inconsiderable body, confined in a wilderness: the commerce, arts and sciences, were all with their enemies. They had the same raiment they wore out of Egypt forty years before; and had no provisions beforehand for a single day. But their peculiar *greatness* arose from their nearness to God: in having Him, they had all. He possessed, and could immediately produce the supplies their necessities required: they had only to ask and have. When David was plundered, and stripped of all he had in Ziklag, it is said, he "encouraged himself in the Lord his God"—*He* was left.

Thus, a Christian who has nothing possesses all things. Creatures may abandon him; but his God will never leave nor forsake him. Friends may die; but the Lord liveth. His "heart and his flesh may fail; but God is the strength of his heart, and his portion forever" (see Ps. 73:26).

"The heavens shall pass away with a great noise, and the elements shall melt with fervent heat, the earth also and the works that are therein shall be burned up" (2 Pet. 3:10)—he stands upon the ashes of a universe, and exclaims, I have lost nothing! Yea, he has gained "new heavens and a new earth, wherein dwelleth righteousness!"

Oh, Hurry!

Oh, hurry to the refuge before the storm breaks.

Oh, hurry to get off the track of wrong before the engine of sin runs over you.

Oh, hurry to get in a lifeboat before the ship sinks.

Oh, hurry to take the antidote before the poison kills.

Oh, hurry to take medicine before disease masters you.

Oh, hurry to answer His call lest He call no more.

Oh, hurry to get aboard the ship before it leaves, never to return.

Oh, hurry to lay hold on eternal life.

Oh, hurry to the city of refuge ere the avenger overtake thee.

Oh, hurry to turn your boat before it plunges over Niagara. *Yes*—hurry!

Now is the accepted time; now is the day of salvation

CHAPTER TWELVE

Roses Will Bloom Again

The desert shall rejoice, and blossom as the rose.
Isa. 35:1

When we go back and see what people have written about the rose and roses, we find a great many wonderful things.

Emerson said, "The sea opulent, plentiful and strong, as beautiful as a rose on a June day."

And Mrs. Browning, the woman Shakespeare of England, wrote: "Roses aplenty, roses aplenty, and nightingale, one for every twenty, and when you put it in a drawer and try to give it a name, all these things just bring it to shame."

Showing us the inadequacy of words really to describe the rose.

Another poet said: "The finest, the frailest kind of rose is more beautiful than the most skillful production of the rose by the sculptor's chisel."

And Keats said: "When they bring roses to me, when you brought roses to me, they had voices that whispered of peace and truth and love."

And another great poet said: "The rosebuds that put their crimson lips together."

Another poet said: "The wayside rose holds out its fragrant arms, and with its beauty our eye it charms."

Then, of course, we remember what Robert Burns said in his sweet Scotch language. He said: "I pluck the rose when Phoebus comes in view, And to pluck it is like a kiss from her bonny mou." ("Mou," which means, of course, mouth.)

We could say many things that the poets have said about the rose. But we know that when we come to think of the beauty of the rose, that it puts the poet's pen to test adequately to describe it, and it puts the orator's eloquence to a test to see if it can really see and say what the rose merits.

We remember, too, that the sculptor, who sometimes brings children unto God, raises children unto God from the sterile womb of stone, has spent hours trying to carve from marble the beauty of the rose.

We remember when we've come to think of the symmetry, fragrance, and softness of the rose amid the thorns, that the painter's brush sometimes is held in a hand that hesitates because of its woeful inadequacy fully to portray all the rose is and has ever been in the thoughts and minds of men.

Sometimes we see the roses adorning the little cottage in the pines, and sometimes adding beauty to the king's palace, and sometimes the rose is put upon beauteous brow, and so many times we have seen the rose at the wedding altar, and many times we have seen roses placed upon the tomb.

When we come to think of all that philosophers have said in their meditations about the rose, and all that singers have sung about the rose—like "My Wild Irish Rose" and "Moonlight and Roses" which always delight my heart and bless my life—we come to understand something, just a little bit of something of what Isaiah meant when he said: "The desert . . . shall blossom as a rose."

The Desert

The desert, the desolate desert, the dreary desert, with the cracks in the ground that seem like parched lips that cry for rain; the desert, desolate without a flower or fountain in all of its weary miles; the desert, with its hot sands that burn the eyes as the wind blows across them; the hot desert, the desolate desert, the dreary desert, the desert without pools of water, the desert without flowers, the desert with the jackals that howl and the wolves that prowl, and the serpents that crawl.

The desolate, dead desert, without any flowers or fountains in all its vast areas.

And Isaiah said: "That desert shall rejoice, and blossom as a rose."

Where the hiss of the serpent was heard, and where the howl of the wolf disturbed the stillness of the night, and where the coughing of the coyotes was unpleasant to hear, and where you could find nothing but dust when you wanted water, and nothing but some kind of gravel bareness when you wanted food, that desolate desert, said Isaiah the prophet, shall blossom, shall rejoice, and blossom as the rose.

That's a wonderful thing that Isaiah said. But what sort of person was Isaiah? Among the constellation of the prophets, Isaiah was very mighty and very beautiful. His smallest whisper was as loud to the ears of the people as a thunderclap in the time of storm. His sweetest words were like breezes laden with honeysuckle fragrance. In his preaching always were the thunders and the lightnings of Sinai and the foregleams of Calvary and the growl of the Assyrian wolf, God's instrument of judgment against His people who had failed to love Him and failed to serve Him and who had forsaken Him.

God came to the place where He said: I'm bored with your sacrifices and your empty worship times. I'm tired and sick of you because you have forsaken Me and have gone out after the idolatries of the day.

We find how Isaiah fought very strongly against these kings who had led the people away from God into the idolatries of his day. They wouldn't listen to him. They even laughed at him.

Then Isaiah, somewhat in despair but guided by the Holy Spirit, telling them about the Assyrian nation that would come and take them into captivity, showed how one day, even though that should be, a remnant should behave, should be saved, and God who demanded holiness should, with this remnant, build a new house of holiness and truth upon the dead ashes of their wrecked life, as it was as a desert.

So we come to find that he talked about how roses should bloom again. There had come to that nation the wintertime, and the religious life of the people had been like trees frozen by the breeze and stripped of their foliage by the terrible blizzardy winds.

As he thought of that, he thought of how the streams, the voices of the streams, frozen beneath the ice, had nothing to say to bird or beast or man, and how spring and summertime were asleep beneath the heavy blankets of snow, and how the desolate desert of national life should someday blossom; he spoke very hopefully about the time when the roses should bloom again, when he said that God would put in the wilderness the fir and the cedar and the oil tree and the pine and He would also put the box tree together and they shall rejoice together (Isa. 41:19).

Then he said that God would comfort Zion. God would comfort her waste places. God would make the wilderness to be as Eden. He would make the desert to be as the garden of the Lord, and in the desert there would be joy and thanksgiving and rejoicing.

Oh, what a dread, desolate picture on the one side and the very beautiful picture on the other side! The desert and then the garden of the Lord. The wilderness and then Eden. The voice of despair and the voice of rejoicing. The voice of ingratitude and the voice of thanksgiving. He said that day will come through the remnant that God shall bring back from captivity after the

Assyrian scourge has finished with you, and He shall build His house of holiness and truth upon the desolate desert places and it shall rejoice and blossom as the rose.

Let's see how that has been true in so many instances.

The Desert and Then the Roses

It was true in Noah's day when, after the terrible time when God hurled oceans over mountain ranges and drowned a world that had hated Him where they should have loved Him and should have obeyed Him, where they had forsaken Him and defied Him, the roses bloomed again.

I think of Abraham, when God told him to take his century plant, his century flower, his only son, Isaac whom he loved, and offer him there on the mountaintop.

When Abraham did what God said, making the three days' journey, he came in sight of the mountain, and he said to his servant: "Abide ye here with the ass; and I and the lad go yonder and worship" (Gen. 22:5).

That was a night, an hour of despair, an hour of night, an hour of hopelessness, an hour when they should worship God but one half of the congregation would kill the other half.

Oh! That was a desert in so many ways to Abraham. But when Abraham had the knife ready to take Isaac's life, God called Abraham's name, and after Abraham answered God told him not to kill Isaac.

And then Abraham turned and saw a ram with his horns caught in the thicket, and he took that and offered it instead of Isaac.

In other words, the desert became an Eden, a garden of the Lord, and where there had been nothing but desolation, there now the roses were blooming again.

I think of David, pursued by King Saul.

David, an outlaw, running from King Saul as a hare would run from the hound, and as a mouse would seek to hide itself from the eagle's talons, and as the lamb sought refuge from the wolf, and David said: "I shall now perish one day by the hand of Saul."

That was a desert for David, but there came a time when the roses bloomed for David, and they bloomed around a throne, and they bloomed clustering around a scepter and a crown when they crowned him King of Judah, and then a little bit later, King of Israel and Judah.

The roses bloomed again!

Then I think of Joseph's being sold into slavery into Egypt, and put in jail because of the lying of Potiphar's wife.

I think of Jacob, who had seen the coat that his sons had brought to him, stained with an animal's blood, and he said: "It is my son's coat; an evil beast has devoured him."

And for twenty years Jacob had been in the desert because of the loss of Joseph whom he loved very much. But when his sons in the time of the famine went down to Egypt and found that Joseph was the governor of the land and wearing the keys of the kingdom at his girdle, then Jacob found that his desert had been made an Eden; his desert had been made the garden of the Lord; and in his desert there was thanksgiving and the voice of joy and rejoicing and prayer.

Yes, these men went back after they found out that Joseph was the governor, and he had made himself known to them, and they went back to Jacob, who for twenty years had had a desert without any roses to bloom in it. They said: "Joseph is yet alive, and he is governor over all the land of Egypt."

And Jacob's heart fainted within him at the news, but when he saw the wagons loaded with the corn that they had brought back from the land of plenty to the land of famine, he said: "I will go and see him."

And, so Jacob, in one of the most beautiful stories in all the Bible to me, old Jacob made that journey and saw his boy whom he hadn't seen for twenty years, and saw him as governor and saw him as a man of power.

In the desert, Jacob found that God changed it to an Eden, to a garden of the Lord, and there was the voice of thanksgiving and rejoicing.

And I think of those four hundred years that are set forth after the prophecy of Malachi before we have any Gospel of Matthew.

Four hundred years, it was a desert time, a time of desolation, a time when the wilderness and not the flower garden prevailed!

And then came a man clothed in camel's hair!

And then came a man descending upon the iniquities of his day with a torch in one hand and a sword in the other!

There came a day when this wilderness preacher came, interpreting the voice of betrothal as a friend of the Bridegroom, pointing out Jesus as the Lamb of God!

Then came Jesus at a time when religion and idolatry were holding hands and when the hands of hypocrisy were playing upon the harp of formalism and ritualism and icy nothingness!

Oh, what a time it was!

Then came some shepherds and worshiped at a manger above which heaven had put out a bright star.

And at that time, at that very time, old Athens, the intellectual center of the world, was drunk with the wine of skepticism, and old Rome was asleep yonder by the river, asleep under the music of a tyrant's voice and the Roman Colosseum tied the cruelty of the Roman Empire and when the Roman fist was upon the purse of the Jewish nation and the Roman heel upon its chest.

At that same time, old Persia was wearing on her brow a funeral wreath, and old Egypt was asleep with her head in the lap of the sphinx, Egypt, where God had wrought His marvelous miracles through the plagues, and yet they had not believed so very much in God at all amidst all their gods.

Then came some shepherds to worship at a cattle trough in a barn.

Then came some Wise Men with their gifts of gold and frankincense and myrrh.

And for this world, so long a desolate waste, the roses bloomed through Him who was called the Rose of Sharon, the Lily of the valley, the fairest of ten thousand, the One altogether lovely.

Then you remember how this Rose of Sharon was put under the terrible heel of death yonder on the cross, how Jesus died. And the day when Jesus died, nobody called Him Lord except a dying thief, and the kingdom about which He had talked, in the minds of the disciples, had shrunk to the narrow dimensions of a grave. Death, with his skeleton heel, had crushed out the life of the Lily of the valley and the Rose of Sharon fair; death, whose only pleasure is fountains of falling tears, had closed the eyes that shed tears over Jerusalem. Death, whose only music is the sob of broken hearts, had hushed the mouth that spake as never man spake.

And the disciples saw all their hopes go down beyond that bloody hill where the crosses were and where the earthquake rolled forth its dirge, and where darkness came down at midday and midnight said to noonday, "Get off the throne of the universe and let me sit there." And noonday did midnight's bidding.

The roses were all dead, it seemed.

The Rose of Sharon seemed to be dead forever and would never bloom.

Resurrection!

But on that third day morning, up from the grave He arose!

The roses bloomed again, and the desert was as Eden, and the desolate place was as the garden of the Lord, and the disciples had their voice of thanksgiving and rejoicing when they said to Thomas: "We have seen the Lord," and they were glad that they saw Him.

Now, can we make this a very practical thing to apply to your own heart and life?

Is your life a desert place?

Is your life a wilderness?

Do you want it to be an Eden?

Do you want it to be the garden of the Lord?

Well, it can be if you will only let the Master have His way with you.

Is it an ill-health blizzard that has taken the roses out of your life's garden?

Well, God cares because God knows.

And He knows our downsitting and our uprising, and He is acquainted with all of our ways.

Is it a loneliness desert where you seem not to have companionship?

Remember what a friend you have in Jesus.

Is it a misunderstanding, desolate desert. Desert, desert. Desert of desolation, desolation, desolation, where the roses of kindness have died?

Is it a desolate desert of abuse, where joy has breathed its last and no roses bloom? There are just thorns for you and maybe some of the devil's poison ivy?

Well, remember this: Jesus is alive, and Jesus cares.

Is your family circle broken? Has it been broken and you wonder about some things?

Has bereavement come and torn some tender flowers you loved so much from your garden? Have you followed the hearse? Have you stood by the grave? Have you heard people sob?

Well, maybe it's a kind of a blizzard like that that has left you in the wintertime.

Perhaps you are not today as great a Christian as God wanted you to be, and somehow you have let the winter blizzards of skepticism, doubt, infidelity, and worldliness blight all the flowers in your life's garden.

Well, where are you going to find any help for a time like that?

Hear these words of Isaiah:

> Come now, and let us reason together, saith the LORD: though your sins be as scarlet, they shall be as white as snow; though they be red like crimson, they shall be as wool (1:18).

What did He do that that should be?
He bore our sins in His own body on the tree.

Has sin gotten the best of you? Has something crept into your life, gnawing at it and blighting it like a frost? Is something corroding your life like rust, and dulling the edge of your spiritual weapons?

Is your life a kind of a desert swept by the blizzard where no flowers bloom?

Well, there is One to whom you can go.

And remember that the rags will be changed into riches, and the pewter will be changed to gold, and if you've lain among the pots and have become blackened and smutty, smut-covered, as Isaiah, the prophet, spoke about it: "You shall be as a dog whose wings are silver."

That's what God says, talking about the time when the roses shall bloom again.

Roses Shall Bloom Again

Jesus came to this earth, and He knew what it was to have roses for awhile.

Robert Browning pictured that in his wonderful poem called, "The Patriot." The poet said that that day they gave him a great parade, just like they gave Jesus a triumphal entry. He said:

> Was roses, roses all the way
> and myrtle mixed in my path
> Like mad, mad, and all the
> Housetops were gay. I could
> Have asked for the Sun yonder
> in the sky and the people would
> have said, "You could have it."

But another day the patriot rode down the street and he said:

"I feel the blood flowing down my face from the bricks they throw at me."

It was like that with Jesus. He came with the galleries of heaven giving Him applause.

He came with the sweetest, purest of a woman to be His mother.

He came, with a man who has never had the praise he should have had, with Joseph to take care of Mary.

He came with the tender ministrations of her love.

He came when the Wise Men worshiped Him and the shepherds worshiped Him.

Those were rose days for Jesus.

But there came the day when Herod wanted to kill Him, and in order to try to kill Him, killed all the boy babies under two years of age.

And then it was that later on the Sanhedrin was deployed against Him.

The army of Rome was against Him.

Forces, evil forces from the palaces of the Caesars were against Him, and these ragged folks of the mob of the streets joined in with the gentlemen of the palace to cry: "Away with Him! Kill Him! Kill Him!"

One day they picked up stones to stone Him to death, and Jesus said:

> For which of My works do you stone me? Would you stone Me because I made the blind to see and the deaf to hear and the fevers to leave bodies that wracked with pain? Would you stone Me because I cleanse lepers and make crazy men have their minds restored? Would you stone Me because I went into sick rooms and healed the sick and in the cemeteries and raised the dead? For which of My works would you stone Me?

But in their hearts they stoned Him long before they crucified Him.

Great forces rode out from hell against Him. Then against these assaulting forces Jesus lifted up His own banner of love; and who gathered at this banner of love? A few shoremen, fishermen gathered. A woman with a broken alabaster box gathered under His banner, and a widow with two mites gathered under His banner. And a rich publican called Zacchaeus gathered under His banner. And a few men, positionless and moneyless and with no political power, gathered.

And it is no wonder, it is no wonder that people asked Him why He didn't surrender to these forces.

But He wouldn't take a step backward. He said:

> I have come to seek and to save the lost. I have come to bring people out of their bondage and sorrow and night into My freedom, gladness, and light. I have come to cut the shackles off the wrists of people. I will not take a step back. I will not refuse to go to the cross. I will tread out the last grape of the last cluster. I will take the last step

> of the last mile. Though every step be punctured with pain, I will take it because I came to seek and to save that which was lost.

Oh, it seemed that these were all thorns. It seemed they were all thorns for Jesus. And He had His enemies who watched in the house into which He went and when He came out.

They watched Him when He ate and with whom He ate.

They watched Him when He drank and what He drank.

They listened to what He said and then found fault with what He said.

And He who went about doing good was followed by the hounds of hell in the person of His enemies until Jesus had to say one day to His disciples: If the world hates you, just remember, it hated Me before it hated you.

Oh, there were thorns amid all the roses that Jesus ever had upon this earth.

And, oh, I couldn't begin to tell you how I feel toward that woman who came and washed His feet with her tears and wiped them with the hairs of her head.

Oh, what roses were they amid the thorns that Jesus had to pierce Him nearly every step of the way. "He was wounded for our transgressions, he was bruised for our iniquities" (Isa. 53:5).

Wounded For Me

I remember reading years ago about how Lady Kincaid talked about the Prince of Wales, who later became King George. One day after the First World War they took the king to visit the hospital. They said, "There are thirty-six men more wounded and maimed than anybody else, and we would like for you, if you will, to see these men." And the Prince of Wales said: "Gladly will I."

And so the doctor guided him into one place and there were thirty men, all maimed and wounded, and he shook hands with some of them and spoke to many of them and was sympathetic with all of them.

He said: "But you told me there were thirty-six. I see only thirty."

They said: "Well, there were six others more maimed than are these, and we keep them in a ward to themselves, because it's best so to do."

The king said, "Well, let me see these six." And he went into this ward where the six men were, and he saw them, more maimed than the others, and he spoke to everyone of them kindly, and then he said: "But you said there were six here. Where's the other man."

They said: "Well, the other man was so maimed and marred we didn't want anybody to see him."

The king, the prince, who later became king, said: "Let me see him."

And they took him into a room where was one man by himself, blind and deaf, armless, legless.

When the prince of the nation saw him, he was stilled in his tracks. He looked at him, this blind and deaf man without any legs, without any arms, and he went over and stooped down and kissed him.

He said, as he kissed him: "Wounded for me. Wounded for me."

Oh, I think of how the Bible tells us how mercy and truth have met together and kissed.

I think of how this Book says: "Kiss the Son, lest he be angry" (Ps. 2:12).

And so, we can think of Jesus, who walked amid the thorns as the Rose of God.

We can look at Him and say: "He was wounded for me. Those thorn punctures in His brow, that terrible hole in His side, where the savage spear drank its precious libation of His blood. It was for me He died. For me He was bruised for my transgressions and with His stripes I shall find healing."

Oh, so many times we think that the roses will never bloom again.

Sometimes in the storm, when the storm is on, and the thunder crashes, the sky is inky black, danger and fear and death, it seems, ride the clouds. Not a bird to be seen or heard, only that thunder and lightning.

But, when the morning dawned, the earth was wonderful. Its air was fresh and washed, and the grass and leaves and flowers were clean and greener than ever, since God washed the world.

The roses bloomed again.

And sometimes we thought when we heard the tramp of the soldiers and saw them go away into the night, and the whole divisions of trained men slipping away, while women wept and while mothers and children wept, the nation stricken with the necessity of armed conflict! How far away seemed the days of peace.

How far away roses seemed when Pearl Harbor came on us that December day. Yes, how terrible it was and how uncertain the future.

But peace did come and roses bloomed again, and somehow, since I know that we will never hear of God's death, and, somehow, since I believe we will never have any newspaper heralding the funeral of Christ Jesus, this world now that's hanging on an abyss, on a thread above an abyss, a world of desolation and Communism and hatred taught us of many people in the nations of the world, people today, fighting, killing each other, somehow, I believe that the roses will bloom again!

And then you remember that day when you thought you could never laugh again? That afternoon late in the day when you turned away from the cemetery alone, you left a loved one behind, and all black and shadowed as you went back, brokenhearted, to the vacant house where kind neighbors came in, preparing the lonely supper?

But, life crowded in the next morning with its cares and duties, very fortunate for all, and, lo, after awhile the roses bloomed again!

The disciples thought the roses would never bloom again when they knew that Jesus was in the grave.

But the roses did bloom!

And after the stress, after the stress and storm, the roses bloomed.

And after the storm, the sun shone.

And after the night, the dawn.

And after the trial, the glory after the struggle, and the victory!

The roses bloom again!

And sometimes I think I would like to get my people to see what the old guide said to a tourist in the Alps mountains. They went to sleep. They slept pretty well that night, covered with their blankets. In the morning about four or five o'clock a great thunderstorm came. The lightning burned its zigzag paths and tearing to shred the vestments, the black vestments of the storm clouds. The thunder boomed and the rocky mountains trembled under it.

And the tourist awoke the guide, and said: "Are we safe? It's terrible, this storm!"

And the old guide lifted up his face and said: "Friend, this is the way the morning dawns a lot of times in this land."

Oh, sometimes it's the way the morning dawns, these storms.

Sometimes it's the planting and blooming of the roses after the desert God's dealing with us!

And so if you are in the desert of unbelief and you are not saved, let Jesus have His way with you, and the roses of salvation will bloom in your life if in Him you trust with repentance toward God and faith in the Lord Jesus Christ.

And so this is the invitation to any who have never trusted Christ. Trust in Him, and the roses of salvation will fill your garden, and the roses of redemption will bloom in your desert place. Yes, they will!

Questions for Group Discussion and Personal Reflection

Chapter One

1. What kind of man was Naboth?
2. What kind of king was Ahab? Do the words "vile human toad" relay somewhat his character?
3. Who was Jezebel? Describe her character.
4. Describe the prophet Elijah.
5. What happened in the real estate request?

6. Why did Naboth refuse to sell this vineyard? See Leviticus 25:23; Numbers 36:7, 9.
7. How did Naboth's refusal affect Ahab?
8. When his wife, Jezebel, found Ahab sulking in his room, what did she do? What did she say?
9. What was Jezebel's promise to Ahab?
10. Do you agree with this statement? Why or why not? "The truth that the spiritual life of a nation, city, town, school, church, home never rises any higher than the spiritual life of women."
11. To take control of Naboth's land, what scheme did Jezebel put into action?
12. What did fasting mean in that day? Why was a fast proclaimed?
13. Why could a criminal not be executed within the city's walls?
14. What happened during the "fatal fast"?
15. How was Naboth killed?
16. Why were Naboth's sons also killed?
17. How does Dr. Lee believe Jezebel received the news of Naboth's death?
18. What happened when Ahab visited the vineyard to claim it as his own?
19. Who was Jehu? What was his job?
20. What was Elijah's message from God to Ahab?
21. Contemplate and discuss the following: "'Payday—Someday' is written in the constitution of God's universe. The retributive providence of God is a reality as certainly as night follows day, because sin carries in itself the seed of its own fatal penalty."
22. What does the name "Ichabod" mean?

23. Discuss the meaning of Exodus 20:7.
24. Discuss the meaning of Emerson's *Compensation*?
25. Ponder the story Dr. Lee tells of the young man who called himself "the chief of the Kangaroo Court."
26. Describe Ahab's death.
27. Before Jezebel's death, explain what happened to Elijah and who followed him as God's prophet.
28. Describe what happened at Ramoth-gilead.
29. Read 2 Kings 9:16–26 and describe the event in your own words.
30. Describe Jezebel's death. How was God's Word revealed in her death?
31. Of what significance is the fact that Jezebel's body was gone (when Jehu ordered its burial) except for her skull, feet, and the palms of her hands?
32. Discuss the following statement: "'Payday—Someday!' God said it—and it was done! Yes, and from this we learn the power and certainty of God in carrying out His own retributive providence, that men might know that His justice slumbereth not. Even though the mill of God grinds slowly, it grinds to powder."
33. Contemplate the words in which the author ends his sermon: "And the only way I know for any man or woman on earth to escape the sinner's payday on earth and the sinner's hell beyond—making sure of the Christian's payday—is through Christ Jesus, who took the sinner's place upon the cross, becoming for all sinners all that God must judge, that sinners through faith in Christ Jesus might become all that God cannot judge."

Chapter Two

1. What does Dr. Lee mean when he quotes: "the Scripture cannot be broken," and "the Word of God is not bound"?

2. Ponder this statement: "This wonderful Book of sixty-six books, a vast library in one volume, written by forty men of different capacity and temperament and position over a period of sixteen hundred years, has one message, progressive, constructive, complete."
3. Do you agree with the description of the Bible as "a miracle Book of diversity in unity, of harmony in infinite complexity"?
4. How does the author describe the "masterpiece of God"?
5. The following are Scripture verses that support verbal inspiration. Look up and contemplate. Can you add to this list? 1 Thessalonians 2:13; 1 Corinthians 14:37; Luke 1:70; Hebrews 1:1; Exodus 24:4; Jeremiah 1:9; 30:2; 1 Corinthians 2:13; John 3:34, and 2 Samuel 23:1–3.
6. To what is the author referring when he writes of that which "prostitutes inspiration to the level of human genius"?
7. Describe the various theories of inspiration to which Dr. Lee refers.
8. What does the author mean by "God-breathed" Scripture?
9. The author writes: "The apostle Paul pulled in the poles of the world of his day and bound them to the Cross." How did the apostle Paul "sacrifice and suffer" as a result of proclaiming the gospel?
10. Paul writes: "But what things were gain to me, those I counted loss for Christ. Yea doubtless, and I count all things but loss for the excellency of the knowledge of Christ Jesus my Lord: for whom I have suffered the loss of all things, and do count them but dung, that I may win Christ" (Phil. 3:7–8). What did Paul mean by these words?
11. Why does the author call the Bible a "living Book"?
12. What did Paul mean by these words: "I would to God, that not only thou, but also all that hear me this day, were both

almost, and altogether such as I am, except these bonds" (Acts 26:29)?

13. Contemplate the following statement by Dr. Lee: "God is the authority. Men who summon the Bible to appear at the bar of human reason and substitute a 'Thus saith the mind of man' for a 'Thus saith the Lord' forget that fact. The Word of God is the voice of the Almighty."

14. What does the following statement mean? "Since God is infinite, His Book will be independent of those finite limitations which characterize man's work."

15. Dr. Lee continues to write about the authority of God. Address each one of the characteristics he attributes to God:

    - God as immutable:
    - God as one:
    - God as omniscient:
    - God as wise:
    - God as almighty:
    - God as creator:
    - God as righteous:
    - God as holy:
    - God as benevolent:
    - God as mysterious and incomprehensible:
    - God as superhuman and supernatural:
    - God as unimpeachable:
    - God as absolutely faithful:
    - God as a God of purpose:
    - God as omnipresent:
    - God as a God of divine providence:
    - God as judge:
    - God as sovereign:
    - God as Spirit:

16. What is meant by this statement? "The Bible has had and still has many enemies. Considering the persecution the Bible has encountered, its survival is the miracle of history and the history of miracle"?

17. Who are the enemies of the Bible? Describe each one as addressed by Dr. Lee.

18. What does the author mean by this phrase: "infidelity with a fancy name"? Do you agree?

19. Discuss the quotes made by the following:

    - Dr. D. S. Fisher
    - Dr. Grayce
    - Dr. Robert Dick Wilson
    - Sir William Ramsey

20. What is "practical indifference"?

21. What is "biblical indifference"?

22. How would you respond to this question? "How long will it take us to learn that in homes, in churches, in schools, in nations, tragedies are enacted because so many fail to read the Bible and refuse to fashion their lives by its precepts?

23. Why is "Jesus" described as the Bible's "great attraction"?

24. Do you agree with this statement? "You cannot believe in the Cross and surrender the infallible authority of the Bible"?

25. Why is this true? "The center of the Book is the Cross of Christ. The circumference of the Book is the glory of Christ."

26. Why do the "promises to fallen man in Eden and the ceremonies of Judaism mean Christ"?

27. Ponder the meaning of John 5:39, 45–47.

28. The Old Testament, the New Testament—what does the author say about both Testaments concerning Christ?

29. Do you agree with the following? "The Bible truths we should apply to every interest in life, whether personal, social, commercial, political, domestic, civil, or religious." What difference would it make if we, as a nation, could do this? Discuss.

30. Ponder the meaning of Deuteronomy 6:7 and Proverbs 6:21-23.

Chapter Three

1. Describe, in summary form, what Dr. Lee writes about the "sad face" of Jesus.
2. What made Jesus sad?
3. Discuss the following reason Jesus was sad: "He saw men making poor choices between things of value and things of no worth—emphasizing the things that matter but little, if at all, neglecting the things that matter most in eternity and in time."
4. In what ways was Jesus "a man of sorrows and acquainted with grief"?
5. What does the author mean by the following: "But the sadness of His face was not the sadness that takes on the stamp of a heart torn with remorse. Not the sadness of a face that takes on the hue of a heart that holds some abiding bitterness. Not the sadness of a face that gives reflection from a heart that nurses some bitter resentment. Not the sadness of a face that testifies to a heart that stamps itself in cynicism and doubt and unbelief on the face."
6. Describe, in summary form, what Dr. Lee writes about the "shining face" of Jesus.
7. Describe the experience that happened in Matthew 17:1–2.
8. Reread Hebrews 1:2–3 and ponder.
9. Describe the appearance of Jesus as recorded in Revelation 1:13–16.
10. Describe the experience of Saul as recorded in Acts 9:1–4.
11. Reread Acts 9:3–6. What was Saul's response to Jesus' question?
12. Describe, in summary form, what Dr. Lee writes about the "stained face" of Jesus.

13. Tell what happened in Luke 19:41. What does this action tell us about Jesus?

14. With what was the face of Jesus stained?

15. Tell in your own words what took place in Luke 22:41–44.

16. Describe, in summary form, what Dr. Lee writes about the "smitten face" of Jesus.

17. What does this passage of Scripture, written eight hundred years before the birth of Christ, mean to you? "I gave my back to the smiters, and my cheeks to them that plucked off the hair: I hid not my face from shame and spitting" (Isa. 50:6).

18. "Then Pilate therefore took Jesus, and scourged him. And the soldiers plaited a crown of thorns, and put it on his head, and they put on him a purple robe, and said, Hail, King of the Jews! and they smote him with their hands" (John 19:1–3). What is the process of scourging? Why was this cruelty used? What significance does the crown of thorns have? The purple robe?

19. What does the author mean when he writes: "Some of us have forgotten the scars."

20. Describe, in summary form, what Dr. Lee writes about the "set face" of Jesus.

21. Discuss the meaning of Isaiah 50:7.

22. Why is this statement true? "Jesus came to die—not to teach, not merely to live a beautiful life, not merely to be a miracle worker, but to die, and He would not be turned aside."

23. What was the cause of Jesus' remark to Peter in Matthew 16:21–23?

24. In this paragraph, to what does Dr. Lee refer? "And long, long centuries had His face been set. Mysterious but true it is that His face was set toward Calvary before light ever came from the sun, before any wave ever broke in white

foam on any shore. Before any wind ever murmured among the forests of earth, the blessed face of Christ was set for our salvation—set bravely toward a bloody hill."

25. Describe, in summary form, what Dr. Lee writes about the "scorching face" of Jesus.
26. What happened in John 2:15–17.
27. Why is this statement true? "In popular thinking much is thought of His tenderness and of His sympathy and of His joyfulness and of His prayerfulness, but little evidence of thought of His severity is shown."
28. In what ways was Jesus a "man of indignation"?
29. Describe, in summary form, what Dr. Lee writes of the "shrouded face" of Jesus.
30. Describe, in summary form, what Dr. Lee writes of the "seen face" of Jesus.

Chapter Four

1. Read and discuss the following verses: John 1:14; Romans 8:3; Isaiah 7:14; Galatians 4:4–5; Hebrews 7:22; and 2 Corinthians 5:21.
2. What does the author mean by this statement? "We make bold to say that none of the days gone forever into the tomb of time had or held more glorious opportunities and more stupendous responsibilities than do these days in which you and I are privileged to live." Do you agree?
3. Ponder: "While the forces of righteousness are alive today—and powerful—so also are the forces of evil."
4. What does Dr. Lee say about the evil of our day?
5. What does Dr. Lee say about the Bible?
6. Ponder and discuss: "[Bible] Book which the dissecting knives of modernistic intellectuals have whacked at, like butchers, and do whack at now like savages on a midnight raid! Book against which snipers from behind some pulpit

stands and some college chairs have aimed their ill-grounded propositions."

7. How was Jesus made flesh? Why?
8. "And the Word was made flesh, and dwelt among us" (John 1:14). Describe and discuss the incarnation of Christ.
9. What is meant by "the preexistent Christ"?
10. Discuss the following: "For by him were all things created, that are in heaven, and that are in earth . . . and he is before all things, and by him all things consist" (Col. 1:16–17).
11. Describe the physical sufferings, as well as the spiritual sufferings, of Jesus on the cross.
12. Ponder and discuss the Virgin Birth: "Therefore the Lord himself shall give you a sign; Behold, a virgin shall conceive, and bear a son, and shall call his name Immanuel" (Isa. 7:14).
13. What does this Scripture mean to you personally? "But when the fullness of the time was come, God sent forth his Son, made of a woman, made under the law, to redeem them that were under the law, that we might receive the adoption of sons" (Gal. 4:4–5).
14. Describe how the author compares Jesus' humanness with His divineness.
15. Reread Galatians 4:4–5. What does "the adoption of sons" mean?
16. How was Jesus "made a curse"?
17. What is meant by this Scripture? "His body shall not remain all night upon the tree, but thou shalt in any wise bury him that day; (for he that is hanged is accursed of God;) that thy land be not defiled, which the LORD thy God giveth thee for an inheritance" (Deut. 21:23).
18. Explain "God was in Christ" (2 Cor. 5:19).

19. In your own words, explain this Scripture: "For he hath made him to be sin for us, who knew no sin; that we might be made the righteousness of God in him" (2 Cor. 5:21).

20. Why is Sin, "the darkest, saddest fact in God's universe"?

21. Discuss the meaning of Romans 5:12: "By one man sin entered into the world, and death by sin; and so death passed upon all men, for that all have sinned."

22. How does the Creator, Himself, view sin?

23. Ponder and explain the following: "He was made for us all that God must judge AND we are made in Him by faith all that God cannot judge."

24. Discuss the righteousness of God.

25. Meditate on this thought and discuss: "And this Christ Jesus, who was 'made flesh,' 'made of a woman,' 'made a curse,' 'made sin,' and 'made alive from the dead' is the same Christ Jesus 'who of God *is* made unto us wisdom, and righteousness, and sanctification, and redemption.' 'Christ in you the hope of glory' (Col. 1:27)."

Chapter Five

1. In the case of Jesus' body, why does Dr. Lee so strongly emphasize the use of the past tense instead of the present tense?

2. Ponder the following statement and discuss: "And there is only one tomb that has imperishable glory. It is the tomb of Joseph of Arimathea 'where never man before was laid' till therein was placed the body of Jesus, marred and scarred with the stigmata of the Cross, where for the first time in thirty-three years the cruel world left Him alone."

3. What is the significance of this Scripture in John 19:25? "Now there stood by the cross of Jesus his mother, and his mother's sister, Mary the wife of Cleophas, and Mary Magdalena."

4. Discuss the implications of this statement: "I am he that liveth, and was dead; and, behold, I am alive for evermore, Amen; and have the keys of hell and of death" (Rev. 1:18).

5. Reflect on the following: "Until the day in which he was taken up, after that he through the Holy Ghost had given commandments unto the apostles whom he had chosen: to whom also he showed himself alive after his passion by many infallible proofs, being seen of them forty days, and speaking of the things pertaining to the kingdom of God" (Acts 1:2–3).

6. Why do we, as believers, "rejoice in the triumphant tense of this Triumph of Scripture"?

7. Why does Dr. Lee call the empty tomb the "triumphant tense"?

8. Dr. Lee makes an interesting statement when he writes "false religions must stop at the tomb." What does he mean? Do you agree? Why or why not?

9. Reflect on the Lord's statement: "I am the resurrection!" What does this mean to you personally?

10. Reread the following passages of Scripture and discuss the significance of each:

    Luke 7:15

    Luke 8:54–55

    John 11:43–44

    Luke 15:24

    Revelation 1:17–18

11. The author asks the question: "What is it that distinguishes Christianity from all man-made religions?" How does Dr. Lee answer the question he poses?

12. Why must we "accept the miracle of the literal bodily resurrection" of Jesus Christ?

13. Why is the resurrection the "foundation and pivotal point of Christianity"?

14. Dr. Lee uses some extraordinary words and images when he writes of the resurrection of Jesus Christ. Ponder and discuss at least two of the words and images listed below:

    - The greatest evidence of Christianity
    - The greatest exhibition of God's power
    - The greatest truth of the gospel
    - The greatest reality of faith
    - The greatest assurance of coming glory
    - The greatest incentive to holiness
    - A fact thrillingly touching the human heart
    - A truth powerfully influencing human character and human destiny
    - A fact mentioned directly more than one hundred times in the New Testament
    - The whole alphabet of human hope
    - The certificate of our Lord's mission from heaven
    - The heart of the gospel in all ages

15. "He comes first to break up our tomb, then to set up His throne." What does the author mean by this statement?

16. Reread Romans 10:9-10 and reflect on its meaning.

Chapter Six

1. Discuss this statement: "Leviticus gives the detail of the walk, worship, and service of that people. In Exodus God speaks out of the mount to which approach was forbidden."

2. Why is "holiness" the "keyword of Leviticus"?

3. How were Aaron and his sons "publicly set apart" and "inducted into the office of the priesthood"?

4. Discuss the meaning of each of the holy garments stated in Exodus 28. What was their individual purpose? What were they used for in that time?

- breastplate
- ephod
- robe
- broidered coat
- miter
- girdle

5. What is the significance of "the washing" in Leviticus 8:6?
6. Discuss the following statement: "The washing of Aaron and his sons *together* sets forth *unity* in sanctification—even as Christ and His church are a unit in sanctification before God."
7. Reflect upon the Scripture found in Hebrews 2:11.
8. What does Dr. Lee mean by the expression "the crimson cash"?
9. What does the author mean when he calls Aaron a "God-clothed man"?
10. Concerning the eight holy garments, why was it important that the people see the "intricate worth of these garments of glory and beauty"?
11. What does it mean to be "set apart" from the people, "exalted" above the people, yet *for* the people?
12. Discuss the following questions:
    a. Why does the breastplate signify the *loving* Christ?
    b. In what way does the ephod speak of the *human* and *divine* Christ?
    c. How does the robe speak of the *heavenly* and *gracious* Christ?
    d. Why do the linen coat and breeches set forth the truth of the *sinless* Christ?
    e. How does the girdle speak of the *serving* Christ?
    f. Why do the shoulder pieces declare the truth of the *strengthening* and *sustaining* Christ?

g. Why is the mitre emblematic of the *obedient* Christ?

h. In what way does the golden plate symbolize the *holy* Christ?

13. In speaking of Christ, why does Dr. Lee say that He "has been set forth in His aloneness upon the consciousness of the world"? What does this mean?

14. Oil was poured on Aaron's head. What significance did this action have? (Reflect on Lev. 8:10–12.)

15. Discuss the following statement: "The centuries from Adam to Christ were crimson with the blood of innocent victims killed as types of the slain Lamb of God."

16. Why do men "label God and label the Bible a lie by believing anything contrary to the truth, or by preaching or by teaching anything contrary to the truth that the blood stream was ordained of God"?

17. Ponder the three-fold consecration of the holy priesthood. Why was the blood of the sacrifice applied to Aaron and his sons in this unusual way? (The blood was put upon the tip of the right ear, upon the thumb of the right hand, and upon the big toe of the right foot.)

18. What does the author say about our "hearing, our service, our walk" for Christ? How does he so beautifully and graphically illustrate this point?

19. What are some of the extraordinary word pictures the author gives us to describe the *ear*?

20. Ponder this statement and discuss: "There is even more peril in listening than in looking and seeing."

21. "A blood-anointed ear is required to hearken to divine communications," writes Dr. Lee. Discuss.

22. "Do not expect the natural man to find pleasure in the voices of the Scriptures," states the author. What does he mean by this statement?

23. Reflect on this statement: "To handle holy things the blood-sprinkled hand alone is worthy. For the worship and service of the heavenly sanctuary, to which we belong, it only is competent."
24. What does the author say about the "consecrated hand"?
25. According to Dr. Lee, what is the literal meaning of Exodus 32:29?
26. How can we "yield" our hands to God as "instruments of righteousness"?
27. Explain why blood was put upon the great toe of the right foot?
28. What does Dr. Lee mean when he writes: "Blood answers blood"?
29. How was the blood on the ear, on the thumb, and on the big toe a "perfect picture" of Jesus?
30. "To die a martyr's death is not so difficult as to live a consecrated, definitely-devoted, Christ-honoring life." Do you agree with Dr. Lee's statement? Why or why not?
31. How do we "speak with our feet"?

Chapter Seven

1. Discuss Dr. Lee's description of the Bible: "That Book which is divine in authorship, human in penmanship, universal in scope, infallible in authority, validated and confirmed by the Holy Spirit with a divine certainty that is incommunicable by reason and impervious to the assaults of doubt, the miracle Book of diversity in unity."
2. Why do you think the Epistle of James devotes a whole chapter to the "loose tongue"?
3. The sacred writers described the tongue in the following terms. Choose at least two of these terms and discuss.
   - The tongue is a fire.
   - The tongue is full of deadly poison.

- The tongue is a little member (of the body) and boasteth great things.
- The tongue is an unruly evil.
- The tongue is a world of iniquity.
- The tongue defileth the whole body.
- The tongue setteth on fire the course of nature.
- The tongue can no man tame.

4. What did Job say about the tongue?
5. Why did the psalmist describe the tongue as an "instrument of unrighteousness"?
6. What did Peter say about the tongue?
7. Why would the psalmist and the author of Proverbs compare the tongue to "a sharp razor" and "a sword"?
8. What does Paul say about the tongue?
9. Discuss the following statement: "People who say there is no personal devil should explain about the someone or the somewhat that gets into men and women and dehumanizes them, makes them hurt people and have little regret as to wounds made."
10. Ponder the interesting word pictures Dr. Lee gives us when he describes the tongue as a tormentor. He calls the tongue:

    - a dagger
    - a scourge
    - a whetted sword
    - a mortar
    - a razor
    - a battering ram
    - a thunderbolt
    - an instrument of "all conceivable pain"

    Choose at least two of these descriptions and discuss the reason for that particular word picture.
11. Consider this strong statement made by the author: "I think the tongue may be indicted as the worse criminal in the world with all the guilt of the devil, since by blasphemy

of God and by blasting human life with its devastating power, it is a satanic mischief."

12. Reread James 3:5–6, and comment on the writer's description of the tongue as a fire.
13. What is the definition of the word *traduce*?
14. Consider the strong language of Plautus: "Those who carry about, and those who listen to slander, should, if I could have my way, all be hanged—the tattlers by the tongue, the listeners by their ears."
15. "The traducing tongue steals a good name which is rather to be chosen than great riches. A man's name is himself." What does the author mean by this statement: "To rob him of his good name is fundamentally to violate the eighth commandment." Do you agree? Why or why not?
16. Discuss the following statement: "George Meredith said: 'Gossip is a beast of prey that does not wait for the death of the creature it devours.'"
17. Consider the strong language of Dr. Adam Clarke when he says: "The word 'backbite' was intended to convey the treble sense of knavishness, cowardice and brutality. He is a knave who would rob you of your good name, a coward who would speak of you in your absence what he dared not do in your presence—and only an ill-conditioned dog would fly at and bite your back when your face was turned. Hence, the backbiter's tongue is the tongue of a knave, a coward, a dog." What is your impression of this statement?
18. How are backbiters classed in the Bible? With whom are they compared?
19. Dr. Lee suggests we pray about a fault-finding tongue. He offers the following prayer: "Keep thy tongue from evil, and thy lips from speaking guile" (Ps. 34:13). God keeps us from having the tongue that "speaketh proud things," that "frameth deceit," and "deviseth mischiefs like a razor," that is "bent like a bow for lies," that is as "an arrow shot out,"

that "boasteth great things." How can this prayer help "tame a tongue" and offer healing? Can you suggest other prayers that would help?

20. Reread the following passage of Scripture and discuss: "For every kind of beasts, and of birds, and of serpents, and of things in the sea, is tamed, and hath been tamed of mankind: but the tongue can no man tame; it is an unruly evil, full of deadly poison. Therewith bless we God, even the Father; and therewith curse we men, which are made after the similitude of God. Out of the same mouth proceedeth blessing and cursing. My brethren, these things ought not so to be" (James 3:7–10).

21. Do you agree with this statement? Why or why not? "The tongue is the greatest power for good in the world."

22. Describe the benefits of a "virtuous tongue rather than a vicious tongue."

23. Discuss Dr. Lee's closing appeal: "What shall I more say? Nothing more say I except to beg you by the tongue of Jesus that spake words of tenderness, of righteousness, of holy and scathing denunciation, of praise, of commendation of right and condemnation of wrong, of comfort, of purity, of truth—by the use He made of His tongue, I beg you to yield your tongue to God as an instrument of righteousness."

24. Contemplate Dr. Lee's closing Scripture: "If any man among you seem to be religious, and bridleth not his tongue, but deceiveth his own heart, this man's religion is vain" (James 1:26).

25. In summary, what does the author say about . . . ?

    - The terrible tongue
    - The tormenting tongue
    - The tongue as a torch
    - The traducing tongue
    - The tar tongue

Chapter Eight

Discuss the meaning of this passage of Scripture: "For the love of Christ constraineth us . . . he died for all, that they which live should not henceforth live unto themselves, but unto him who died for them, and rose again" (2 Cor. 5:14–15).

2. What does the author mean by the term *Cross constraint?*

3. What does the "constraint of the Cross" bid us to do? What does it bid us not to do?

4. Dr. Lee asks the question: "What urged early Christians along life's highway?" How would you answer that question?

5. How does Jesus warn us regarding the "atrophy of heroism"?

6. What does this statement mean to you: "By His Cross [Jesus] shows us how poor many things we count great, how shoddy our splendor, how tawdry our luxury, how worthless many things about which we boast"?

7. Why is the following statement true? "Fearsomely easy it is to take the Cross for granted, to be no different because of that tremendous fact."

8. What is the "crucified life"? How can it be lived in today's society?

9. Do you agree with this statement? "But let us not forget that the Cross should also stand between us and the great world system of sin and pleasure. We need to think in terms of the Cross, in all things applying it as our standard, carrying it daily through life's multitudinous details, meeting our tasks in its spirit."

10. Why is this statement true? "Ornamental cross *wearing* is more popular than sacrificial cross *bearing*."

11. What does Dr. Lee mean when he writes about "the weakness of modern Christianity"?

12. Do you believe that Christians have disgraced Christ, as mentioned by a Jewish Rabbi? Why or why not? If so, in what ways?

13. Consider this remark made by Robert Speer: "After thirty years of leadership in missionary work it is my conclusion and conviction that the greatest missionary problem is just the failure of Christian people to live up to their professions." Do you agree or disagree? Why or why not?

14. Consider this statement made by "Mr. Johnston": "The chief obstacle to the spread of Christianity is not Hinduism, not Buddhism, not even paganism, but the rotten behavior of people who call themselves Christians." Do you agree? Why or why not?

15. Contemplate this statement and then discuss its meaning: "The only marks of victory Christ bears are the wounds of Calvary."

16. What did the apostle Paul mean when he said: "I bear in my body the marks of the Lord Jesus"?

17. The author calls this world "unreconciled, alienated, dislocated, sin-troubled, sin-saddened. . . ." What would you call the present-day world?

18. As Christians, what is our commission, according to the author?

19. When we "go and disciple," what is our assurance?

20. Dr. Lee asks that "the cross ________ us, ________ us, and ________ on us." Do you agree?

21. Ponder the following and discuss: "Nothing is won without sacrifice, nothing held without blood."

22. Laying down our lives for Christ, Dr. Lee writes, will lift us:

    - from ________________ to ________________
    - from ________________ into ________________
    - from ________________ to ________________.

23. Dr. Lee writes: "With the Cross our experience, not a mere historical statement, we will be lifted:

    - from ________ to __________,
    - from ________ to __________,
    - from ________ to __________,
    - from ________ to __________,
    - from ________ to __________."

24. Do you agree with this statement? "So long as Southern Baptists have a passion for the salvation of sinners everywhere, there is little danger of our drifting into materialism—little danger of our frittering away our energies in 'the ethical development of the world.'" Why or why not?

25. What does the author mean by "bloodless gospels"?

26. What does Dr. Lee mean by these phrases? "Molluscous liberalism" and "self-satisfied complacency."

27. Ponder the truth of the following statement: "At Christ's Cross is the solution for our indebtedness problem, the sufficient stimulus for our lowered morale, the adequate replenishing for empty treasuries."

28. According to Dr. Lee, what is it that Baptists believe?

    a. ______________________________

    b. ______________________________

    c. ______________________________

    d. ______________________________

    e. ______________________________

    f. ______________________________

    g. ______________________________

29. According to Dr. Lee, what are those things that Baptists do not believe?

    a. ______________________________

    b. ______________________________

c. ________________________________

d. ________________________________

e. ________________________________

f. ________________________________

g. ________________________________

30. What are "the tragic terms of the Cross"?

Chapter Nine

1. From Dr. Lee's description of Nineveh, what was the city like?
2. What was the main theme of Nahum's prophecy?
3. Discuss the city of Nineveh regarding:
   - her power
   - her pride
   - her sin
   - her degradation
4. Discuss the significance of the following statement: "The eternity of God is duration without beginning or end, a *continuing* fact. The eternity of God is existence without bound or dimension, a *continuing* existence. The eternity of God is present, without past or future, a *continuing* present."
5. What does the author mean when he writes: "And God is the first Cause, absolutely"?
6. What does the author mean when he writes: "God is the first Cause, universally?"
7. What does Dr. Lee mean by: "God is the first Cause, everlastingly?"
8. Discuss the following: "What [God] was, He is. What He is, He will be. What He will be, He ever has been. He changes not."

9. Ponder and respond to this statement: "God's immutability and eternity are pledged for the perpetuity of His church. God's immutability and eternity are pledged for the immutability of His church."

10. Contemplate the meaning of the poem"Fear."

11. When "man asks a harder question: 'What shall I do with my sins?'" what is the response given to him?

12. In light of the question above, ponder the meaning of this statement: "And, depend on it, verily, if Jesus, Son of man and Son of God, had never come into the world, that sad question would have echoed around the world, up and down the corridors of all the centuries, unanswered and unanswerable until this very day."

13. What does the author mean by this statement: "In the day of accusation, when conscience rises as a strong man armed, we shall need a defense far more substantial than a man-made refuge."

14. Reread Hosea 8:7 and discuss.

15. What does the author write about "the chamber of growth"?

16. "Like produces like," writes Dr. Lee. What does he mean by this? Give some of the examples he used to explain.

17. Contemplate the following: "I think it was Mr. Moody who, in his own matchless way under God's Spirit, kept saying to the hearts of men and women the truth that though the worldling may look with contempt upon Christians, the time is coming when the worldlings will give anything to exchange places with the meanest Christian that walks the streets." Do you agree with this statement? Why or why not?

18. Reread Ecclesiastes 8:11–13. What does this passage of Scripture say to you?

19. What does Dr. Lee say about "sowing the seed"?

20. Why is it "dangerous to do wrong"?
21. According to the author, why must we not make a "pet" of sin? Did you find his rattlesnake story an effective way to illustrate this point?
22. Recall the story told by Dr. Lee Rutland Scarborough. What did this story say to you?
23. Reread 2 Kings 2:1-11 and discuss.
24. What does the author say about "separation"?
25. Reflect on the author's use of "whirlwind" throughout this chapter.

Chapter Ten

1. Discuss the following quotes made by various men:
    - Carlyle: "History is the essence of innumerable biographies."
    - Voltaire: "History is little else than a picture of human crimes and misfortune!"
    - Kaufman: "History is making a collection of autopsy reports!"
    - Kossuth: "History is but the development and revelation of providence!"
    - Napoleon: "History is a fable agreed upon!"
    - Bancroft: "Each generation gathers together the imperishable children of the past, and increases them by new sons of light alike radiant with immortality!"
    - Lanahan: "God is in the facts of history as truly as He is in the march of the seasons, the revolutions of the planets, or the architecture of the worlds!"
    - Cromwell: "All histories are but God manifesting Himself, shaking down and trampling underfoot whatsoever He hath not planted!"
2. Comment on the following Scripture passages. What do they tell you?

"Thou, Lord, in the beginning hast laid the foundation of the earth" (Heb. 1:10).

"Before the mountains were brought forth, or ever thou hadst formed the earth and the world, even from everlasting to everlasting, thou art God" (Ps. 90:2).

"For by him were all things created, that are in heaven, and that are in earth, visible and invisible, whether they be thrones, or dominions, or principalities, or powers: all things were created by him, and for him: and he is before all things, and by him all things consist" (Col. 1:16–17).

3. What does Dr. Lee say about "Before the World Is God"?
4. What does Dr. Lee say about "God's Presence in the World"?
5. Is God "an absentee God, a God detached from the lives which men and women are living here"? Discuss.
6. Contemplate God's guiding hand in history as illustrated by the author.
7. Ponder this statement: "Take God from nature, and this universe would indeed be 'a fortuitous concourse of atoms'—and worse."
8. What do you think about this statement: "There is purpose, mind, design—the presence and activity of God. God is active in all things in the realm of nature. God is manifest in all things?"
9. What does the author mean when he says: God "is no law-limited God"?
10. What meaning does this statement hold for you: "God *in* His world means God *throughout* His world"?
11. Reread Psalm 139 and ponder.
12. What does Dr. Lee say about "God in Human Experience"?

13. What does Dr. Lee say about "God in Human History"?
14. Do you believe this statement to be true and why? "And if God is with the world at all times, most certainly shall we not believe He is with it during its *crises* of history?"
15. In your own words, what is the meaning of Revelation 19:6?
16. What is meant by the term *anonymous powers?*
17. Discuss this statement: "But if we believe in God as a moral being, as the moral governor of the universe, then it follows that we must believe that He rules and governs and that His plan is beneficent and just."
18. What does the author believe about God's will and America? What points does he make to illustrate his point?
19. What does Dr. Lee say about "God's Use of Little Things In History"?
20. What is meant by the term (used to describe Jesus): "The Lamb slain from the foundation of the world"?
21. What does the author include regarding "God's Judgment upon the Nations"?

Chapter Eleven

1. Why does the author begin his sermon in this way? "I am no photographer of sordid spots, no driver of a garbage wagon, no prober of abscesses, no seeker after carrion." What does he mean by this?
2. What is meant by this statement? "The Bible is summoned to appear at the bar of human reason."
3. Discuss the effect of the vivid language used to describe the following: "This is a day of invertebrate theology, of jellyfish morality, of India-rubber convictions, of see-saw religion, of somersault philosophy."
4. What do these terms/names mean and what is the purpose of each?

- Moloch
- Belial
- Mammon

5. Discuss the following statement: "There is the notion that ethics, religion, soul and God, are only concepts—having their origin in man's experience with shadows, dreams, trances, storms, seasons, and other natural forces."

6. Reread Psalm 94:16 and ponder.

7. Contemplate and answer the following: "What road shall we take when 'civilization is undergoing the frightful processes of self-burial'"?

8. Does the author give apt description to our present-day world when he writes about "this poor, head-dizzy, heart-saddened, sin-smitten, war-blooded, hate-blackened, hell-bound world"? Discuss.

9. What does the author mean by "Christlike conduct"?

10. When Dr. Lee describes "the white flower of a blameless life," of whom is he speaking?

11. Ponder the following strong statements and discuss:

    - "Is it not true that if the virtues productive of good citizenship are lost by the people, free government may give place to despotism without conquest by a foreign foe, and even without any change of political structure?"
    - "Has not corruption, as often as conquest, caused the loss of human rights and liberties?"

12. Do you believe the following statement to be true? Why or why not? "History tells but one story about the downfall of the world's great nations. Strong at first because of the virility of its people, a nation rises to world power, then by its power acquires wealth, and through wealth sinks into luxury, by luxury becomes soft and spiritually-decadent, and then falls an easy victim to a strong aggressor."

13. What is "our first line of defense"?

14. "Jesus taught us to live by dying." Why is this statement true?

15. "For if men are not in the path of truth and righteousness, they are in peril." Do you agree?

16. How does the author describe the attributes of Christ?

    - Christ is the ________.
    - Christ is the ________.
    - Christ is the ________.
    - Christ is the ________.
    - Christ is the ________.
    - Christ is the ________.

17. What is meant by this statement: "Great are the symbols of being, but that which is symboled is greater."

18. Ponder this strong statement made by Spurgeon: "We shall not see any great change until we have some men in our ranks who are willing to be martyrs. That deep ditch can never be crossed till the bodies of a few of us shall fill it up."

19. What does Dr. Lee write about "compassion"? What does "compassion" mean?

20. Do you agree with this statement? "One of the dangers of the present time is the paralysis of compassion."

21. What is Dr. Lee's definition of "heroism"? Do you agree?

22. What statements does the author make for the importance and urgency of prayer?

23. A statement to ponder: "Our greatest need is prayer that is strong, prevailing, believing—prayer that takes all we have and are to offer it to God, as it took all Jesus had on Calvary to give us the right to pray."

24. Do you agree with the following statement? Why or why not? "It is only the prayer born in the very heart of God, shot through with the very blood and passion of the Son of God, filled with the power and persistence of the Holy Ghost and loaded with a deep and heavy sense of the

Church's plight and the world's appalling need that sets the wheels of revival in motion."

25. Discuss the following: "Apart from the salvation that is in Christ Jesus, the most comforting doctrine in our day and generation is the absolute sovereignty of our omniscient, omnipotent, omnipresent God."
26. Study Revelation 6:10 and interpret in your own words.
27. Discuss Revelation 21:4.
28. Ponder the following statement: "Thus a Christian who has nothing possesses all things."

Chapter Twelve

1. What did Isaiah mean when he said: "That desert shall rejoice, and blossom as a rose"?
2. How does the author describe the person of Isaiah? How would you describe him in your own words?
3. What was Isaiah's message to God's people?
4. Reread and comment upon Isaiah 41:19.
5. Describe the "Assyrian scourge."
6. "And then Abraham turned and saw a ram with his horns caught in the thicket, and he took that and offered it instead of Isaac." What does this statement mean in light of Christ, the Lamb?
7. The author uses the stories of Noah, Abraham, David, Joseph, and Jacob to illustrate the point of "Roses Will Bloom Again." Do you consider these stories effective in illustrating the point? What stories or illustrations could you add?
8. Describe the four-hundred-year silence of God after the prophecy of Malachi and before the ministry of John the Baptist.

9. Describe the society into which Jesus came according to the author: "a time when religion and idolatry were holding hands and when the hands of hypocrisy were playing upon the harp of formalism and ritualism and icy nothingness."

10. At Jesus' birth, what was happening politically in . . .

    - Athens
    - Rome
    - Persia
    - Egypt

11. Why was Jesus referred to as the "Rose of Sharon"?

12. Reread and discuss Isaiah 1:18. How does Dr. Lee use this verse to minister to his listeners/readers?

13. What was the prophet Isaiah talking about when he said: "You shall be as a dog whose wings are silver"?

14. Discuss the meaning of Browning's poem, "The Patriot."

15. Referring to Jesus, what does this statement say to you: "But in their hearts they stoned Him long before they crucified Him."

16. Consider the meaning of Jesus' statement to His disciples: If the world hates you, just remember, it hated Me before it hated you.

17. Describe the effect of using the image of "roses" to illustrate the sermon in the ways that the author used it. Was it effective? How was it effective?

18. What effect do you believe this sermon or chapter had upon its hearers or readers?

19. At this time in your own life, or in the lives of your loved ones, do you (or they) desperately need to hear the assurance that the "roses will bloom again"? Ponder this and reflect either silently or with a group.

Index